DATE DUE

APR 16 2004		
GAYLORD		PRINTED IN U.S.A.

Goodbye, Descartes

Goodbye, Descartes

THE END OF LOGIC AND THE SEARCH FOR A NEW COSMOLOGY OF THE MIND

KEITH DEVLIN

John Wiley & Sons, Inc.
New York • Chichester • Brisbane • Toronto • Singapore • Weinheim

Copyright © 1997 by Keith Devlin
Published by John Wiley & Sons, Inc.

Library of Congress Cataloging-in-Publication Data:

Devlin, Keith J.
    Goodbye, Descartes : The end of logic and the search for a new cosmology of the mind / Keith Devlin.
       p.   cm.
    Includes bibliographical references and index.
    ISBN 0-471-14216-6 (cloth : alk. paper)
    1. Philosophy of mind.   I. Title.
BD418.3.D48   1997
128'.2—dc20   96-25493

Printed in the United States of America
10 9 8 7 6 5 4 3 2 1

CONTENTS

PREFACE

Bookstore managers and librarians are going to hate this book. They may enjoy *reading* it—I hope they do. But they will still hate it, because they will find it almost impossible to catalogue. Where do you put it? Nonfiction, certainly. 'General market' is probably also an appropriate classification. But then what? In what section of the bookstore or the library should the book be placed? Science? Mathematics? Logic? Philosophy? Linguistics? Computer Science? Artificial Intelligence? Psychology? Sociology? Cognitive Science? Every one of these traditional categories is appropriate. And there lies a paradox: Because the contents of this book cover all those categories, no single one of them is really appropriate.

Bookstore managers and librarians are not the only people who might be annoyed by this book. If you are a psychologist, linguist, or sociologist who feels uneasy about mathematics, you might be unhappy with my prediction that your discipline will become steadily more mathematical. And if you are a dyed-in-the-wool hard scientist or a mathematician, you might not like what I have to say about the limitations of the scientific and mathematical methods.

But don't blame me. As far as the concepts in this book are concerned, I am only the messenger. The plain fact of the matter is that the traditional borders between all of those separate intellectual disciplines listed above are rapidly breaking down. The degree of analytic precision that is nowadays achieved in the human sciences of psychology and sociology is increasing their need for, and dependency on, mathematics. At the same time, the humanistic nature of such studies is forcing scientists and mathematicians to face up to the fact that there are definite limitations to what can be achieved using mathematics and science. Indeed, in order to make further progress in our understanding of human reasoning and communication, we may well have to abandon some of the most fundamental assumptions that underpin the modern scientific method, assumptions that go back to Aristotle and Plato in ancient Greek times and to the seventeenth-century intellectual giants Galileo, Bacon, and Descartes.

Since I am a mathematician by inclination and by training, this book is inevitably written from a mathematician's perspective. However, it is *not* a mathematics book. Its subject matter is the human mind, in particular, the mind when it reasons and when it communicates with another human mind. A mathematical approach, however, can help us to understand what goes on when people reason and communicate. Plato and Aristotle knew this, as have generations of thinkers in the centuries since then who have worked in the intellectual tradition of logic begun by those two great philosophers.

Though the conclusion I eventually draw is that the existing techniques of logic and mathematics—indeed of the traditional scientific method in general—are inadequate for understanding the human mind, I do not see this as a cause for dismay. Rather, I rejoice to be living in an age when a major intellectual challenge is forcing us to develop new analytic techniques. My previous book, *Mathematics: The Science of Patterns,* published in 1994, was a celebration of the breadth and the enormous success of mathematics as an intellectual discipline. With the aid of mathematics, mankind has been able to understand, explore, and, on occasion, even adapt, control, and conquer the physical universe and the physical environment we live in. During the two-and-a-half-thousand-year period in which mathematics has grown from a study of numbers into today's widely applicable 'science of patterns', a number of attempts have been made to apply the techniques of mathematics to the human domains of reasoning and communication. Though such attempts have met with a certain degree of success, it has been far short of the success achieved in applying mathematics to the physical world. Our putative 'sciences of reasoning and communication' are not nearly as precise and reliable as physics or chemistry.

But things are changing. As with advances in mathematics and science in the past, the new developments are in response to changes taking place in society at large. Arithmetic arose in response to the needs of commerce in the early Sumerian civilizations. Geometry had its origins in earth measurement and navigation. Calculus was developed to meet the needs of astronomy and physics, and so forth. Today's world is based, in large part, on information, and it is in response to the needs of information technology and a society built around that technology that much of the work described in this book is being carried out. Attempts to meet the challenges of the information age led at first to advances in technology, in particular, computer and communications technology. Indeed, in many ways it was the development of the technology that *produced* the information age. More recently, however, mathematicians and scientists have come to realize that the truly difficult problems of the information age are not technological; rather, they concern *ourselves*—what it is to think, to reason, and to engage in conversation. Meeting these challenges will almost certainly require new kinds of science—or, if you want to reserve the title 'science' for the traditions begun by Galileo, Bacon, and Descartes—new analytic techniques, new conceptual tools with which to analyze and understand the workings of the human mind.

What do you need in order to read this book? Curiosity, and nothing more. Curiosity about science, logic, and mathematics, but most of all, curiosity about ourselves, about what it is to be human. You will not find complete answers to all the questions raised between the covers of this book. You won't find answers to these questions in any book. No one has all the answers. What we have are partial answers, pieces of a giant puzzle whose solution we have not yet found—indeed, we may never find the complete solution.

Though the approach I take is that of a mathematician—particularly a logician, as logic is my specialty—there is little in the way of difficult mathematics in these pages. You will find a few formulas here and there and the occasional technical discussion. Nothing is included that requires any prior knowledge of mathematics beyond the high school level—and all you need from that is to have encountered the use of algebraic notation. On the other hand, it is not an easy book to read. The mathematics may be minimal, but the topic itself is difficult. After all, if the workings of the human mind were not difficult to study, we would be little different from rocks or vegetables. Ultimately, the complexity lies not in the science I describe but in the nature of the human mind.

People I meet sometimes ask me how long it has taken me to write a particular book. I usually give the only truly honest answer, "N months," where N is my age in months on the day the book is completed. Any book is the product of a lifetime of experiences. It is also true that any book is the product not just of one mind but of a great many minds, the minds of the people with whom the author has interacted. Among those whose interactions have contributed significantly to this particular book are my many colleagues at Stanford University's Center for the Study of Language and Information (CSLI), which has provided me with an excellent environment to pursue my interests over the past nine years. Various parts of the manuscript for this book have benefited enormously from feedback from my colleagues Stanley Peters, Livia Polanyi, Duska Rosenberg, and David Israel. My editor at John Wiley & Sons, Emily Loose, was enthusiastic about this project before the first words were written. She continued to be enormously supportive throughout, providing constant feedback and advice as I struggled to find ways to make a mountain of highly technical, abstract science accessible to that mythical creature, 'the general reader.'

Finally, a word about footnotes. In this book, except for some chapter openings, there aren't any. Though footnotes are appropriate in a book intended for heavy-duty study, I find them an annoyance in a book designed to be read from cover to cover. Their use is a distraction exceeded only by the even worse practice of endnotes—footnotes relegated to the back of the book. If I think a particular piece of information is important to the development of my theme, I include it as part of the main text, and where I need to make reference to a specific source, I do so in the text. At the end of the book I provide a list of suggested further reading. Any reader who wishes to use this book as the start of a serious, in-depth study should begin by looking at some of the books listed there.

Keith Devlin

Moraga, California
January, 1996

Goodbye,
Descartes

1

PATTERNS
OF MIND

Question: How many psychotherapists does it take to
to change a lightbulb?

Answer: One. But only if, deep down, the lightbulb
is willing to change.

—Anonymous

WE ALL DO IT

The quotation above is yet another in the seemingly endless stream of lightbulb jokes. It is, of course, just a joke, and not particularly brilliant as those jokes go. But for all its triviality, it illustrates two fascinating—and far from trivial—features of the human mind: our abilities to use language and to think.

Practically every mature person can use language to communicate. Moreover, it takes no conscious effort to use language, at least for everyday conversation and reading. We use language to transfer thoughts or ideas from one human mind to another easily and, generally, with great precision. The information or idea transferred may be fairly straightforward, or it may be more complicated, as with the lightbulb joke. With that joke, reading the words and knowing what each word means is only a small part of what it takes to understand it. Almost certainly, you recognized at once that it was a joke and not something to be taken literally. How did you do that? If you had not seen this joke before, you probably found it amusing. Why? What is it exactly about this sequence of sentences that makes it a 'joke'? How much general knowledge of the world do we need in order to recognize the quotation as a joke, to be amused by it, and to explain why it is amusing? And how can we access and process that knowledge so quickly and without any perceptible effort? What is it

1

that leads us at once to the appropriate two meanings of the word *change* out of the many different meanings this word has—two meanings that are in general unrelated, but that have to be brought together and contrasted in order for the joke to work? And finally, how is it that you almost certainly failed to observe that one of the quoted sentences is ungrammatical? You don't believe me? Take another look. You still don't see anything wrong? Most people don't. *Not* seeing anything wrong with the quotation is yet another illustration of our incredible facility with language. We are so good at it that we generally read what we *think* is there, rather than what is actually there. In this case, among the things that are actually there is a repetition of the word *to* in the first sentence. (Ah, now you see it. And from now on, you will never fail to see it. We are also very good at learning from our mistakes.)

If you are reading these words, then you must be a member of the animal species known as *Homo sapiens*—the thinking hominid, man. You possess a brain that, thanks to a million years of evolution, is equipped to reason, to reflect, to make decisions and guide your actions in a rational manner, and to use language to communicate. Your survival in the world, and the survival of your fellow humans, long ceased to depend upon raw strength, speed, and a thick coat of fur. Instead, you rely, often subconsciously, on your brain. For the most part, you act rationally. This is why people so often comment when someone behaves in a way that seems irrational. The two things that distinguish us from our fellow creatures are our ability to communicate and our ability to reason. These two facilities are the very essence of what it is to be human. And since the dawn of the Age of Reason in ancient Greece, mankind has sought to understand these abilities—to explain how we communicate and how we reason.

PATTERNS OF THOUGHT

Efforts to provide a scientific explanation of 'rational thought' have led to the large and impressive body of learning known as *logic*. Of course, logic is not the only product of all that effort—sociology, psychology, and cognitive science also have their origins, at least in part, in the study of rationality. However, though we shall encounter each of these other disciplines along the way, logic is the central theme of this book.

As a scientific theory of reasoning, logic tries to explain how people make 'perfect' deductions (when they do). Aristotle and Plato were two of the earliest pioneers of the field. Aristotle tried to analyze logical thinking—and thereby logical discourse—in terms of simple inference rules called *syllogisms*. These are rules for deducing one assertion from exactly two others. An example of a syllogism is:

All men are mortal.
Socrates is a man.

Socrates is mortal.

The idea is that the third assertion, the one below the line, follows logically from the previous two. In the case of this simple example, this deduction certainly seems correct enough, albeit pretty obvious. But as with any scientific explanation, the idea is to uncover general patterns that apply in many instances. In the case of the above syllogism, it is obvious that there is a general pattern, namely:

All M are P.
S is a M.

S is P.

This *general deduction rule* is true whatever M, P, and S may be. Some of the other syllogisms Aristotle formulated are less obvious. For example, the following rule is valid, but you have to think quite a bit to convince yourself that this is so:

No M is P.
Some S is M.

Some S is not P.

Aristotle's proposal was that any logical argument can, in principle, be broken down into a series of applications of a small number of syllogisms, and he set out to find all the syllogisms involved in logical reasoning. He listed a total of nineteen, though as we shall see in Chapter 2, some of the ones on his list were subsequently shown to be invalid.

As it turned out, the syllogism was found to be too restrictive. There are logically valid arguments that cannot be broken down into a series of syllogisms, no matter how finely those arguments are analyzed. Nevertheless, Aristotle's attempt was one of the first to analyze logical thought, and for that alone his prominent place in history is well deserved.

In the centuries following Aristotle, various people tried to extend his theory, including, notably, Gottfried Leibniz in the seventeenth century, George Boole in the nineteenth century, and Gottlob Frege in the early twentieth century. More recently, the twentieth century has seen a veritable explosion of such efforts.

As logic developed, it gained in stature, and by the beginning of the twentieth century, there was a growing belief that logic could provide a single, all-powerful, and fundamental framework for precise explanations of all reasoning and rational behavior. This view was adopted with particular force by an intellectual group that emerged in the 1930s called the logical positivists. It arose again in a slightly different guise in the 1950s with the birth of the disciplines of artificial intelligence and cognitive science.

Artificial intelligence (AI) sets out to build computer programs that can reason and make 'logical' decisions. Such programs work by encoding rules of logic into the language of the computer, in much the same way computers can be made to solve mathematical equations by encoding the rules of algebra and arithmetic. Cognitive scientists try to use AI programs to help understand how the brain works—the computer program provides a model of various thought processes that can be examined in greater detail, and with more precision, than can be done with the human mind.

Behind most of the major advances in logic throughout its two-thousand-year history lay the following view of the way the mind works: Rational ('logical') thought is a kind of mental calculation that follows certain prescribed rules, in many ways not unlike arithmetic. Plato thought this, as did Leibniz and Boole. It is the key motivating idea for artificial intelligence and much of cognitive science. And the view of the mind as a calculator following certain rules also led to recent attempts to use logic to describe language.

LOGIC AND LANGUAGE

There has been a connection between logic and the analysis of language ever since logic began. Because logical deductions are expressed using language, it follows that practically all of logic must involve a study of language in some sense. For example, Aristotle's syllogisms describe how sentences of certain forms follow logically from pairs of sentences having certain other forms. That is, Aristotle's logical patterns depend on certain linguistic patterns.

Twentieth-century logic—described in Chapter 4—likewise seeks to describe patterns of reasoning in terms of patterns of language. Approaching reason through language seems unavoidable. Thought takes place in our minds, and we cannot (at least not yet) see inside the mind. (We can, of course, think about what is going on in our minds, but that just leads to more thought that we cannot see!) What we can see are the outputs from the mind, namely, the words we speak and the actions we perform. Our thoughts can be expressed in language, and it is through language that they take observable shape. Sometimes we even think directly in language, hearing an internal voice in our minds. Thus, language provides us with a kind of window to the mind, and one of the goals of logic throughout its history has been to investigate patterns of language as a way to uncover patterns of thought.

Starting with the work of the American linguist Noam Chomsky in the 1950s, contemporary linguists have tried to go in the other direction: Instead of looking at language to understand reasoning, as the logicians did, they have tried to use techniques of logic to study language. This approach rests on the assumption that language is generated and understood according to rules much like the rules of logic—indeed, that language is a logical phenomenon.

For instance, Chomsky's own early work involved the formulation of rules that determine when a particular sequence of words is a grammatical sentence. This is analogous to Aristotle's attempt to write down rules that said which sequences of assertions constitute a valid deduction. Chomsky referred to such sentence-formation rules as constituting a *grammar.* This use of the word should not be confused with *style grammar,* which stipulates the etiquette of correct speech or good writing. An example of a rule in a Chomsky-style grammar would be if you write down the definite article *the* followed by a noun, then a verb followed by another *the,* and then another noun, the result will be a sentence. For example:

The + train + approach + the + station = The train approach the station.

As this example demonstrates, Chomsky's concept of a generative grammar is quite different from our standard notion of grammar. Though the resulting sentence is understandable, it is not grammatical. To obtain a genuinely grammatical sentence, the rule needs some modification, to address issues of verb tense or case agreement. In Chapters 5 and 6 we will see how Chomsky developed more sophisticated rules to account for such issues and how his ideas provide a powerful framework for studying the underlying mental ability that makes language possible.

Thus, by the middle of the twentieth century, logicians were basing their work on studies of linguistic patterns, and linguists were using ideas and techniques of logic in order to study language. However, there was little attempt made to explore the underlying mental connections between reasoning and language ability—to study reasoning and language as two aspects of a single human phenomenon. That step was only taken within roughly the last twenty years.

Contemporary researchers have probed more deeply for a single, unifying theory of reasoning and language ability as a result of a growing awareness that the rules that had been proposed for reasoning and for language use were severely limited in their ability to generate anything close to the actual reasoning and language abilities of the human mind. It became clear that following the rules was just not enough. There had to be more going on in the human mind than a rule-based, logically structured thought process. Logicians and linguists were forced to face this fact when they tried to use their specified rules to generate artificial versions of human abilities. Both groups, logicians and linguists alike, ran into seemingly insurmountable obstacles. After a forty-year period when logic seemed on the verge of providing a scientific understanding of reasoning and language—perhaps comparable to the way physics provides a scientific understanding of the universe—high, solid walls suddenly barred the way to further progress.

The Language Wall

In linguistics, by the late 1950s, increasingly sophisticated logic-based theories of language offered the prospect of programming computers to understand and produce ordinary language. Computers are logic machines, and if we could describe ordinary language using logic, the argument went, we could instruct computers to understand and produce humanlike language—a goal known as *natural-language processing*. By the early 1960s, predictions were made that before the end of the century, people would communicate with computers by speaking to them and listening to them, just as we do with each other. However, those predictions did not come true, and the greater the attempts, the more it became clear that they probably never will. Thousands of hours of effort by brilliant computer scientists, mathematicians, linguists, and systems engineers have yet to produce an interactive help facility on a photocopier that is even remotely as good as an office junior, just out of high school, who has had an hour's instruction on using the machine. Within a few months of first learning to talk, a small child can produce and understand sentences that baffle the most sophisticated computer system.

This does not mean that work on natural-language processing systems was a waste of time. For one thing, considerable improvements in computer system design have resulted from such work. For another, the failure to re-create the linguistic abilities of even a small child has increased our understanding of just how complex language is—both in its structure and how we use it. Every piece of data we encounter that defies our existing understanding of language leads to greater insight and comprehension, as we examine the data in greater and greater detail. For instance, though each of the linguistic examples listed below involve phenomena that have defeated attempts to develop natural-language processing systems, examination of such examples has helped linguists develop better theories of language:

- Faced with a sign that says

    SAFETY GOGGLES MUST ALWAYS BE WORN INSIDE THE BUILDING

who would have any doubt as to what to do when entering the building? And yet, faced with the superficially similar sign

    DOGS MUST ALWAYS BE CARRIED ON THE ESCALATOR

a person sensible enough to look around for a pair of goggles to put on when faced with the first sign would surely not head off in search of a dog before stepping onto the escalator.

- Imagine a computer system that has been programmed to read newspaper announcements of marriages and update its database of married couples. Presented with the headline

    JOHN SMITH TO MARRY MARY JONES

the computer would record, correctly, the forthcoming union of Smith and Jones. But how would the system cope with the headline

    RETIRED PRIEST WILL MARRY BRUCE SPRINGSTEEN

that actually appeared a few years ago?

- People have no difficulty identifying the subject and verb in the two sentences

    Time flies like an arrow.
    Fruit flies like an apple.

but how do they do it? More specifically, how do they do it when they encounter these two sentences for the very first time? For that matter, how is it that practically every day we manage to correctly produce and understand sentences that we have never uttered or encountered before, in some cases sentences that nobody else in the world has ever uttered before, such as the very sentence you are now reading?

- If you started to read a story that began

    Noam set off on a trip to the beach.
    The car ran out of gas.

and I asked you what mode of transport Noam used, you would have no
trouble in providing the answer: by car. And yet this information is not
explicitly provided by the two sentences. Nowhere is anything said about
the manner in which Noam traveled to the beach; rather you *inferred*
your answer. What would your answer have been if, just before you
started to read the story, you were told that Noam and Linda had just
had an awful row and Linda had taken the car to drive to her mother's?
Or, what would your reply be if the story started this way:

    Noam set off on a trip to the beach.
    The car was still in the repair shop.

- The following sentence was proposed by Chomsky:

    Colorless green ideas sleep furiously.

Most people would agree with Chomsky that this is a sentence, even
though it is quite meaningless. What exactly is it that distinguishes a
sentence from a nonsentence sequence of words? Most people would
agree that the following is a much 'better' English sentence than the one
above:

    Many biologists are fascinated by the A-spinelli Morphenium.

And yet, it could be argued that whereas the 'green ideas' sentence is nonsensical, this new example is not even a sentence of English at all. For the
fact is, *A-spinelli* and *Morphenium* are not words of the English language;
I simply made them up. It seems that the entities we recognize as 'sentences' do not have to have any meaning, nor do all the constituents have
to be genuine words. So what does it take to make a sentence? Since the
human mind is able to distinguish sentences from nonsentences without
effort, any light we can throw onto the issue of what constitutes a sentence will surely tell us quite a lot about our minds.

- The following two sentences differ only in the last word.

    The boys drank two cups of cocoa because they were warm.
    The boys drank two cups of cocoa because they were cold.

One would expect that changing *warm* to *cold* alters the meaning of a
sentence (and perhaps whether it is true or not), but in this case it also

alters the entire grammatical structure. In the first sentence the pronoun *they* refers to the cocoa, and in the second, *they* refers to the boys. The examples given earlier might suggest that sentence structure is independent of meaning, but this example suggests that things are not quite so simple. Here is another example where the grammatical structure changes when we alter one word:

> *Susan saw the man in the park with a dog.*
> *Susan saw the man in the park with a statue.*
> *Susan saw the man in the park with a telescope.*

These all have the general form *Susan saw the man in the park with a X.* But where is, or who has, the X? It depends on what the X is—dog, statue, or telescope. A fascinating aspect of these three sentences is that, once again, the differences in sentence structure are quite obvious to us. The fact that in general we understand such sentences without having to reason them out suggests that the method by which we understand sentences of our language is a fundamental feature of our minds. The same general remark also applies to our next example.

■ How is it that the sentence

> *The sun was already setting when a small*
> *sailboat slipped into the harbor.*

conjures up a visual image in the mind, but the following sentence does not?

> *Linguistics is a fascinating subject that interests*
> *a number of mathematicians.*

■ Our final example. Jan looks up from her book and says

> *Are you cold?*

and Keith gets up and closes the window. Both agree that Keith's action was a reasonable response to Jan's remark. But why? On the face of it, Jan was asking a question. And yet, had Keith simply answered the question, looking back at Jan and replying, truthfully, "yes," his response would be judged by most observers as inappropriate. Though the words Jan utters constitute, on the face of it, a question about Keith's physical state, what Jan *means,* and what her words convey, is that she wants Keith to perform a certain action, namely, to close the window. And yet Jan makes no direct reference to either the window or the action of closing it. How is it that language functions in this way?

It seems, then, that there is a lot more to language than strings of words, whether those words are printed on a page or riding through the air on a wave of sound. The examples listed above are all ones that have caused immense problems for linguists trying to develop scientific theories of language and for computer scientists attempting to write computer programs to 'understand' everyday human language. And yet they are extremely simple examples. How can such simple sentences cause so much difficulty?

Modern science has been remarkably successful in understanding the inner workings of the atom, the structure of the distant stars, and the origins of the universe. And yet we have been far less successful in understanding the thought processes involved in the everyday use of language. Why?

One possibility is that we have been approaching the task in the wrong way. During the past decade, an increasing number of linguists have begun to consider that possibility.

At the same time, cognitive scientists have run into similar doubts about the way they had been using logic to understand reasoning. For they too suddenly came up against a wall—the logic wall.

THE LOGIC WALL

By the 1970s, artificial intelligence and cognitive science—both based on logic—had chalked up a number of impressive successes. Many people predicted still further advances in the application of logic, to the point where it could be used not only to explain logical behavior in humans but even to enable us to design computers that could think and act like a human. For instance, in the book *The Micro Millenium,* published in 1979, Christopher Evans made the following prediction:

> We are about to embark on a massive programme to develop highly intelligent machines, a process by which we will lead computers by the hand until they reach our own intellectual level, after which they will proceed to surpass us. . . . It is unlikely there will be any serious objections to this apart from those of an emotional or doctrinaire nature. (p. 195.)

In a similar vein, Robert Jastrow, writing in *Science Digest* in June of 1982, presented the following vision of a world where we each had a personal robot:

> Just pick them up, tuck them under your arm, and go off to attend to your business. They will be Artoo-Deetoos without wheels: brilliant, but nice personalities, never sarcastic, always giving you a straight answer—little elec-

tronic friends that can solve all your problems. ("The Thinking Computer,"
p. 107.)

A year later, Marvin Minsky, head of the Artificial Intelligence Laboratory at the Massachussetts Institute of Technology, had similar things to
say:

> Today our robots are like toys. They do only the simple things they're pro-
> grammed to do. But clearly they're about to cross the edgeless line past
> which they'll do all the things we are programmed to. . . . What will happen
> when we face new options in our work and home, where more intelligent
> machines can better do the things we like to do? What kinds of minds and
> personalities should we dispense to them? What kind of rights and privileges
> should we withhold from them? (*Omni,* April 1983.)

Besides these predictions, there were grand expectations for military
applications. In the United States, in the 1980s, billions of dollars were
thrown into the Strategic Defense Initiative, the Star Wars nuclear defense
shield that would entrust the safety of two hundred million Americans—
and in the nuclear age, millions more elsewhere in the world—to a computer program. In its March 11, 1985 issue, *Time* magazine described the
Star Wars system like this:

> Humans would make the key strategic decisions in advance, determining un-
> der what conditions the missile defense would start firing, and devise a com-
> puter system that could translate those decisions into a program. In the end
> the defensive response would be out of human hands: [I]t would be activated
> by computer before U.S. commanders even knew that a battle had begun.

With the stakes so high, it is a sobering fact to realize that today, as
the computer age approaches its fiftieth birthday, the interactive, com-
puter-controlled, electromechanical system generally regarded as the most
reliable and the easiest for humans to use—and then only because of an
enormous human effort that has gone into its design and repeated im-
provement—is the automatic teller machine outside your bank. You
know, the machine that tells you that it is "unable to carry out your trans-
action at the present time" but which cannot be persuaded to tell you
why.

The difficulty in designing such a seemingly simple device as an automatic teller machine is one of the things that has made it increasingly
clear over the past twenty years just how hard it is to simulate even very
simple and routine human thought processes. Computers are extremely
good at following precise instructions. They follow the rules of logic with
impeccable accuracy. Unfortunately, many aspects of what we generally

refer to as logical thought and logical behavior do not follow rules of logic at all—at least, this is unfortunate for those whose dreams of a utopian future were based on the breathless prose of all those 1970s and 1980s books and magazine articles.

Teenage smoking provides a familiar example of a human activity that seems to defy logic. Smoking is known to be seriously detrimental to health. It is clearly logical to want to remain healthy. On those grounds, it would appear to be logical not to start smoking. But many young people take up smoking. Are they being illogical? Not necessarily. It is important to young people in particular to be accepted by their peers, to appear adult and cool, and occasionally to do things that are frowned upon, and perhaps even forbidden, by their parents and teachers. From that standpoint, it is perfectly logical to take up smoking. The point is, in human terms logical behavior is not an absolute notion; it is relative. It depends on what the individual wants to achieve. What is logical to the teenage smoker is not what is logical to his or her physician.

Here is another example of seemingly illogical behavior, one we shall return to later. About twenty years ago, the French magazine *Le Nouvel Observateur* published the results of a national survey on the subjective factors that contribute to happiness and unhappiness. Despite its seeming similarity to the superficial surveys published regularly in the United States in *Cosmopolitan* and similar magazines, this particular survey was a well-constructed, scientific investigation, designed according to the most reliable statistical techniques. According to the poll, the most important single factor that contributed to personal happiness was "another person." Second was "the full realization of one's own potential." Money was ranked well down on the list, and in last place was "to be in good health." All of this probably strikes you as quite reasonable. However, what seems on the surface to be contradictory was that the same poll put *not* being in good health as the most important factor in causing *un*happiness.

Were the respondents in the French survey being illogical? Well, if by 'illogical' you mean acting in a fashion that violates strict adherence to the rules of logic, the answer is yes. But the respondents were surely not being illogical in an everyday sense. Rather their rankings reflected a common human tendency to devalue things that are considered 'givens', part of the status quo. If we are in good health, we rarely reflect on the matter. But if we are ill, we are constantly aware of the fact and of how it affects everything we do. When asked what contributes to our happiness, we generally *presuppose* good health—the normal state. On the other hand, when asked to list factors that cause us to be unhappy, then ill health—an abnormal state—is a very significant factor, and indeed, the French respondents ranked it number one.

The following pair of scenarios provide still another example where seemingly rational people act in a manner that is contrary to the rules of logic.

■ You spend $100 on a (nonrefundable) ticket to a concert you particularly want to attend. (The figure of $100 is not in itself important. What counts is that it is an amount that you regard as 'significant', and would generally reflect on carefully before spending.) The concert is in a city sixty miles away, and on the day of the concert, there is a fierce snowstorm. You know that it will take at least two hours of difficult driving to get there, and two more equally difficult hours to return home afterwards. What do you do? Most people would go anyway, justifying their decision on the grounds that the ticket has already been bought and it would be silly to waste that expense.

■ You missed buying a ticket in advance. On the day of the concert a friend, a very timid driver who will do anything to avoid driving in bad weather, offers to give you his ticket for free, with no strings attached. What do you do? Most 'rational' people would refuse, saying to themselves, "Hey, the weather is terrible, and it's not worth the effort, even though I have the offer of a free ticket."

Both decisions would seem quite reasonable to most people. And yet they cannot both be logical in any absolute sense. In the first case, your decision to attend the concert indicates that you think it is worth $100 plus four hours of difficult driving to attend the concert. In the second case, your decision not to attend indicates that you think it is not worth $100 plus four hours of difficult driving. True, in the first case the $100 has already been spent, whereas in the second case you are simply rejecting a gift worth $100. In both scenarios, however, by the morning after the concert you are down $100, either because you spent the money on the ticket in the first scenario or because you turned down an offer of a ticket worth $100 in the second scenario. In the strictly monetary terms of profit and loss, the two scenarios are entirely equivalent. But in the first scenario you go; in the second, you don't. Just what is it that leads you to make this decision? We can assume that your underlying desire to attend the concert is the same in both cases—it is, after all, the *same* concert in the two scenarios—so that's not the reason.

In fact, the answer is not to be found in a simple mathematical or economic analysis. Rather, the issue seems to be one of making a commitment to yourself. Having committed to themselves to attend the concert in the first scenario, most people are extremely reluctant to change their plans, and are generally prepared to invest further resources in order to be able to fulfill the commitment. To stay at home having bought the ticket leaves them with a feeling of having wasted the original expenditure of $100. On the other hand, if there is no prior commitment, as in the second scenario, people generally find it easy to simply say no and forego the gift of a $100 ticket. Moreover, in this case they are not left with any sense of having wasted $100; when they turn down the offer of the ticket, they do not think of the $100 as ever having been their money to waste.

"Aha," you say, "so there you have the missing factor that results in the two seemingly contradictory behaviors. It is self-commitment." That's a fair observation. The question is, how can this insight be incorporated into a scientific theory of rational behavior? Answering questions such as this provided one of the key leads to the emerging new science of human reasoning described in the latter part of this book.

ROGER: THE IRRATIONAL MAN OF LOGIC

I once had a colleague—I will call him Roger—who had adopted the idea of logical thought in a big way. A competent mathematician and a veritable whiz at computing, Roger believed in using the principles of logical reasoning in all aspects of his professional and everyday life. Whenever he was faced with making a decision, he would collect all the available evidence, weigh it carefully, and then look for the course of action that logically followed. In the absence of sufficient evidence, he would, whenever possible, avoid the issue altogether, claiming that he could not make any decision at all. In short, Roger tried to run his life along the clear, unambiguous, logical lines of a digital computer.

Do you know, he kept running into obstacle after obstacle. Things kept going wrong for Roger. Whenever this happened, he would carefully analyze his reasoning to see where he had gone astray, to see at what point he had violated one of the rules of logic. Generally finding nothing amiss with his line of reasoning, he would lament the fact that other people, the people he had to deal with, had not functioned to the same computer level of logical precision as he had, and that the problem lay with them.

For example, the occasion arose when he did not submit a case for promotion at his job on the grounds that the instructions asked that the employee list "all relevant activities" but left it to the individual to decide what should count as relevant. In the first of a lengthy series of carefully crafted memos, Roger asked for clarification of the term *relevant*. "Relevant to what?" he asked. He was informed that he should provide information on activities relevant to his performance, and hence to his professional advancement. In response, he argued at great length that everything he had done in his entire life surely had some relevance. Needless to say, Roger's superiors quickly tired of this exchange, and no promotion ensued.

It would be tempting to think that Roger was simply trying to make some kind of point—though it is hard to see what exactly that point might be—except for the fact that this kind of behavior was typical for him. Whenever he was asked to perform some task, he would first consult the job handbook to see how to proceed, and then would try to follow the handbook's procedures in a completely literal fashion. As soon as he encountered a word or term in the instructions that was open to interpretation (which was on almost every occasion), he would be thrown into a turmoil of indecision.

'Illogical Roger' and 'black-and-white Roger' were the names given to him—in his absence—by many of his colleagues. He was valued for his skill with computers, but in the category of common sense he was a nonstarter. Those who had witnessed his prowess at resolving problems with their desktop PCs explained his strange, 'illogical' behavior as resulting from his continuous attempt to operate like a computer.

There seems to be a paradox here. Anyone familiar with the basic principles of computing knows that the modern digital computer operates by following to the letter the rules of logic. And yet when a person tries to function in the manner of a computer, as Roger did, the result is often behavior that strikes most people as illogical.

The source of this computer-age conundrum lies in the distinction between logic and rationality. At the micro level, computers do indeed operate according to the rules of logic, but that does not mean that their resulting behavior will be *rational* in human terms. Strictly speaking, logical behavior means behavior that follows certain prescribed rules—the rules of logic. Rational behavior refers to activities that make sense to a person in terms of the goals, desires, and capabilities of that person, based on the prevailing circumstances. As a result of two thousand years of development in logic, it is quite common for logicians, and others having some familiarity with logic, to assume that rational actions can be captured by various formal rules. This was precisely the mistake made by Roger. The odd thing was that he continued to make the same mistake, even though he rarely achieved the goals toward which his rule-based behavior was supposedly directed. On the other hand, maybe Roger's persistence, though extreme, is not so incredible. After all, the confusion of logic with rationality and the mistaken belief that logic can capture or explain rationality continue to this day, despite the growing evidence to the contrary that has been amassed during the last forty years.

Against all odds

Given the examples in the previous sections, should we continue to use the two words *rational* and *logical* as if they mean the same thing? According to the definition given in the *Oxford English Dictionary*, rational means

> . . . endowed with reason, reasoning; sensible, sane, moderate, not foolish or absurd or extreme; of or based on reasoning or reason, rejecting what is unreasonable or cannot be tested by reason in religion or custom.

Logic is defined as

> . . . the science of reasoning, proof, thinking, or inference.

The definition given for rational seems to agree with both the everyday and the scientific uses of the word, but there is a problem with the definition for logic. Since at least the early twentieth century, logic has been understood, by scientists at least, to mean the formulation of precise rules of inference. In this widely used sense of the word, logic is a well-established scientific discipline that provides a precise definition of what it means to be logical. That is, behavior or thought is said to be logical if it obeys the rules of logic. On the other hand, as we saw in the previous two sections, there are many cases where a person behaves in a way that does not follow the rules of logic, but where the behavior is clearly 'rational', from that individual's perspective. Recognizing the possible confusion caused by the modern, technical meaning of the word logic, the professionals in the logic world generally use the word logical to mean 'according to the rules of logic' and rational to mean 'rational from the perspective of the individual'.

Unfortunately, the waters are still muddy, since there are occasions when a rational person will act in a way that is not only illogical (in the strict sense), but is not at all in the person's best interest.

The example described below shows that a person's presumed rational behavior can fly in the face of both cold, hard logic and rational self-interest. It is generally referred to as the 'Monty Hall problem', after the host of a now defunct but once popular American TV quiz show, *Let's*

Make a Deal. A particularly intriguing aspect of this example is that, even when the correct choice is explained and justified, many otherwise rational and intelligent people continue to feel 'in their bones' that the argument must be wrong and that their ingrained instincts are more reliable.

To begin with, imagine yourself a contestant on a quiz show. At a certain moment in the show, the host, Monty, directs your attention to three doors. You are told that behind one of them is a chest containing ten thousand dollars; behind each of the other two doors is a banana. You can pick one door and keep what you find behind it. From his position on the stage, Monty can see behind the doors. He knows where the money is, but you do not. He is skilled at his job and gives you no clue as to which door leads to the money.

If you were to make a random choice, what would be your chances of picking the door shielding the ten thousand dollars? Everyone answers "one-in-three" to this question, and that is correct (assuming everything is set up as I have described it).

But that is not the way the game is played. What happens is this. After you tell Monty your choice, your chosen door is not opened. Instead, Monty opens one of the remaining two doors to reveal a banana. Since he knows the location of the money, he can, of course, always do this—you are choosing randomly, but he is not. (I should stress that you, the contestant in the show, are aware that Monty knows where the money is located. This is a crucial piece of information.) Having eliminated one of the other two doors as concealing the money, Monty now makes you an offer: Do you want to stick with your original choice of doors, or would you rather switch to the other unopened door? It will cost you ten dollars to make the switch.

The most common response people give when presented with this scenario is that changing their original choice does not make any difference to their chances of winning the money. "The odds remain the same," they declare. So they decide not to pay the ten dollars to make the switch; they stay with their first choice.

What would you do in the same situation: switch or stay? Would you agree with the majority of the people presented with this problem, who believe there is nothing to be gained, and ten dollars to lose, by changing doors? If you did, then you would be wrong. Switching doors *doubles* your chance of winning the ten thousand dollars. That's right, your chance of winning increases by a factor of two if you switch doors: The odds leap up from the initial one-in-three of your first choice to a very favorable two-in-three. A participant in the real quiz show would be crazy not to switch!

This example is notorious for leading otherwise sane and rational citizens to heights of frenzied argument. I have known people who could never be convinced by the rock-solid mathematical argument that switching doors changes the odds in your favor from 1/3 to 2/3.

For the record, here is that argument. (If you don't want to know, just skip to the next section.) After you make your first choice, there is a 1/3 chance that you have chosen the door that hides the money. Since the probabilities of all possible outcomes must add up to 1, the probability that the money lies behind one of the other two doors is 2/3. If you had to choose between those two doors *at random,* then that 2/3 would split into two 1/3s, one for each door. In that situation, namely, making a random switch, your odds would not change. But things are not random. Monty opens one of the two doors to reveal a banana. The probability that the money lies behind one of the two doors you did not originally choose remains 2/3, but Monty eliminates one of those two as leading to the money. He is able to do this because he knows where the money is located. (Remember, I told you this was a crucial piece of information.) Since the opened door may now be eliminated as the one hiding the money, those attractive 2/3 odds in favor of the money being behind one of the *two* doors you did not choose now amount to 2/3 odds in favor of the *one* unopened door not chosen. Hence, you should jump at the chance to change your choice of doors. Of course, you may lose by doing so. This is, after all, a game of chance. If your first guess had been correct, then switching will change your position from winning to losing. But in terms of the odds, it is always better to switch. If you were to play this game repeatedly and consistently adopt the switching strategy, then while losing approximately one-third of the time, you would win, on average, two out of three times. You would win twice as often as you would lose.

The Monty Hall problem is one in which the person who wants to win ten thousand dollars *can* act in an entirely rational way. The mathematical analysis of the problem just given is completely correct and tells you exactly what to do, namely, switch on every occasion. Yet the majority of rational people not only adopt the wrong strategy, the illogical one of staying with their original choice, they also have great difficulty in coming to terms with the fact that switching is always advantageous. So what is going on? In the final chapter, I'll say exactly what I think the issue is. In the meantime, here are some initial thoughts.

Though few people bother to calculate odds mathematically in their daily lives, evolution has equipped most of us with the ability to make estimates of odds. We do it all the time. Instead of stating numerical odds, we often use phrases such as 'a considerable risk', 'too risky', 'about fifty-

fifty', 'better than even', or 'a near certainty'. Such estimates can be reliable, but numerous studies have shown that they are generally far less reliable than we might imagine.

In the case of the Monty Hall problem, there is something about the way our minds evaluate chances that is *highly* misleading; in that case, it is not a question of a minor change in odds, since switching doors changes the odds from being two-to-one against you (probability 1/3) to being two-to-one in your favor (probability 2/3).

What the Monty Hall problem tells us is that, on occasion, our so-called rationality not only leads us to make decisions that contradict the hard facts of logic, it can make it extremely difficult for us even to see where we have gone wrong when it is pointed out to us.

THE MORAL OF THE LOST CAR KEYS

The development of logic during the twentieth century has made it not more, but steadily less, suitable as a framework to analyze and explain human behavior. These days, logic tends to be presented and studied in a highly mathematical way. Moreover, much of the development of logic over the last one hundred years has been guided in large part by *mathematical* applications, in particular the desire of mathematicians to understand mathematical (as opposed to everyday) reasoning. Rational behavior, on the other hand, is essentially a psychological or sociological notion. This is not to say that mathematical techniques cannot be used in psychology or sociology; indeed, in the latter part of this book I describe some new mathematical techniques that can be applied in these disciplines. However, it would be surprising indeed if a mathematical theory designed to handle the issues of mathematical reasoning were appropriate for the task of understanding rational human behavior. It is not.

Nevertheless, each new generation of researchers seems to produce a group who are convinced that they can succeed where all before have failed. Inspired by the apparent scope and power of logic, they make new attempts to build computer systems that can carry out simple, everyday reasoning or can understand simple, everyday language. At first, such attempts produce some hopeful signs—or at least some claims—that the long-elusive breakthrough is, at last, just around the corner. Then, despite the clever new ideas, those attempts eventually run up against a wall—the logic wall or the language wall. Faced with such a record of failures, you might wonder why anyone continues to make the attempt. Well, one perfectly reasonable reason would be that you don't abandon a method just because you haven't got it to work so far; maybe you just need to work harder. But there is another explanation, one that a growing number of people suspect is closer to the truth: This explanation might be termed *conceptual momentum*. This phenomenon was nicely summarized by the physicist J. Robert Oppenheimer, who directed the project to develop the atomic bomb during the latter years of the Second World War. In 1963, in an article entitled "Communication and Comprehension of Scientific Knowledge," he wrote:

> We come to our new problems full of old ideas and old words, not only the inevitable words of daily life, but those which experience has shown to be fruitful over the years. . . . We love the old words, the old imagery, and the old analogies, and we keep them for more and more unfamiliar and more unrecognizable things. (*Science,* vol. 124, p. 1144.)

Not only do we feel comfortable with logic—"the old words" and "the old imagery"—but it has an impressive pedigree. Beginning with the work of Aristotle and other Greek thinkers, and developing through the ages to the work of Boole and others in the nineteenth century and a small army of logicians in the twentieth century, logic has developed into a rich and powerful subject with many successful applications to its credit. Faced with such credentials, it is hard to face the fact that if we really want to understand how people reason and how they use language to communicate, then we may have to abandon many of our cherished notions of logic.

But abandon those old notions we must. In recent years, faced with failure after failure in trying to apply logic in AI and cognitive science, a growing number of experts have become convinced that attempts to apply logic to reasoning and communication are misguided. To such people, those continued attempts are reminiscent of the man who, upon losing his keys as he steps from his car late one night, walks along the road a bit and starts to crawl around on the pavement under the street light. He knows, of course, that he is unlikely to find his keys there. After all, he dropped them by the car. So why does he continue to look where he does? "Because," he says, "the light is better here."

In the chapters that follow, we will discover why we need to start looking for the keys where the light is poor. But in order to understand why such a move is necessary, we first need to become familiar with the developments that led to such a powerful light shining in one particular location. For some of the very features that are measures of success in the two-thousand-year development of logic turn out to be the very sources of its limitations.

2

A PASSION
FOR ORDER

*Bachelors and Masters of Arts who do not follow Aristotle's philoso-
phy are subject to a fine of five shillings for each point of divergence,
as well as for infractions of the rules of the* Organon.

—Statutes of the University of Oxford, fourteenth century

The modern study of logic—the science of thought—begins, like many of
today's arts and sciences, with the ancient Greeks. Among the Greek
scholars who played a major role in the early development of logic was
the mathematician and mystic Pythagoras.

THE SQUARE ON THE HYPOTENUSE

Fame is often achieved for the wrong reason. Pythagoras is one of the
most famous scholars of all time, and his fame rests on the most famous
mathematical theorem of all time. Indeed, for most people, not only do
they know about the Pythagorean theorem, it is the *only* mathematical
theorem they can both name and quote. The words trip off their tongue in
a familiar poetic rhythm: "The Pythagorean theorem: In any right-angled
triangle, the square of the hypotenuse equals the sum of the squares of the
other two sides." But in all probability, Pythagoras simply picked up the
theorem from the writings of earlier Babylonian mathematicians.

So if Pythagoras is to be famous, it should be for something else.
Rather than for discovering the theorem that now bears his name, he
might be lauded for appreciating and advocating the pursuit of abstract

order and the definite knowledge that the theorem exemplifies. On the other hand, if that were to be the ground for his fame, he would have to share it with others. For Pythagoras, who lived some time around 570–500 B.C., was just one of many Greek scholars for whom the search for order and abstract patterns was regarded as the highest form of intellectual pursuit.

The Pythagorean theorem exhibits all the features of mathematical knowledge that so appealed to the ancient Greeks: abstraction, precision, certainty, and eternity. The notion of 'a triangle' in the theorem is of a purely abstract 'triangle concept'. The theorem does not refer to some particular triangle; rather it speaks of *any* right-angled triangle, large or small, squat or elongated. Moreover, the theorem makes a precise claim about right-angled triangles: In each and every case, the square of the length of the hypotenuse is equal to the sum of the squares of the lengths of the other two sides. Not just approximately equal, or equal in most cases, but absolutely equal, for every right-angled triangle. And finally, once the truth of the theorem has been established, it remains true for all time. For the most part, the growth of human knowledge is not a cumulative process. The scientific 'truths' of, say, physics, chemistry, or biology known to one generation are often discarded by the next. But that does not happen in mathematics. Mathematical knowledge is knowledge for all time.

For the ancient Greeks, with their love of learning and their passion to find order in the world, mathematics offered the path to the surest knowledge of all. They looked for mathematical ways to describe the order in the world around them, the order in the movement of the sun and the moon above them, and order in the patterns of thought and language by which people reasoned and communicated.

What is it about mathematical knowledge that makes it so certain? How was Pythagoras able to assert with such confidence the theorem that today bears his name? The answer is, he could *prove* it by means of a logically convincing argument (whoever's argument it was initially). The original discovery of the Pythagorean theorem is remarkable on two counts. First of all, the discoverer was able to discern a relationship between the squares of the sides, observing that there was a regular pattern that was exhibited by *all* right-angled triangles. Second, that unknown discoverer—or maybe someone else, since discovery and proof are not the same—was able to come up with a rigorous *proof* that the pattern observed held for all such triangles.

Observation → abstraction → understanding → description → proof. That is the essence of the mathematical method. First, some general pattern is observed. It might be a physical pattern that can be seen with the eyes or heard with the ears, or it might be an abstract pattern, such as a pattern of reasoning or of language. Then comes abstraction: The sun and moon each appears to trace a circle across the sky, the phases of the moon appear to come around in a regular fashion, there seem to be systematic ways to deduce a valid conclusion from two given premises, and so forth. Next comes understanding, where an explanation is sought for the abstract patterns that have been observed. The final goal is proof, a conclusive argument that establishes the truth of what has been observed. But before there can be a proof, the abstract patterns have to be described in a clear, unambiguous language—the language of mathematics.

The mathematical method dominated the Greeks' approach to all knowledge. Aristotle looked for and found numerical patterns in music. Both Aristotle and Zeno studied patterns of reasoning. And mathematical proofs dominated Euclid's thirteen-volume treatise *Elements,* written around 350 B.C. In this mammoth work, Euclid developed geometry and arithmetic in a systematic fashion, starting out with formal definitions of the terms to be used and a list of basic assumptions and proving all subsequent assertions from those initial assumptions.

Again, one of the most striking features of mathematical proofs that distinguish them from 'proofs' in other walks of life is their finality. It might take some effort to follow one of Euclid's geometric proofs, but once the proof has been understood, that is the end of the matter. A mathematical proof leaves no room for doubt. There is no other area of human learning that provides such complete certainty, not physics, biology, chemistry, politics, law, psychology, or economics, nor any other area. This is part of the reason why, when mathematics *can* be applied to a phenomenon, it can lead to a level of precision and certainty that would otherwise be unattainable. It is this absolute certainty of mathematical knowledge that motivated the ancient Greeks and generations of thinkers ever since to try to find *mathematical* explanations of human reasoning.

THE ARROW AND THE TORTOISE

Most people today, if they think about mathematical arguments at all, generally regard them as the means to prove mathematical theorems or perhaps to establish a technical result in physics. But the Greeks used them for far more than that. They applied mathematical arguments to investigate the nature of existence and to understand human nature. The *dialectic method* is the name we give today to the use of pure reason—as opposed to observation, measurement, or experiment—in order to analyze a phenomenon.

Zeno of Elea made dramatic use of the dialectic method to investigate the nature of space and time. Zeno, who lived circa 450 B.C., was a student of Parmenides, the founder of the Eleatic school of philosophy that flourished for a while in Elea, in Magna Graecia. By means of the "paradox of the arrow," he challenged the atomic conception of space and time, which viewed space as consisting of a multiplicity of adjacent points and time as a succession of instants.

Zeno asked his contemporaries to imagine an arrow in flight. If time consists of discrete instants, then at any particular instant of time, the arrow must be at a particular location, a certain point in space. At that instant, the arrow is indistinguishable from a similar arrow at rest. But this will be true of *any* instant of time, Zeno argued, so how can the arrow move? Surely, if the arrow is at rest at every instant, then it is always at rest.

The arrow paradox strikes a blow against the view of space and time as atomic. Zeno further demonstrated that the nature of space and time were not well understood by formulating a second paradox that challenged the alternative prevailing conception of space and time—that they are infinitely divisible. This was the paradox of Achilles and the tortoise, perhaps the best known of Zeno's arguments. Achilles is to race the tortoise over, say, 100 meters. Since Achilles can run ten times faster than the tortoise, the tortoise is given a 10-meter start. The race starts and Achilles sets off in pursuit of the tortoise. In the time it takes Achilles to cover the 10 meters needed to reach the point from which the tortoise had started, the tortoise has covered exactly 1 meter, and so is 1 meter ahead. By the time Achilles has covered that extra meter, the tortoise is 1/10 of a meter in the lead. When Achilles gets to that point, the tortoise is 1/100 of a meter ahead, and so on, ad infinitum. Thus, the argument goes, the tortoise remains forever in the lead, albeit by smaller and smaller margins; Achilles never overtakes his opponent to win the race.

The purpose of these paradoxes was certainly not to argue that an arrow cannot move or that Achilles can never overtake the tortoise. Both of these are undeniable, empirical facts. Rather, Zeno's puzzles presented challenges to the existing analyses of space, time, and motion. The Greeks themselves were not able to meet Zeno's challenges. Indeed, truly satisfactory resolutions to the paradoxes were not found until the end of the nineteenth century, when mathematicians finally came to grips with infinity.

Notice in particular the way Zeno sets up his two paradoxes. The arrow paradox starts with the *assumption* (or *premise*) that space and time are atomic; the paradox of Achilles and the tortoise starts with the opposite assumption that space and time are infinitely divisible. In each case, a seemingly logical argument then deduces, from that initial assumption, a conclusion that is quite obviously false. Now, if a rigorous argument leads from an initial assumption to a false conclusion, then that initial assumption must be false. This is the logical principle known as *proof by contradiction* or by the Latin phrase *reductio ad absurdum.* By starting with pairs of complementary assumptions, as Zeno did, and deriving logical consequences of them in search of a contradiction, one has a method to discover truths about the nature of the universe. (In fact, both of Zeno's arguments were faulty—though the Greeks were not in a position to see what the problem was—so on this occasion the dialectic method does not lead to any valid conclusion.)

It was the dialectic method applied not to metaphysics but to aspects of everyday life that the great debater Socrates used to such great effect in his marketplace dialogues, described in Plato's writings. Of course, when applied to human situations, the dialectic method does not have the certainty of a mathematical proof, and it is clear that the kinds of argument put forward by Socrates were often intended as a kind of verbal exercise. Thus, in Book I of Plato's *Republic,* Socrates engages in the following dialogue:

> And undoubtedly a man is well able to guard an army, when he has also a talent for stealing the enemy's plans and all his other operations.
>
> Certainly.
>
> That is to say, a man can guard expertly whatever he can thieve expertly.
>
> So it would seem.
>
> Hence, if the just man is expert at guarding money, he is also expert in stealing it.
>
> I confess the argument points that way.
>
> Then, to all appearance, it turns out that the just man is a kind of thief: a doctrine which you have probably learnt from Homer . . . because, as the poet says, he outdid all men in thievishness and perjury. Justice therefore, according to you, Homer, and Simonides, appears to be a kind of art of stealing, whose object, however, is to help one's friends and injure one's enemies. Was not this your meaning?
>
> Most certainly it was not, he replied; but I no longer know what I did mean.

Now, Plato warns against the use of the dialectic method for mere amusement. So it seems likely that the purpose of examples such as the one just given, where the reasoning is obviously flawed, was to serve as exercises to help clarify various points concerning valid inference. Aristotle referred to arguments that have the appearance of being valid, and yet lead to an obviously false conclusion, as *sophisms*. In his book *Euthymedus*, Plato describes a dialogue between Euthymedus and Dionysodorus in which they prove by means of sophisms such nonsensical propositions as: no one can tell a lie; Socrates knows everything; and the father of Ctesippus is a dog.

This, then, was the mathematical and philosophical environment in which the Greeks founded the science of proof or rational argument, the science that third-century A.D. scholars would name *logic*.

In fact, there was not one school of logic in ancient Greece but two—Stoic logic and Aristotelean logic—and these two schools adopted very different approaches to the analysis of reasoning. Before we look at the specific theory of each school in turn, it will be helpful to prepare the ground by making some general observations about logical reasoning that are common to both approaches.

Bricks in a building

Logic begins with the observation that certain kinds of sentences make claims. For example, each of the following sentences does so:

- *The angles of a triangle add up to 180 degrees.*
- *The arrow is at rest.*
- *The world is flat.*
- *Athens is the capital of Greece.*

In contrast, none of the following sentences makes a claim:

- *What is the capital of Greece?*
- *Do the angles of a rectangle always add up to 360 degrees?*
- *Lay down your arms and surrender!*
- *I now declare you man and wife.*

Logicians call sentences of the first kind *propositions*. At least, that is almost right, but not quite. Remember, what we are after when we study logic are the abstract patterns of reasoning, not the patterns of the particular language in which the reasoning is expressed. For example, the English sentence *It is raining* and the German sentence *Es regnet* are different sentences, in different languages, but they both express the same proposition, namely, a claim about the weather. It is that claim—that abstract notion—that is called the proposition. Thus, in each of the first four examples above, the proposition is the claim made by the sentence, not the sentence itself.

The distinction between sentences and the abstract propositions that they express is one of the key ideas of logic. For propositions are the constituents that make up a logical argument. Just as a building may be built from bricks, assembled together in a systematic fashion, so too a logical argument consists of propositions, assembled together in a systematic fashion. The task facing the logician is to examine that systematic fashion in which the constituent propositions of an argument fit together.

For example, from the two propositions

- *The capital of Greece is Athens.*
- *Athens is a beautiful city.*

you can deduce the proposition

- *The capital of Greece is a beautiful city.*

For all its simplicity, this three-line deduction involves some pretty sophisticated notions: the geographical concepts of city and country, the geopolitical concept of a nation's capital, and the aesthetic notion of beauty. In order to understand what the deduction *says* you have to know about all of these notions, and that means you have to know quite a lot about the world, both physical and sociological. But do you have to know all of this stuff in order to say whether or not the deduction is logically valid?

The obvious (though incorrect) answer to this question is yes. It seems reasonable to imagine that, in order to check if the argument is valid, you have to examine each step in turn, and see if the claim is true. For the first sentence, *The capital of Greece is Athens,* either world knowledge or reference to an encyclopedia can be used to establish if this claim is true. Having established that this is the case, you could then turn to the second sentence, *Athens is a beautiful city.* Is this true? Opinions vary, but for the sake of argument let's suppose it is true. Then you can combine these two observations into one: *Athens, the capital of Greece, is a beautiful city.* And this tells you that the capital of Greece is a beautiful city.

The approach just described, to verify an argument by verifying each step in turn, is certainly not incorrect. But it is not necessary. To try to verify an argument by verifying each step is to confuse two issues. Whether the *overall argument* is correct is quite a separate issue from whether each step is true, or even whether the conclusion is true. The only connection of any significance between these two separate issues is that *if* the argument is valid and *if* all the assumptions in the argument are true, *then* the conclusion is true. Or, to put it another way, whether or not an argument is valid has to do with the overall *structure* of the argument, not the truth or falsity of each claim in the argument.

The situation is the same as the one for the sentences considered in the previous chapter: Whether or not a certain sequence of words (or even nonwords such as *A-spinelli* and *Morphenium*) is a sentence is largely independent of any meaning the sentence or its constituent 'words' may or may not have. Rather, it is a matter of the abstract structure.

The argument about Greece and Athens has the following abstract form:

- *G is A.*
- *A is B.*

Therefore

- *G is B.*

Here, the letter G denotes *The capital of Greece*, A denotes *Athens*, and B denotes the property of being *a beautiful city*. We arrive at the abstract, logical pattern of the argument by asking if the argument would be true *whatever the letters G, A, and B referred to.*

The answer is yes. In fact, having already introduced algebraic notation, we may as well go the whole way and write the argument in a completely mathematical way:

- $G = A.$
- $A = B.$

Therefore,

- $G = B.$

To most people, writing the argument in terms of equations in this way would suggest that it is about numbers. Indeed, it could be about numbers. In fact, it could be about absolutely anything in the world, and this is precisely the point. The argument is valid *whatever it is about*—cities, nations, beauty, numbers, whatever. And it is valid *however you write it*—in words, as a mixture of letters and words, or as equations. What makes the argument valid is not what it is about, or how it is written, but its *structure*. The structure of an argument stripped of all reference to what it is about is what we call the *logical structure* of the argument.

One tricky point about logical arguments is this: The fact that an argument is logically valid does not necessarily mean that the conclusion of the argument is true. If you start with true premises, then the conclusion of a valid argument is true. But if one or more of the premises is false, then there is no guarantee that the conclusion is true (though it may be). For instance, there are people who think that Athens is not at all beautiful. (The nice thing about examples involving aesthetic issues is that you can use them both ways.) If you are one of those people, then for you the conclusion *The capital of Greece is a beautiful city* is not true, even though the *argument* is true for everyone. In this case one of the two premises of the argument is false.

Most everyday arguments are, of course, considerably more complicated than the example above, though in many cases the increased complexity of those arguments is essentially one of length, not of fundamental structure. However, no matter how long an argument may be, and how complicated it may seem, when it is broken down into individual steps, each step has a simple logical structure. It is much like constructing a building out of bricks. Overall, the building may be large and impressive, but when you look at it brick by brick, you see that the structure is largely the same throughout, for the most part consisting of one brick stacked upon two others.

Logic, then, sets out to describe the abstract patterns whereby propositions may be combined to produce valid arguments. Those patterns should be patterns of logical structure, independent of what the individual propositions are about. What distinguishes Stoic logic from Aristotelean logic, and what distinguishes either form of Greek logic from the logic that followed, is the *kind* of pattern singled out for analysis. We have met one such pattern, Aristotle's syllogism, in Chapter 1. However, Aristotle's logic was just one of two major Greek attempts to develop a science of reasoning. The other approach was due to the Stoics.

THE FIRST AND THE SECOND

The Stoic school of logic was founded some 300 years before the birth of Christ by Zeno of Citium (not to be confused with Zeno of Elea, discussed earlier in this chapter). After Zeno's death in 264 B.C., the school was led by Cleanthes, who was followed by Chrysippus. It was largely through the copious writings of Chrysippus that the Stoic school became established, though many of these writings have been lost.

The Stoics were enthusiastic believers in the dialectic method. Indeed, they placed so much importance on the power of pure reason that, if their reasoning led them to adopt a particular course of action, they would pursue that course even if it involved pain or suffering—a characteristic that led to our modern usage of the word *stoical.*

With logical reasoning playing such an exalted role in their lives, it was natural that the Stoics made a study of the logical process itself. The patterns of reasoning described by Stoic logic are the patterns of interconnection between propositions that are completely independent of what those propositions say. Thus, in Stoic logic, propositions are treated the way atoms are treated in present-day chemistry, where the focus is on the way atoms fit together to form molecules, rather than on the internal structure of the atoms. In terms of constructing a wall of a building, Stoic logic investigates the way the wall may be constructed when no attention is paid to the shape or size of each brick, and when the bricks come in all shapes and sizes.

It was possible for the Stoics to analyze arguments in this way because you can recognize a given sentence as expressing a proposition just by looking at the sentence, without knowing whether it is true or not. For example, *Keith Devlin has a mole on his left foot* clearly expresses a proposition, but the average reader of this book will not know whether this proposition is true or false.

The Stoics commenced their analysis by examining a number of ways in which two propositions can be combined to give a third, more complicated proposition. One simple way that two propositions may be joined to form a single, new proposition is by means of the connective *and.* The operation of combining two propositions in this way is called *conjunction.* For example, the conjunction of the two propositions

John ordered ice cream   Mary ordered mousse

is the single proposition

John ordered ice cream and Mary ordered mousse.

Present-day logicians bring out the abstract pattern of connective operations such as conjunction by using algebraic notation. The letters p, q, and r are generally used to denote arbitrary propositions, and the symbol $\wedge$ is used to abbreviate the word *and.* Thus, $p \wedge q$ denotes the conjunction of the propositions p and q. (The formula is read as "p and q.")

It is of interest to note that at no time did the Stoics themselves hit upon the idea of using algebraic notation, with letters denoting arbitrary propositions and symbols denoting connecting words. They wrote everything out in ordinary language. As we shall see, this often resulted in their having to write down long and complicated sentences that are difficult to follow. For anyone who feels comfortable with algebra, the modern way of expressing the notions of Stoic logic is much better—the algebraic expressions are far shorter and much easier to read. (It is one of life's many ironies that a linguistic device introduced to make things clearer and simpler, namely, algebraic notation, should have precisely the opposite effect on so many people.)

As we have observed, the key idea behind the Stoics' approach to logic was that you do not know what the constituent propositions are about, or even whether each constituent proposition is true or false. All that you know is that any proposition must be *either* true *or* false. So, when the Stoics came to analyze the combining of two propositions by conjunction, they did so by looking at the pattern of truth and falsity. The pattern is straightforward: If both p and q are true, then the conjunction $p \wedge q$ will be true; if one or both of p and q are false, then $p \wedge q$ will be false.

Modern logicians generally display this pattern of truth in the tabular form shown below, using what is known as a *truth table,* a nineteenth-century device not available to the Stoics.

p	q	$p \wedge q$
T	T	T
T	F	F
F	T	F
F	F	F

In the table, T denotes the *truth value* 'true' and F denotes the truth value 'false'. Reading along a row, each right-hand listing indicates the truth value of the compound that arises from the truth values of the components. For example, reading along the third row tells you that if p is false (entry F) and q is true (entry T), then $p \wedge q$ is false (entry F).

Here is how the Stoics would have expressed the truth pattern for conjunction:

> *If the first and if the second, then the first and the second. If not the first, then not the first and the second. If not the second, then not the first and the second.*

If you replace *the first* by the letter p, *the second* by the letter q, and abbreviate p *and* q by $p \wedge q$, this rather perplexing looking sentence becomes:

> *If p and if q, then $p \wedge q$. If not p, then not $p \wedge q$. If not q, then not $p \wedge q$.*

And from this version, it is but a small step to the truth pattern for conjunction as expressed above (or to the truth table for conjunction).

Another way to combine two propositions is by the connective *or*. The operation of combining two propositions in this manner is called *disjunction*.

For example, the disjunction of the two propositions

> *Alice captained the team*   *Sam played for the defense*

is the single proposition

> *Alice captained the team or Sam played for the defense.*

The present-day algebraic way to express the disjunction of the propositions p and q is: $p \vee q$. (This is read as "p or q.")

However, when Stoics came to analyze the truth pattern of disjunction, they met with a difficulty. In everyday language, the word *or* has two meanings. It can be used in an exclusive way, as in the sentence "The door is locked or it is not locked." In this case, only one of these possibilities can be true. Alternatively, it may be used inclusively, as in "It will rain or snow." In this case, there is the possibility that both will occur. In everyday communication, people rely on their general knowledge to make the intended meaning clear. But in the logic of propositions, as studied by the Stoics, there is not supposed to be any reference to general knowledge. All you have is the bare knowledge of truth or falsity of the constituent propositions. So, in order to write down the truth pattern of disjunction, they had to make a choice. Though they were never able to fully agree on the matter, they preferred the exclusive version. For technical reasons, present-day logicians always choose the inclusive version. Since this book is being written in the twentieth century, I take the inclusive-or as basic, which means that the disjunction $p \vee q$ is true if p is true, q is true, or both.

Here is the truth pattern for disjunction expressed as a truth table:

p	q	$p \vee q$
T	T	T
T	F	T
F	T	T
F	F	F

Here is how the Stoics would have expressed this pattern:

> *If the first, then the first or the second. If the second, then the first or the second. If not the first and if not the second, then not the first or the second.*

Another logical operation the Stoics examined is *negation*. The negation of a proposition p is the assertion that p is false, an assertion that may be written *not-p*. For example, the negation of the proposition *Athens is the capital of Greece* is the proposition

not-[Athens is the capital of Greece.]

Of course, in ordinary English, this would be written as *Athens is not the capital of Greece*.

The symbolic expression for the negation of a proposition *p* is ¬*p*, which is read as "not *p*." In terms of truth and falsity, the proposition ¬*p* is true whenever *p* is false and false whenever *p* is true. The truth table for negation is therefore extremely simple:

p	¬*p*
T	F
F	T

So far, we have identified three logical operations that may be used to combine propositions together to give more complex propositions: the two connectives *and* and *or* and the negation operator *not*. Moreover, we have discovered the truth patterns that each of these gives rise to. For their study of reasoning, the Stoics examined one further connective: the *conditional*.

Suppose that *p* and *q* are any propositions whatsoever. Then it is possible to form the compound proposition

If p then q.

Such a compound proposition, constructed from two given propositions *p* and *q* in this way, is called the *conditional* of *p* and *q*. For example, suppose *p* is the proposition *The Democrats are in power* and *q* is the proposition *Taxes will rise*. Then the conditional "*If p then q*" is the proposition

If the Democrats are in power then taxes will rise.

What is the truth pattern of the conditional? It turns out that it is not as easy to answer this question as it was in the previous cases. Before we look for the general pattern and embroil ourselves in algebra (to say nothing of *the first* and *the second*), let's see what happens with the example.

Many Americans believe that this conditional proposition is true. Without wishing to enter into that particular political debate, let us assume for the sake of argument that they are right and the conditional is true. Then surely it will be true whoever happens to be in power at the time, the Democrats or the Republicans. For it says something about the Democrats' policies in general, regardless of who won the last election.

Thus, it appears that the truth or falsity of the conditional does not depend on the truth or falsity of the two constituent propositions—the truth table will have a T everywhere in the last column. But wait a moment. Suppose that the Democrats are in power (p is true) but that taxes do not rise (q is false). Then a Democrat supporter can point to the constant tax level and say to her Republican opponent, "See, your conditional was wrong; the Democrats are in power, but taxes are not rising." Thus, at least for our Democrats-and-taxes example, if p is true and q is false, then the conditional "*If p then q*" is false.

So what is going on? Answering this question turns out to be a difficult task. I propose to proceed in the following fashion. First, we'll fix our terminology and introduce another abbreviation to avoid a plethora of *if*s and *then*s. Then, skipping the Stoics's analysis, I'll jump ahead and *give* you the resulting truth pattern for the conditional. Once we have that pattern, we will be able to complete our tour of Stoic logic without too much trouble. Then, for those who really want to know, tucked away at the end of the chapter, I'll give the 'fine print'—the intricate reasoning that uncovers the truth pattern of the conditional. As with all fine print, it's up to you whether to simply take it on trust or check all the details for yourself.

As defined already, given two propositions p and q, the conditional of p and q is the compound proposition

If p, then q.

The standard abbreviation used by present-day logicians is

$$p \rightarrow q.$$

(This is read "p arrows q.") The proposition p is called the *antecedent* of the conditional; q is called the *consequent*.

The truth pattern for the conditional is:

1. If p is true and q is true, then $p \rightarrow q$ is true.
2. If p is true and q is false, then $p \rightarrow q$ is false.
3. If p is false (and q is true or false), then $p \rightarrow q$ is true.

Here is the truth table:

p	q	$p \rightarrow q$
T	T	T
T	F	F
F	T	T
F	F	T

And here it is in Stoic language:

If the first and if the second, then if the first then the second. If the first and if not the second, then not if the first then the second. If not the first, then if the first then the second.

Once again we see the enormous advantages of algebraic notation, and it is perhaps surprising that the Stoics did not take such a step.

As far as logical reasoning is concerned, the crucial fact about conditionals is that it captures an important pattern of inference. Namely, if you know that the conditional $p \rightarrow q$ is true, and if you also know that the antecedent p is true, then you can conclude that the consequent q is true. Thus, the conditional provides a means for deducing one proposition from two others. The proposition q is deduced from the propositions p and $p \rightarrow q$. This rule of deduction is still known today by its original Greek name, *modus ponens*.

As an illustration of *modus ponens*, let's look again at our Democrats-and-taxes example. For this example, p is the proposition *"The Democrats are in power,"* q is the proposition *"Taxes will rise,"* and the conditional $p \rightarrow q$ is the proposition

If the Democrats are in power then taxes will rise.

Suppose that this conditional proposition ($p \rightarrow q$) is true. Suppose further that the Democrats *are* in power (i.e., p is true). It then follows, by *modus ponens*, that q is true (i.e., taxes will rise). (Of course, since this conclusion follows by Stoic logic, you should endure the rising taxes in true stoical fashion.)

Leaving Democrats and taxes aside from now on, we should observe again that an important feature of the entire Stoic approach to logic is that it does not require that you know anything about the constituent propositions p and q in an inference. They can be about Democrats, Republicans, watermelons, bicycles, negative numbers, right-angled triangles, taxes, taxis, or taxidermists. *Modus ponens* is a valid rule of inference whatever the constituent propositions may be.

Here is another example, one where the truth of the conditional can vary from one circumstance to another:

If it rains at noon today, then I will get wet.

Some days this may be true, such as when I have to cycle to the library during my lunch hour to return a book. However, on a day when I will be stuck indoors throughout my lunch period, it will be false. Thus the truth or falsity of the conditional depends on what I will be doing at lunchtime.

(This is one of the reasons why the analysis of the truth patterns of the conditional is so tricky.)

Modern logicians generally use the symbol ⊢ to indicate a valid inference. Adopting this notation, *modus ponens* may be expressed like this:

$$p \rightarrow q, p \vdash q.$$

To the left of the ⊢ symbol (which is generally referred to as a 'turnstile') are listed the premises for the inference, separated by commas; on the right is the conclusion.

Here is how the Stoics themselves expressed the *modus ponens* rule:

If the first then the second, and if the first, then the second.

(Does anyone still need convincing that algebra can be better than words?)

Modus ponens is just one of five different inference rules (i.e., general patterns of inference) identified by the Stoics. For the record, I list them below in present-day algebraic notation, using the symbol $\vee$ to denote the exclusive-or that the Stoics favored. (So $p \vee q$ is true if exactly one of p, q is true.) *Modus ponens* is the first of these.

1. $p \rightarrow q, p \vdash q$
2. $p \rightarrow q, \neg q \vdash \neg p$
3. $\neg(p \wedge q), p \vdash \neg q$
4. $p \vee q, p \vdash \neg q$
5. $p \vee q, \neg q \vdash p$

If you were a Stoic logician, you would have to work hard to convince yourself that these five inference rules are correct. (You would also have a hard time simply figuring out what they say, since there would be *first*s and *second*s all over the place.) However, present-day logicians can verify the rules in a simple fashion using truth tables. (The idea is to build a truth table that includes all of the compound propositions that appear in the inference to be checked, and check that every entry in the final column is T.)

Starting with their five inference rules, the Stoics were able to deduce a number of other patterns of reasoning. For example, they showed that the following deduction is valid:

$$p \rightarrow (p \rightarrow q), p \vdash q.$$

Using the Stoics's own terminology:

If the first then if the first then the second, and if the first, then the second.

Given algebraic notation and the modern technique of truth tables, much of Stoic logic reduces to some simple algebraic manipulations together with the filling in of truth values in a table. However, it took over two thousand years for mankind to reach that stage. Not having access to such modern tools, the Stoics had a much harder time establishing their results. But establish them they did. By singling out propositions as the building blocks for reasoning and identifying some of the abstract patterns involved in reasoning with propositions, including *modus ponens,* the Stoics's contribution to logic was a major intellectual achievement. Together with Aristotelean logic considered next, it paved the way for all subsequent work in logic to the present day and led to much of twentieth-century linguistics and computer science.

The all and the some

The other great school of logic in ancient Greek times was the one founded by Aristotle. By and large, the two schools adopted quite different approaches to the study of reasoning, and developed independently of one another. Indeed, it was only with the development of predicate logic in the late nineteenth century (see Chapter 4) that the two Greek approaches were superseded by a common extension.

Aristotelean logic was by far the more dominant approach in the centuries following the development of the two schools. This was not so much due to any inherent superiority, but was a consequence of the widespread availability of all of Aristotle's writings on the subject. In particular, shortly after Aristotle's death in 322 B.C., his pupils grouped together a collection of his works and published them under the title *Organon,* meaning 'instrument of science'. The *Organon* was widely disseminated through Latin and Arabic translations, as well as the original Greek. In medieval times, with the founding of the early European universities, it soon achieved high status as a 'required text'. In 1159, an English logician called John of Salisbury wrote *Metalogicon,* the first of what were to be many logic books based on the *Organon.* By the fourteenth century, Aristotle's teachings had become such a central feature at Oxford University that adherence to the 'rules of the *Organon*' was codified in the university statutes. (See the quotation at the start of this chapter.)

Both Stoic logic and Aristotelean logic are based on particular patterns of language. The Stoic logicians began with an initial collection of basic, unanalyzed propositions p, q, r, et cetera, and looked at various ways these propositions can be combined to give more complex propositions, $p \wedge q$, $p \vee q$, $p \rightarrow q$, and $\neg p$. They then looked for general patterns of reasoning that arise from the forms of those more complex propositions. The patterns they studied do not depend on what the initial propositions say. In contrast, Aristotle's logic concentrated instead on finding general patterns in what the propositions actually say.

For instance, each of the following propositions says something quite different:

All apples are fruit.
All men are mortal.
All philosophers like mathematics.

However, there is an obvious general pattern to the three propositions. They are all of the form

All S are P

for some properties S and P. (For the third example, you have to rephrase it as *All philosophers are mathematics-likers.*) This is the kind of abstract pattern of language that Aristotle examined.

However, Aristotle took the abstraction one step further in order to develop his logic. He observed that there is an abstract pattern common to all the following propositions:

All men are mortal.
Some musicians like mathematics.
Some animals are not carnivores.

Propositions of these general forms are called *subject–predicate propositions*. These are the kinds of propositions with which Aristotle developed his logic. He examined the logical rules whereby one subject–predicate proposition can be deduced from other subject–predicate propositions.

When you think about it, few logical arguments in everyday life (or in science and mathematics) are expressed using (only) subject–predicate propositions. However, you can say an awful lot with such propositions, and many (though not all) everyday arguments may be recast in such terms. Rewriting an argument in terms of subject–predicate propositions might make it very long and hard to follow, but it can often be done, at least in principle. This is why Aristotle's logic was a major advance in our understanding of logical reasoning.

A subject–predicate proposition is composed of two entities, a *subject* and a property (or *predicate*) ascribed to that subject. Aristotle began his analysis of such propositions by abstracting away from the particular references, say to men or to mortality, to obtain a more general pattern. (Note that Aristotle's patterns are patterns *of* propositions, whereas the Stoics studied patterns that *connect* propositions.) Following Aristotle, let us use S to denote the subject of any subject–predicate proposition and P to denote the predicate. For example, in the case of the proposition *All men are mortal, S* denotes *men* and P denotes the predicate *being mortal.*

Abstracting from the subject and predicate reveals the following general pattern:

(All/some) S (have/have not) the property P.

Of course, in moving to this level of abstraction, we lose some of the grammaticality—or at least the naturalness—of ordinary language. If we express the first of the above examples in the general form just given it reads

All men have the property being mortal.

This sentence is stilted. Others can look just as bad, if not worse. For example, the proposition *Some musicians like mathematicians* becomes:

Some musicians have the property liking mathematics.

Some animals are not carnivores becomes

Some animals have not the property being carnivores.

The last one is reminiscent of those old, low-budget cowboy movies where the Indian chief says "Me no like paleface." However, the whole purpose of this process of abstraction is to get away from ordinary language and work with the abstract patterns expressed in the language, so some awkwardness is allowed.

The initial *all* or *some* in a subject–predicate proposition is called the *quantifier* of the proposition, because it quantifies the subject. Since there are two kinds of quantification of the subject (*all* and *some*) and two ways to combine the subject with the predicate (*have* and *have not*), there will be four (2 × 2) possible quantified subject–predicate propositions:

All S have P.
All S have not P.
Some S have P.
Some S have not P.

We have seen examples of the first, third, and fourth of these general patterns, but what of the second, *All S have not P*? In ordinary English, it would be more natural to write this in the form

No S has P.

You might have to think for a moment to convince yourself that this says the same thing. For example, *All Englishmen are not German* is equivalent to *No Englishmen are German*. (Using the more awkward terminology that emphasizes the general pattern, these two propositions read: *All Englishmen have not the property 'being German'* and *No Englishmen have the property 'being German'*.)

However, all issues of grammaticality disappear with the next step in Aristotle's abstraction process, which is to write the four subject–predicate patterns in abbreviated form:

> *SaP* : *All S have P.*
> *SeP* : *All S have not P. (No S have P.)*
> *SiP* : *Some S have P.*
> *SoP* : *Some S have not P.*

With this final step in the abstraction process, Aristotle succeeded in expressing the general patterns of subject–predicate propositions in purely algebraic notation.

Yet this is only the first stage of the analysis. The purpose of the abstraction process is not simply to find general patterns in subject–predicate propositions, but to uncover general patterns of reasoning. What Aristotle was searching for were inference rules.

The inference rules he identified are the syllogisms, already mentioned in Chapter 1. These are rules for deducing one assertion from exactly two others. For example, we have the syllogism

> *All mathematicians are perfect.*
> *Some students are mathematicians.*
> ___
> *Some students are perfect.*

This syllogism has the general pattern

> *All M have P.*
> *Some S have M.*
> ___
> *Some S have P.*

This general form is a valid inference, no matter what *M*, *P*, and *S* denote.

However, we now appear to have a problem. The syllogism given in Chapter 1 is:

> *All men are mortal.*
> *Socrates is a man.*
> ———————————
> *Socrates is mortal.*

This does not seem to fit the mold captured by Aristotle's rule, which requires that the subject be quantified, either as *all S* or as *some S*. In this example, there is just Socrates.

On reflection, though, this is not a problem. Due to the fact that there is only one Socrates, to say just "Socrates" is equivalent to saying "All Socrateses" or "Some Socrateses."

Having described the abstract structure of the particular kinds of propositions that may be used in an Aristotelean argument, the next step is to identify the valid syllogisms that may be constructed from such propositions. In other words, what are the valid rules for reasoning with syllogisms? Once again, we are involved in a search for general patterns.

A syllogism consists of two initial propositions, called the *premises* of the syllogism, which we generally write above the line, and a *conclusion*, drawn below the line, that follows from the two premises. If S and P are used to denote the subject and predicate of the conclusion, then in order for inference to take place, there must be some third entity involved with the two premises. This additional entity is called the *middle term*; denoted by M.

For the example

> *All men are mortal.*
> *Socrates is a man.*
> ———————————
> *Socrates is mortal.*

S denotes Socrates (more precisely, the property of being Socrates), P denotes the predicate of being mortal, and M is the property of being a man. In symbols, this particular syllogism thus has the form

$$MaP$$
$$SaM$$
$$\overline{}$$
$$SaP$$

The premise involving M and P is called the *major premise,* and is always written first; the other one, involving S and M, is called the *minor premise,* and is written second.

A syllogistic inference amounts to elimination of the middle term—you start out with a proposition relating P and M and another proposition relating S and M, and you eliminate M to end with a proposition relating S and P.

How many different possible syllogism patterns can there be? The question can be approached purely as a problem in algebra.

M and P can appear in the different orders MP and PM. Then, S and M can appear in the two orders SM and MS. Combining these possibilities, we get the four basic forms below:

I	II	III	IV
MP	PM	MP	PM
SM	SM	MS	MS
SP	SP	SP	SP

Aristotle called these four classes the *figures* of the syllogism.

Note that we have so far ignored whether each proposition is prefaced by *all* or *some* and whether each is of the form *has the property* or *has not the property*. We now have to add these distinctions.

For example, in the first figure, where the pattern is

$$MP$$
$$SM$$
$$\overline{SP}$$

the major premise can be any one of *MaP, MeP, MiP,* and *MoP*. (In words, *All M are P, All M are not P, Some M are P,* and *Some M are not P*.) These choices similarly exist for the minor premise and for the conclusion. So, there are four possibilities for the major premise, and for each of those possibilities, there are four possibilities for the minor premise. And then for each combination of major and minor premise, there are four possibilities for the conclusion. Altogether then, there are $4 \times 4 \times 4 = 64$ possible syllogisms in the first figure alone.

The same is true for each of the other three figures. For each figure, there are 64 different syllogisms. As there are four figures, there are altogether $4 \times 64 = 256$ possible syllogisms.

However, this figure of 256 is what we arrive at when we just look at all the possible abstract (or *algebraic*) patterns. Not all of those patterns will represent a logically valid inference. To obtain his logic, Aristotle had to identify among those 256 possibilities all the logically valid ones.

According to Aristotle, of all the 256 possibilities, only 19 represent patterns of valid inferences. For instance, the valid inferences in the first figure are:

All M are P.	All M are not P.	All M are P.	All M are not P.
All S are M.	All S are M.	Some S are M.	Some S are M.
All S are P.	All S are not P.	Some S are P.	Some S are not P.

In symbolic form:

MaP	MeP	MaP	MeP
SaM	SaM	SiM	SiM
SaP	SeP	SiP	SoP

For the record, here is the list of the quantifier patterns of all nineteen of Aristotle's valid syllogisms in abbreviated form:

Figure I: *aaa, eae, aii, eio*
Figure II: *eae, aee, eio, aoo*
Figure III: *aai, iai, aii, eao, oao, eio*
Figure IV: *aai, aee, iai, eao, eio*

In fact, Aristotle made some errors. To be more precise, he made one error, but he made that error in a number of his syllogisms, with the result that not all the syllogisms on his list are valid. However, it was not until the nineteenth century that anyone spotted the error. Moreover, the mistake is highly technical, as we'll see in a moment. So, if the last few pages have left you reeling, take heart. Aristotle's theory of the syllogism left people reeling for almost two thousand years.

You get some idea of the difficulty Aristotle faced when you look at some of the more subtle syllogisms. For example, most people find it hard to find any conclusion that fits the following two premises:

No councillors are bankers.
All bankers are athletes.

?   ?   ?

There is a valid conclusion, but it takes quite a bit of effort to find it. Here's how we can solve the riddle, following Aristotle. First of all, let the familiar *P* stand for councillors, *M* for bankers, and *S* for athletes. The two premises then have the pattern:

PeM
MaS

Concentrating for the moment simply on the arrangement of the subjects and predicates in the two premises, the arrangement is:

PM
MS

This means that the syllogism is in Aristotle's fourth figure, and hence must have the form

$$PM$$
$$\underline{MS}$$
$$SP$$

For the two premises given, the quantifier pattern begins *ea*. In Figure IV of the syllogism, the only way to continue this pattern is as *eao*. So the syllogism must be of the form

$$PeM$$
$$\underline{MaS}$$
$$SoP$$

The conclusion *SoP* translates to

> *Some athletes are not councillors.*

There you have it. I didn't say it was easy, but at least with Aristotle's analysis it is possible to come to a conclusion. And once you think about that conclusion for a few moments, it makes very good sense.

But now, just when we think we have got the hang of it, the plot thickens. Take a look at the following syllogism:

> *No horned animal is a unicorn.*
> *All unicorns are horned animals.*
> ___
> *Some horned animals are not horned animals.*

If *P* and *S* both denote the property of being a horned animal and *M* denotes being a unicorn, then this example has the same form as the previous one about the councillors, bankers, and athletes. So, according to Aristotle's analysis, it is a valid syllogism. However, it is not valid, and here we meet an instance of Aristotle's error.

The first premise is obviously true: Since unicorns do not exist, no horned animal is a unicorn. How about the second premise: All unicorns are horned animals? In strict *logical* terms, this proposition is true—it is part of what it means to *be* a unicorn that it is an animal with a horn. Whether or not such creatures exist is a separate issue. In this rather convoluted case, both premises are true. Still, the conclusion to the syllogism is obviously false. Since a valid syllogism cannot lead from two true premises to a false conclusion, it follows that this syllogism is not valid.

"Good heavens," you say, "if that was the nature of Aristotle's error, then there is no wonder he missed it." I would agree. Finding fault with

Aristotle's analysis in this fashion is like the smart defense lawyer who manages to get her obviously guilty client acquitted on a legal technicality. This analogy is a good one, so I shall pursue it a bit further. It is in the best interests of society to have laws and to formulate them as precisely as possible. The price we pay for the law's protection is that occasionally someone may exploit the law's precision to achieve an end for which the law was not intended. Likewise in logic. The purpose of logic is to formulate rules of reasoning in a precise manner. Generally, the precision of logic is to our advantage. Occasionally, however, someone can come along and find a way to exploit that precision in a manner not intended.

In the case of Aristotle's original list of syllogisms, they are all valid provided they are applied to real things like athletes, bankers, and councillors. You only run into trouble when you apply some of them to things that do not exist, such as unicorns.

THE FINE PRINT

Just as the cautious consumer should read the fine print before signing a contract, so too the potential purchaser of Greek logic should read the fine print before using the product. For those of you who are curious, here is the fine print of Greek logic, namely, the thorny issue of the Stoic conditional. As you would expect from fine print, the terrain will be rocky in places. Examination of the conditional turns out to be the mathematical equivalent of delicate brain surgery—I am tempted to call it logic surgery. If you find yourself irretrievably lost, I suggest you skip ahead to the next chapter and try again another time. But for those who stick with it (in true 'stoical' fashion?), the reward is considerable insight into the fine details of logical arguments and the way mathematics can be used in the description of human reasoning. It also shows how the use of mathematics can highlight problematic issues and lead to a new understanding of what at first appears to be a relatively straightforward issue. It's worth the effort.

The task is to uncover the truth pattern of the conditional $p \rightarrow q$. To do this, you can't ask what p and q are about, since the idea of Stoic logic is that all you know about p and q is that each one, being a proposition, will be either true or false. You have only one option: to discover how the truth or falsity of the conditional $p \rightarrow q$ depends on the truth or falsity of p and q, regardless of what p and q say.

This is precisely what the Stoics themselves did. According to their analysis, a conditional proposition

$$p \rightarrow q$$

will be true provided it does not begin with a truth and end with a false-hood, that is, if it is *not* the case that p is true and q is false. This seems a little obscure, so let's try to see what reasoning led the Stoics to reach this conclusion.

By way of an example, imagine that Italy has reached the final of the World Cup soccer tournament. Consider the conditional

> *If Italy loses the World Cup, then the coach will resign.*

This conditional is of the form $p \rightarrow q$ if we take p to denote the proposition *Italy loses the World Cup* and q the proposition *the coach will resign.*

Suppose I make this statement the day before the World Cup final. You disagree with me. What will it take for you to prove that I am wrong? Obviously, we both wait until the game has been played and see what happens. If Italy loses (p is true) but the coach hangs on to his job (q is false) then my prediction is demonstrated to be false.

If you think about it, that is the only way to prove conclusively that my claim is false. For if Italy loses and the coach does resign, then I am proved correct. If Italy wins, then the coach can do whatever he pleases and you are not able to prove me wrong, since I did not make any claim about what happens if Italy wins.

So proving that my claim is false seems straightforward enough, and our finding is in agreement with the Stoics's analysis. What about proving that my claim is true? Again, we wait until the game has been played and see what happens. If Italy loses and the coach resigns, my claim was correct. If Italy loses and the coach hangs on, my claim was wrong. But what happens if Italy wins? As I observed above, my statement makes no claim about this possibility. We are left dangling, not knowing if I had been right or wrong. Here we have the Stoics's dilemma. If the antecedent (i.e., the first proposition, p) in a conditional is false, then we seem to be in limbo, unable to decide between truth and falsity.

Though they were never completely happy with their solution to this dilemma, what the Stoics did at this point, and what all present-day logicians do, is to start with the one circumstance in which we know for sure that a conditional is false, and then *declare* it to be true in *all* other cases. This is the mathematician's equivalent of the legal maxim of presumed innocence unless proven guilty: A conditional is assumed to be true unless proved false.

Just as with the legal equivalent, this is very much an adversarial resolution to the problem. In the case of the World Cup, when I make my claim prior to the game, it is up to you to prove me wrong. If you cannot, then I claim I was right—by default, if you like.

According to this analysis, a conditional $p \rightarrow q$ will be true if either of the following occur:

1. both p and q are true; or
2. p is false (and q is either true or false).

For example, the conditional

If Italy loses the World Cup, then the coach will resign.

will be true if

1. Italy loses the World Cup, and the coach resigns; or
2. Italy wins the World Cup (and the coach does whatever he likes).

If you are feeling a little uneasy about the above analysis of the conditional, then you are in the company of the Stoics themselves and many generations of logicians since then. Presuming innocence is one thing, but truth is supposed to be something else, especially mathematical truth. Surely things are either true or false. How can we find ourselves having to make a presumption of truth? Well, the fact is, in practice we don't, or at least, not very often. The troublesome cases rarely arise. Just as honest, law-abiding citizens do not generally have to depend upon being presumed innocent—because they *are* innocent—so too, if you remain within the realm of true propositions you rarely encounter a troublesome conditional with a false antecedent. In the construction of a logical argument, you would normally only introduce the conditional p → q if you had already established that p is true. If you did not know this, there would surely be no point in introducing this conditional, since it would not lead anywhere. Where the difficult cases do arise is in 'counterfactual' statements, where a false premise is adopted in the course of an argument in order to achieve a particular end, perhaps even to establish the very falsity of the initial assumption. An example is the prosecutor in court who begins a line of reasoning by asking the jury to assume—for a moment—that the defendant's alibi is true and then proceeds to deduce obviously false consequences in order to demonstrate that the alibi could not, in fact, be true.

In the end then, the Stoics did not discover the truth pattern of the conditional. For as the above discussion shows, the conditional does not have a complete truth pattern. The only truth pattern it has is the partial one that if p is true and q is true, then $p \rightarrow q$ is true, and if p is true and q is false, then $p \rightarrow q$ is false. If p is false, there is no general pattern to discover. What the Stoics did—and what we all do today—was decide to *define* the conditional to have a certain truth pattern. The definition chosen is a logician's version of "innocent unless proven guilty." We regard a conditional to be true in all cases except the one that definitely makes it false, namely, a true antecedent and a false consequent.

For all its problems, the formulation of a definition of the conditional that covers all possible combinations of truth and falsity was a major achievement of the Stoics. However, there was a second problem with their analysis. In arriving at a definition of the conditional in terms of the pattern of truth, the Stoics took the conditional away from its original conception of *implication*. To explain what I mean, take a look at the following conditional:

If Keith Devlin is an Englishman, then there are infinitely many primes.

According to the Stoic definition, this conditional is true, since both its antecedent and its consequent are true. Moreover, it is not true by virtue of the "it never happened" condition where the antecedent is false; on the contrary, in this case everything is true, antecedent, consequent, and conditional. But although it is true, this particular conditional is surely quite meaningless. It certainly does not express a valid implication. The infinitude of the prime numbers is in no way a logical *consequence* of my being an Englishman.

So what has gone wrong?

The answer is that nothing has really gone wrong. It is just that the conditional, as defined by the Stoics and by present-day logicians, is not the same as implication. This may come as a surprise, given that the investigation started out looking at everyday if–then propositions, which certainly seems like implication. However, implication involves some form of link or causality between the antecedent and the consequent: Under normal circumstances, a statement of the form *A implies B* tells you that *B* is a definite *consequence* of *A*, that the truth of *B* is somehow *caused by* the truth of *A*. In contrast, the conditional is defined purely in terms of truth and falsity, and says nothing about causation.

This is not untypical of the price that often has to be paid for a precise, mathematical definition of a real-world phenomenon. In formulating a precise definition of some notion, certain features may be lost, and as a result the nature of the notion may be 'corrupted'. If the corruption is really bad, then the precise definition will have to be abandoned and another one sought. However, in the case of the conditional, the Stoics's pattern-of-truth definition does get it right for many cases. Indeed, it works for most of the cases of interest to mathematicians, linguists, and computer scientists, and so it has been accepted as part of mathematical logic from Greek times up to the present day.

Happy? Probably not, despite my attempts to convince you that things are really not that bad. Indeed, the Stoics themselves were never content with their analysis, and they made a number of attempts to define a variant of the conditional that was more like genuine implication. So too have subsequent generations of logicians. Recent efforts in this direction have led to what is known as *relevance logic,* a variant of present-day mathematical logic that attempts to formulate a notion of implication in which the antecedent is relevant to the consequent. However, it is fair to say that there is, to this day, no truly satisfactory mathematical theory of implication.

As the above discussions illustrate, it is a significant challenge to obtain a proper understanding of reasoning. We should not hold it against Aristotle or the Stoics that their products were imperfect. The fact that Aristotle was able to identify—with just one hard-to-spot error—all the valid syllogisms among the 256 possible patterns is a remarkable feat. So too is the intricate logic of the Stoics, who identified the idea of an abstract proposition as a key to the analysis of reason and went on to discover some of the patterns of propositional reasoning. Taken together, the accomplishments of the Stoic and Aristotelean logicians demonstrate the tremendous power of abstraction in finding general patterns of reason. By their efforts, the Greeks established beyond any doubt that human reason could be subjected to rigorous scientific analysis, and they pointed the way to much more powerful attempts in later years.

3

THE LAWS
OF THOUGHT

The design of the following treatise is to investigate the fundamental laws of those operations of the mind by which reasoning is performed; to give expression to them in the symbolic language of a Calculus, and upon this foundation to establish the science of Logic and construct its method.

—George Boole[1]

MATHEMATICAL LOGIC—THE VERY IDEA

The success—and the limitations—of Greek logic presented mankind with an irresistible challenge: to push to the limit the idea of a rule-based analysis of human reasoning. Attempts to achieve that goal led to more rigorous and more mathematical representations of thought. The biggest single advance was made in the middle of the nineteenth century.

In 1854, an Englishman named George Boole published a book called *The Laws of Thought.* The book begins with the passage quoted above. By the phrase *the symbolic language of a Calculus,* Boole meant algebra. Not just the use of algebraic symbols like *x, y, z* or *p, q, r* to denote unknown words, phrases, or propositions. That much had been done by Aristotle and many subsequent logicians. What Boole was talking about was using the entire apparatus of a high school algebra class, with operations such as addition and multiplication, methods to solve equations,

---

1. From the introduction to *The Laws of Thought,* 1854.

and the like. Boole's algebra required the formulation of a symbolic language of thought. Solving an equation in that language would not lead to a numerical answer; it would give the conclusion of a logical argument. His algebra was to be an algebra of thought.

Even at the end of the twentieth century, when we are familiar with computers—the 'thinking machines' that are direct descendants of Boole's logical algebra—it seems an audacious idea: to write down algebraic equations that describe the way we think. What on earth led the young Englishman to propose such a thing, and why did he think it might be successful? Ever since the ancient Greeks, a formal analysis and representation of thought had seemed a reasonable goal. Such an analysis might even make use of some mathematical notions from time to time, as Aristotle had done with his symbolic notations. But mathematical equations that describe thought? An *algebra* of thought? Such notions went way beyond anything the Greeks had done. What happened to logic in the two thousand years after the Greeks that prepared the way for Boole's startling proposal? How did the seeds spread that were eventually to germinate in Boole's work?

Dialectica, dialectica

Contemporary scholars often divide sciences into two camps: the 'hard sciences', such as mathematics, physics, chemistry, and biology, and the 'soft sciences', such as economics, sociology, psychology, and anthropology. The division is an uneasy one; the boundaries are blurred and moreover, the blurring has increased with the introduction of mathematical techniques into the soft sciences. Insofar as the hard/soft distinction is meaningful, it can be used to characterize the degree of mathematical precision employed by a science and the exactness of the results. The soft sciences tend to be 'soft' because they deal with people—people as freewilled and often unpredictable creatures, not the complex biological entities studied by the hard science of biology.

As an attempt to develop a rigorous theory of language and thought, logic seems to fall right on that blurred boundary between the hard and soft sciences. As characterized by the work of the two great Greek schools of logic, the Stoics and the Aristoteleans, logic could claim to be a hard science—or at least to fall on the hard side of the divide. On the other hand, much Greek logic would be classified today as soft, namely, their interest in logic as a form of investigation (*dialectic*) or discourse (*rhetoric*), as displayed in the writings of Plato, in the dialogues of Socrates, and in the paradoxes of Zeno.

Though logic in the post-Boole era has been clearly a hard science, for much of its history it was very much a soft science. The soft side of logic was emphasized by Roman scholars, who first took up logic's mantle after the Greeks.

By and large, the Romans's interest in logic was utilitarian. They regarded the study of logic as part of the training of the mind in preparation for Roman public office, for example, as an orator, politician, or judge. One of the texts that an intending public official would likely find himself having to study was *Topica,* an adaptation of Aristotle's *Topics* (part of the *Organon*) written by the Roman orator and philosopher Cicero in the century before the birth of Christ.

Cicero also wrote about Stoic logic, and in so doing introduced some of the terminology used in present-day logic, though in some cases the modern use differs from the original meaning. For instance, he used the term *propositio* for the leading premise in an argument and *assumptio* for the additional premise. Realizing that in drawing a conclusion from two premises involves a kind of pulling together of those premises, he referred to the conclusion of an argument as the *complexio,* a word that translates literally as "a knitting together."

Arguably the most significant lasting aspect of the Romans's work in logic was in keeping the subject alive; their commentaries and Latin translations of the Greek texts would eventually help to disseminate the ideas of Greek logic around the world. However, toward the end of the Roman period, some scholars did show an interest in logic for its own sake, and not merely as mental calisthenics. In the second century A.D., the book *De Philosophia Rationali sive Peri Hermenias,* generally attributed to a man called Apuleius, presented a comparative study of Aristotelean and Stoic logic. Then, in a later book by the Roman Galen titled *Introduction to Dialectic,* the two streams of Greek logic were brought together into a single subject for the first time. Aristotle's logic was regarded as the logic of geometric reasoning, while Stoic logic provided the basis for what is nowadays known as *dialectic metaphysics.* Dialectic metaphysics is the application of pure reason (the dialectic method we met in Chapter 2) to try to understand the nature of the universe and to question the existence of God. The ensuing centuries were to see many attempts to use logic in this way. Such attempts brought logic into the realm of theology, sometimes at personal cost to those bold or foolhardy enough to follow the pursuit openly and risk annoying the Church.

Roman logic came to an end with the fall of the Roman empire in the fifth century. The last, dying embers of the Roman era in terms of logic were various writings of Saint Augustine and of Boethius, including the latter's Latin translation of Aristotle's *Organon.*

So, in Roman hands logic did not really advance but it did soften. Certainly there was no sign of anything that would set the scene for Boole's algebra of thought. Nor would there be for several hundred years, since the end of the Roman era marked the start of the Barbarian period, during which the pursuit of logic was no more treasured than any other branch of intellectual activity.

Interest in logic was rekindled with the revival of learning in the eighth century. As in Roman times, the main interest in logic in the eighth century was in the soft side—examining the use of language in dialectic analysis. Alcuin of York was the first of many authors to write a book with the title *Dialectica.* Another influential *Dialectica* was written by Garland in eleventh-century Liège. A century later, the Frenchman Abelard wrote yet another *Dialectica* and got into trouble with the Church for trying to use logic to prove the existence of God. Much of Abelard's writing would today be classified as pure linguistics, as he considered the role in arguments played by nouns, verbs, and so forth. Thus, the period from the eighth century to the twelfth saw some modest advances in the applications of logic to dialectic investigations, including the odd bit of linguistics, but still nothing that could be seen to prepare the way for Boole.

The twelfth century brought a development that would in time lead to advances not only in logic but many other intellectual pursuits, namely, the formation of a number of universities in Europe. In the university setting, it was not long before logic was regarded as a standard part of the education of a learned person. Aristotle's *Organon,* translated into Western languages from Boethius's Latin version, became a standard textbook.

The pursuit of logic in the early universities was also very much in the soft science tradition of the Romans. Logic was once again regarded more as part of the training of the mind than as a scientific investigation of reasoning. In particular, there was considerable interest in the logical puzzles of the ancient Greeks. One of the most famous of these was the Liar Paradox, proposed by Eubulides. This tantalizing paradox arises when someone stands up and says "What I am now saying is false." The question is, is this person speaking the truth or is she telling a lie? It is impossible to answer this question. If what she says is true, then what she is saying must be false, since that is exactly what her true statement says. On the other hand, if what she is saying is false, then it must be the case that what she is saying is true—again, this is a consequence of what her statement says. The Greek logicians made their heads spin in attempts to unravel this paradox, as have generations of logic students ever since. Indeed, it is only within the last twenty years that logicians have developed theories of logic that eliminate paradoxes of this kind (see Chapter 10).

For twelfth-century logicians, as for the Greeks and Romans before them, a study of logical paradoxes was supposed to develop an ability to spot a false argument in a court of law. For example, suppose you are a member of a jury. The defense lawyer walks up to you, looks you in the eye and says, "I have demonstrated that my client is a generous man. It is a matter of record that he is the plaintiff's neighbor. Now I ask you, is it likely that a generous neighbor would do what my client is accused of doing?"

Presented persuasively by a skillful lawyer, this argument might work. But if you think about it for a moment, you realize that there is something decidedly fishy about it. The crux of the argument is the step from

My client is generous,

and

My client is a neighbor,

to

My client is a generous neighbor.

Let me refer to this deduction as argument 1. On the face of it, argument 1 seems to have exactly the same form as the following, far less loaded argument:

Argument 2. *This is a pen. This is blue. Therefore, this is a blue pen.*

Argument 2 is surely valid. Faced with an objection that argument 1 was not logical, the lawyer might even use the obviously valid argument 2 to support his case, saying that if argument 1 was invalid, then argument 2 would surely be invalid as well. At this point, the prosecution might bring up the following example:

Argument 3. *That dog is a father. That dog is his. Therefore that dog is his father.*

Argument 3 is obviously nonsense. But here is the rub. All three arguments have the same general pattern, namely:

X is A. X is B. Therefore X is AB.

There is no doubt that argument 1 is more like argument 3 than argument 2. The Greeks knew that, and so would any rational person. (In fact, argument 3 is adapted from an example considered by Plato in

Euthymedus.) The question is, why is this the case? When can this general pattern be applied, and when not? Suppose that, instead of being a member of the jury, you were called as an expert witness—a representative rational person—and were asked to explain the underlying logical principles that made argument 2 valid but arguments 1 and 3 false. What would you say?

False arguments having the same superficial structure as valid ones were referred to as *sophisms* by Aristotle. According to Aristotle, there were men called Sophists who made their living by inventing such arguments and presenting them in public, and in Plato's *Euthymedus,* Euthymedus and Dionysodorous present sophisms that purport to prove that no one can tell a lie, that Socrates knows everything, and that the father of Ctesippus is a dog. The whole point about sophisms is that they are so trivial that their falsity is not in question. Rather, the issue is to explain why they do not follow the valid logical rules that their verbal form seems to suggest.

That the Greeks regarded the study of sophisms as a serious method for understanding the rules of human reason is made clear in Plato's *Republic,* when he warns against the use of the method for mere amusement. He says his warning applies especially to the young, thereby putting the study of logic into the same category of dangerous influences on young minds to which later generations would add pop music, horror comics, television, cannabis, video games, and the opposite sex.

The same point about the purpose of sophistry was made by Adam of Balsham in his book *Ars Disserendi,* published in 1132. This early English logician stressed that one of the main aims of studying logic is to gain a mastery of language adequate to prevent one being deceived by sophisms.

These cautions were all well and good, especially if one felt particularly at risk from sophists, but still were nothing that advanced logic in Boole's direction. Continuing through history, another logician of note in the period spanning the twelfth and thirteenth centuries was Peter of Spain (later to become Pope John XXI), whose book *Summulae Logicales* was the standard logic textbook throughout the Middle Ages. In fact, this book was still is use in the seventeenth century, by which time it had run to 166 printed editions. In England, at about the same time, William of Shyreswood wrote a book entitled *Introductiones Logicam,* in which he described in some detail the theory of the *proprietates terminorum,* which was prominent throughout the period of later medieval logic. This theory, much of which would nowadays be regarded as part of linguistics, deals with the different roles played by words and phrases, depending on how and where they appear in propositions. It had its origins in the work of Abelard mentioned earlier. An investigation of the spurious legal argument and other sophisms presented above would fall within the *proprietates terminorum* theory. Another typical task for the theory would be to explain why the first of the following two deductions is valid and the second false:

> *No man is an ass. Therefore no man is this ass.*
> *Every man is an animal. Therefore every man is this animal.*

A great deal of discussion in *Introductiones Logicam* concerns words such as *man* that can be used to denote both an individual and a species. (More precisely, the equivalent Latin word *homo* was studied, since all learned books at that time were written in Latin.) The medieval logicians reading William of Shyreswood would have been well prepared to analyze one of the most famous quotations of the twentieth century, namely the words spoken by American astronaut Neil Armstrong as he became the first person to set foot on the Moon:

> *That's one small step for Man; one giant leap for Mankind.*

As Armstrong said afterward, what he intended to say, and what he had rehearsed in his mind in the final moments before stepping out from the lunar module to make his historic first step, is

> *That's one small step for a man; one giant leap for Mankind.*

Whether or not he actually did say this planned version (and Armstrong maintains that he did say it), what was heard by millions of people back on Earth, and what was recorded on the tapes, was the version without the indefinite article *a* before the word *man*. Because man can be used both to denote an individual and to be synonymous with mankind, the recorded (and much repeated) passage is perfectly correct English, but makes no sense. In the age of the tape recorder, the history-conscious Armstrong might have been far more cautious had his history education included a study of the *proprietates terminorum*.

THE LOGIC OF WILLIAM OCKHAM AND PSEUDO-SCOT

Logic took a decisive step closer to Boole's eventual algebra of thought with the arrival on the logic scene of William Ockham in the fourteenth century. Ockham was not the first medieval scholar to show an interest in logic as a 'science of deduction', but he was the first person since the ancient Greeks to make any significant progress.

The name given to the investigation of reasoning at the time was *consequentiae*, the Latin term for consequences. In their studies of Stoic logic, medieval scholars used the Latin term *consequentia* to refer to what is nowadays called a conditional proposition, a proposition of the form "If *A*, then *B*," where *A* is the *antecedent* and *B* the *consequent*. In time, the plural *consequentiae* came to be used to denote the entire field of study.

Ockham was an Englishman who lived from 1295 to 1349. In some of his work he examined the behavior of different words in logical arguments, and those investigations would nowadays be regarded as linguistics. But Ockham's linguistic research stemmed from his interest in the methods by which people reason and acquire knowledge, and looking at those activities very definitely classified his work as logic. Thus, Ockham was led from the soft science of linguistics to the hard science of *consequentiae*.

In connection with his investigations into how we come to know the things that we know, Ockham is undoubtedly best remembered for the famous principle known as 'Ockham's razor', which says that in constructing a scientific theory (a body of knowledge) you should pare away as many initial assumptions as possible and make use of the simplest logical base from which you can derive the conclusions you want to make. Oddly enough, no such statement has been found anywhere in Ockham's writings, though it can be inferred from remarks he did make.

Ockham's book, *Summa Totius Logicae,* a three-volume classic, was really the first attempt ever made to cover all of logic in a single, systematic manner, and it had a significant influence on the development of logic in England, France, and Germany into the fourteenth century.

Ockham adopted an axiomatic approach to logic: He described the rules (or *axioms*) of reasoning and applied logic in a scientific manner. Bucking a well-established trend of the time, he was very much against the use of logic to support theological doctrines, a practice for which his contemporary Saint Thomas Aquinas, the great Christian philosopher, was well known. (The question of God's knowledge of future events was one of the issues Aquinas investigated using logic.)

In his book, Ockham listed eleven general rules for valid *consequentiae*. If you were a medieval student of logic, you would probably find yourself having to commit these rules to memory, much as you would a passage from Homer. They are all listed below, but in these more enlightened times, I include them purely to give a sense of how Ockham set about trying to capture the patterns of human reasoning.

1. The false never follows from the true.
2. The true may follow from the false.
3. If a consequentia is valid, the negative of its antecedent follows from the negative of its consequent.
4. Whatever follows from the consequent follows from the antecedent.
5. If the antecedent follows from any proposition, the consequent follows from the same.
6. Whatever is consistent with the antecedent is consistent with the consequent.
7. Whatever is inconsistent with the consequent is inconsistent with the antecedent.
8. The contingent does not follow from the necessary.
9. The impossible does not follow from the possible.
10. Anything whatsoever follows from the impossible.
11. The necessary follows from anything whatsoever.

Here then was a major step toward an algebra of thought. By writing down rules of logic in this way, Ockham was describing the abstract patterns involved in logical thought.

Important additional rules of deduction involving logical connectives—*and, or,* and *not*—were given in the volume *In Universam Logicam Quaestiones,* which reference books will tell you was written by someone named "Pseudo-Scot." As you might imagine, there was no such person. What happened is that the text was originally thought to have been written by John Duns the Scot, who lived from 1266 to 1308. However, there was subsequently considerable doubt as to the real authorship, and from then on the author has been listed, rather quaintly, as Pseudo-Scot. Whether the real Scot or not, the author was a talented logician. Among the rules for *consequentiae* given in the book are the following:

1. From a conjunctive proposition to either of its parts.
2. From either part of a disjunctive proposition to the whole of which it is part.
3. From the negation of a conjunctive proposition to the disjunction of the negations of its parts, and conversely.
4. From the negation of a disjunctive proposition to the conjunction of the negations of its parts, and conversely.
5. From a disjunctive proposition and the negation of one of its parts to the other part.
6. From a conditional proposition and its antecedent to its consequent.

7. From a singular proposition to the corresponding indefinite proposition.
8. From any proposition with an added determinant to the same without the added determinant.

Rules 3 and 4 are interesting, having the appearance of some strange rules of arithmetic. (Using modern symbolic notation, rule 3 looks like this:

$$\neg(p \land q) = (\neg p) \lor (\neg q)$$

and rule 4 is similar.) Modern scholars refer to them as De Morgan's laws, after the nineteenth-century English logician Augustus De Morgan, who rediscovered them. They occur explicitly in Ockham's work and are presupposed by the Pseudo-Scot.

Rule 5 is the logical rule that underpins Sherlock Holmes's famous observation that, when you have eliminated the impossible, whatever is left, however improbable, must be the truth.

Rule 6 is *modus ponens,* explicitly stated.

An application of rule 7 would allow you to infer from the statement "John is awake," the conclusion, "Someone is awake."

Rule 8 tells you that from the statement "A tall man is running" you can infer "A man is running." This seems reasonable enough, but as the medieval logicians themselves observed, rule 8 does not always work when applied to ordinary language. It fails when the 'added determinant' is an adjective such as *imitation, simulated, forged,* or *artificial.* For example, the truth of the statement "My wife has an imitation pearl necklace" does not imply the truth of the statement "My wife has a pearl necklace."

With the work of both Ockham and Pseudo-Scot then, there were definite attempts to develop logic in a rigorous, axiomatic way. Though neither of these two fourteenth-century logicians made use of mathematical notation to express their rules—that development was still well in the future—their approach was reminiscent of that adopted by Euclid in his treatment of geometry and described in his book *Elements.*

To see just how similar in style to Euclid's axiomatic geometry was the work of Ockham and Pseudo-Scot, here are the five basic postulates for geometry that Euclid gave in the first volume of *Elements*—the five basic axioms from which he believed all geometric facts could be deduced by means of pure logical reasoning.

Postulate 1 [It is possible] to draw a straight line from any point to any point.

Postulate 2 [It is possible] to produce a finite straight line continuously in a straight line.

Postulate 3   [It is possible] to describe a circle with any center and [radius].

Postulate 4   All right angles are equal to one another.

Postulate 5   If a straight line falling on two straight lines makes the interior angles on the same side less than two right angles, the two straight lines, if produced indefinitely, meet on that side on which are the angles less than the two right angles.

In formulating axioms for rational thought fashioned after Euclid's postulates for geometry, both Ockham and Pseudo-Scot pushed logic away from the soft sciences toward the hard-science realm of mathematics and prepared the way for Boole's algebra of thought over five centuries later. But the path from Ockham and Pseudo-Scot to Boole turned out to be a bumpy one. Just as there can be difficult times when a young child matures to adulthood, so too was logic to have a painful adolescence. In terms of this metaphor, logic was born in Greece in the fourth century B.C. and became a full-fledged adult with the work of Boole in the nineteenth century. Its adolescence began in the sixteenth century and came to a traumatic head a century later.

Adolescence, English Puns, and a Loss of Favor

In the sixteenth century, the first logic texts written in English appeared. At first, this seemed to be a good thing. Not only did this development make logic accessible to a wider public than before, it also allowed the use of book titles with clever second meanings, a practice that has always appealed to English scholars. Thus, Thomas Wilson titled his 1551 book *The Rule of Reason,* a phrase that nowadays would not look out of place on a T-shirt. Wilson introduced Anglicizations of Latin terms such as *proposition.* Other logic texts written in English at the time were *The Arte of Reason, Rightly Termed Witcraft,* published by Raphe Lever in 1573, and *The Lawiers Logike,* which left no doubt as to the audience Abraham Fraunce was trying to reach with his 1588 volume.

The introduction of English-language logic texts offered another advantage in addition to the possibility of clever puns in titles. In an age when Latin was still the language of the high church, the use of English helped to separate logic from theology, another goal that has been dear to generations of English scholastic hearts. Lever (he of *The Arte of Reason*) took this goal to great lengths by being as Anglo–Saxon as he could, producing prose such as

> *Gaynsaying shewsayes are two shewsayes, the one a yeasay and the other a naysaye, changing neither foreset, backset nor verbe.*

ट

Clever puns aside, by making logic accessible to a wider population and presenting it in a way that separated it from theology, the appearance of English-language texts on logic should have advanced the subject. However, as far as the status of logic was concerned, the writing had been on the wall—in Latin and Greek—long before the appearance of English-language texts. With their rediscovery of the literature of antiquity, fifteenth- and sixteenth-century humanists regarded logic as a dull and largely irrelevant pursuit, fit only for second-class minds. Far from improving logic's status, the rising use of English in logic only made matters worse. At the same time that logic texts were making the transition from Latin to 'common' English, Latin, Greek, and classic literary texts written in those languages were rising in status. As far as the scholarly in-crowd of the Renaissance was concerned, logic was out.

However, a lowered social status was not the only problem for logic. Another blow was struck by the rise in the seventeenth century of what came to be known as the *scientific method,* which changed the notion of what science is. For sixteen hundred years, the dialectic method of the ancient Greeks had been the principal method for establishing scientific truth. That placed logic at the pinnacle of human knowledge. However, after the scientific revolution, scientific truth was determined by empirical observation followed by analysis. Consequently, the dialectic method was no longer regarded as an instrument for the discovery of facts about the world. For instance, when the English philosopher Francis Bacon wrote his famous description of scientific discovery in 1620, he titled his book *Novum Organum (New Organon)*, indicating that the new analytic method was to replace the logic of Aristotle's *Organon.*

The publication of French philosopher René Descartes's book *Discourse of Methode,* in 1637, likewise highlighted the irrelevancy of the dialectic as a tool of discovery by promoting the method of heuristic discovery and analysis, based on observation.

We thus have the seemingly paradoxical situation where the rise of the scientific method—generally regarded as the beginning of the modern age of reason—led to a decline in the status of logic. However, what was being called into question was not the importance of logical thought. After all, science puts a great premium on precise, logical analysis. Rather, with the demise of the dialectic method as the principle tool of scientific discovery, scientists no longer viewed as important the study of abstract formal logic *as a subject in its own right.* For instance, following close on the heels of Bacon and Descartes, the English philosophers John Locke and Thomas Hobbes were very dismissive of Aristotle. In his "Essay Concerning Human Understanding," Locke wrote:

A country gentlewoman that has never heard of Aristotle can reason well enough about her own affairs. Syllogisms are useless for discovery, and serve only for verbal fencing. As for identical statements of the form 'A is A' and statements in which part of any complex idea is predicated of the whole, they are but trifling.

In mathematics too, axiomatic logic suffered a lowering of status with the discovery of the infinitesimal calculus by Isaac Newton and Gottfried Leibniz. With its heavy dependency on handling infinity (the infinitely large and the infinitely small), which nobody knew how to approach axiomatically, Newton and Leibniz's calculus meant that the *analysis* of observed mathematical properties was far more important than the formulation of axioms and the use of axiomatic logic to deduce consequences of those axioms.

Of course, the emphasis on analysis in mathematics did not mean that logic—that is to say, logical thought—was no longer relevant in mathematics. Rather, as in science, it was the study of *formal,* or *axiomatic,* logic that was no longer viewed as an important part of mathematics.

Thus, for the leading thinkers of the seventeenth century, the study of abstract, formal logic was regarded as little more than an idle pastime fit only for children; real men used the scientific method. In that respect, Gottfried Leibniz was a real man. Yet it was Leibniz who made the greatest step toward Boole's eventual algebra of thought, which was to restore the status of formal logic as a discipline in its own right.

THE LOGIC OF LEIBNIZ

With Leibniz, the world took its first recognizable step toward an algebra of thought. The man who (simultaneously with Isaac Newton) developed the *infinitesimal calculus* that made it possible to describe the motions of the planets, also set out to develop a *logical calculus* that could be used to describe human thought.

Born in 1646, Leibniz was a child prodigy whose father was a professor of philosophy. He taught himself Aristotle's theory of the syllogism from his father's books when he was twelve years old, and within a few years had worked out his own version, eventually published in his book *De Arte Combinatoria* in 1666. Whereas Aristotle had catalogued the valid syllogisms into four different figures across which were distributed nineteen patterns, Leibniz's scheme consisted of four figures each having exactly six patterns. With a total of 24 syllogisms versus Aristotle's 19, Leibniz's theory was more complicated than Aristotle's. This was almost certainly the result of a desire for symmetry and perfection on Leibniz's part. Unfortunately, though symmetry and perfection are admirable goals in a theory, if they are achieved at the expense of overall simplicity or faithfulness to the data, they can obstruct progress.

At age fifteen, Leibniz entered the University of Leipzig. Five years later, he had completed his doctorate and was set to embark on an academic career when he decided to abandon university life and enter government service. By 1672, he was a high-level diplomat in Paris, traveling frequently to Holland and Britain. It was those visits that eventually brought him back to mathematics, inspired by the contact he made with some of the leading European scientists of the day. Once he resumed mathematics, Leibniz learned fast. By 1676, he had progressed from being a relative novice in mathematics to discovering the fundamental principles of the calculus.

In his book *De Arte Combinatoria,* Leibniz proposed a radically new approach to a science of reasoning. He envisioned a kind of mental alphabet in which all thoughts could be represented as suitable combinations of symbols, and by which reasoning would be regarded as a process of discovery—a mechanical process of going through a list of possibilities. For Leibniz, the co-discoverer of the calculus, logic was to be a hard science.

Leibniz's proposed new theory was intended to incorporate logic and a great deal more. He set out to develop his own new theory as a very general mathematical framework, which he called *universal mathematics*.

Unfortunately, despite a number of attempts to develop such a theory, Leibniz did not even come close to success. The best he achieved was an algebraic calculus for determining the identity of two concepts. But that in itself was a major advance. For what Leibniz did show was that algebra—part of the language of hard science—could be applied to thoughts in the human mind.

In order to develop his algebra, Leibniz first had to decide what it *means* for two concepts to be the same. There are at least two possibilities. For example, if I make two perfect photocopies of a document on identical paper, are the two copies the same? Assuming they are perfect copies that you cannot tell apart no matter how closely you examine them, it would be perfectly reasonable to say that they are, indeed, the same. On the other hand, as distinct physical objects, they are in an obvious sense different, and hence not the same. Which do you prefer?

In the case of concepts, Leibniz's choice was that two concepts are the same when one can be replaced by the other without altering the truth of any statement. This seems to be in the spirit of the two identical photocopies being declared 'the same', though the reference to 'any statement' in Leibniz's definition tends to push the notion toward the 'truly identical' alternative.

Leibniz used the letters A, B, C, et cetera, to denote concepts and expressed the fact that the concepts A and B are the same by means of the mathematical equation $A = B$. This last step might seem innocent, but the moment you write down that equation, a question arises. Isn't the equation $A = B$ itself a statement about A and B? Obviously it is, in which case, you should be able to replace each of A and B by the other without altering the truth of that statement. What happens if you go ahead and do that? Ah, if only all mathematical equations were as easy to solve. Replacing A by B and B by A in the equation $A = B$ gives the equation $B = A$. And with that one simple observation, Leibniz had proved the first theorem about his new calculus: The equation $A = B$ implies the equation $B = A$.

Written in the form of an equation, this hardly seems like the theorem of the year. In the case of equations in ordinary algebra, everyone knows that it does not matter in which order you write down the two terms. If A and B are numbers, then "A is B" and "B is A" mean the same thing. But remember, Leibniz's letters don't denote numbers; they stand for concepts. There are plenty of examples of equations involving things other than numbers where order does make a difference. Words in an English sentence are an obvious example. If you swap the words *John* and *big* in the sentence "John is big," the result, "big is John," is not only not the same, it is not even a sentence (apart from an unusual poetic reading).

Leibniz wrote $A \neq B$ to denote that A and B are not the same. And then immediately he was able to prove his second theorem: If $A \neq B$, then $B \neq A$. He couldn't prove this theorem by swapping components the way he did with $A = B$ (see above), since there is no general rule about replacing concepts in a not-the-same statement as there is for a sameness statement. Instead, he applied the old Sherlock Holmes approach: Eliminate all the alternatives, and what is left must be the truth. Here is the proof. Start out by assuming $A \neq B$. The goal is to conclude that $B \neq A$. The alternative to $B \neq A$ is $B = A$. If $B = A$, then by Leibniz's first theorem, $A = B$. Since you started out assuming $A \neq B$, $A = B$ is not true. This means you have eliminated $B = A$. Hence $B \neq A$. Again, the result is the same as when A and B denote numbers or expressions in algebra.

Using similar two-line arguments, Leibniz proved two more theorems that are familiar in the case when the letters denote numbers or expressions of algebra:

If $A = B$ and $B = C$, then $A = C$.
If $A = B$ and $B \neq C$, then $A \neq C$.

Leibniz's first four theorems were all related to the basic meaning of sameness (or equality) for concepts. Things become more complicated when you take into account the fact that two or more concepts can be combined to produce a new concept. For example, in the phrase *the big red apple,* the two concepts, *big* and *red,* are combined to produce the concept *big red* and this is then combined with the concept *apple* to produce the concept *big red apple.* Leibniz denoted the combination of concepts A and B by $A + B$. Having demonstrated that his equations between concepts behave like equations in algebra, he now had a notion of addition for concepts.

At this point, it is natural to ask if $A + B = B + A$. This equation holds for numbers and algebraic expressions, where it is called the *commutative property of addition.* Is it also true for concepts? It turns out that it is not possible to prove the equation on the basis of the definitions Leibniz gave. Nevertheless, it is surely a reasonable property to have available. For instance, the two 'sums'

$$big + red$$

and

$$red + big$$

ought to give the same concept, namely, *big red.* Recognizing the desirability of the commutative property for the addition of concepts, Leibniz took it as an axiom.

A striking difference between Leibniz's system and ordinary arithmetic and algebra arises with the one additional axiom Leibniz formulated for his theory of concept sameness, namely the equation

$$A + A = A.$$

This equation is not true for numbers or for expressions in algebra. But it is a desirable property to have in the case of concepts. For example, it is surely the case that

$$red + red = red.$$

Though we sometimes use repetition for stress, perhaps saying that someone is a "big, big person," in terms of the concepts, repeated addition surely makes no difference.

Leibniz proved a total of 21 theorems about his algebra of concepts. We have met the first four already. Two of the others are:

If $A = B$, then $A + C = B + C$.
If $A = L$ and $B = M$, then $A + B = L + M$.

These are also true for arithmetic. (Leibniz's other theorems all involve one additional relation, called *constituent,* which I have omitted from this account.)

To today's observer, all of this may seem pretty superficial. However, Leibniz's algebra of concepts was not only a major step forward in logic, but also the first time in history that anyone had worked out an algebraic theory that did not deal with numbers or space. As such it marked a significant advance for mathematics.

THE CALM BEFORE THE STORM

Following the overture played by Leibniz, there was a period of relative quiet before Boole began the full symphony of logic. The two-hundred-year period after Leibniz saw continued interest in logic, but little by way of real progress. Yet a surface calm can be misleading. Across science and mathematics, a number of events were taking place that would prepare the ground for Boole to make his dramatic proposal of an algebra of thought.

In 1697, the Italian mathematician Gerolmo Saccheri published a book titled *Logica Demonstratia,* in which he joined the long line of logicians who examined Aristotle's syllogisms and their application to Euclidean geometry. He brought little that was new to the subject, but in a later book published in 1733 (the title of which translates into English as *Euclid Freed of Every Flaw*), he closely examined the logical structure of the proofs in Euclid's famous geometry text *Elements* and came close to discovering non-Euclidean geometry (see below).

Leonhard Euler, a Swiss mathematician whose incredible intellect was matched only by his prodigious output of research publications, made a small but decidedly neat contribution to the theory of the syllogism in 1761. He introduced a pictorial way to depict the four different kinds of statement that appear in the syllogisms. Euler's clever innovation, known as *Euler circles,* is illustrated in figure 1.

In his 1881 book, *Symbolic Logic,* the English mathematician John Venn improved on Euler's idea to produce what became known as *Venn diagrams* (Fig. 2; illustrated on page 79). Venn diagrams provide a means of displaying information about classes of objects and are nowadays widely used in logic, computer science, linguistics, cognitive science, decision theory, engineering, and other subjects.

While Saccheri, Euler, Venn, and other mathematicians were slowly developing logic as a hard science, the philosophers were turning away from the soft side that had been dominant for so long. In his oft-quoted

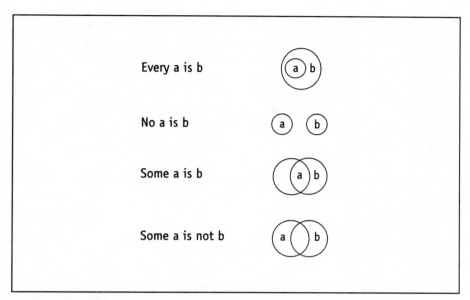

FIGURE 1 The Method of Euler Circles

Critique of Pure Reason, published in 1781, the famous philosopher Immanuel Kant tried to put an end to the dialectic method—the use of logic to derive facts about the universe and/or God.

Kant did not completely succeed, and one of those who ignored the arguments of the *Critique* and continued to seek a "logical theory of everything" was Bernard Bolzano, a Roman Catholic priest and a professor of philosophy of religion at the University of Prague. Bolzano expounded his theory in a mammoth, multivolume book entitled *Wissenschaftslehre,* published in 1837. The title translates into English as *Theory of Science,* which indicates that Bolzano was continuing in much the same spirit as Leibniz. Bolzano acknowledges as much, referring to his predecessor at one point as "the great Leibniz."

Bolzano was an accomplished mathematician, and some of his mathematical results are studied as a matter of course by today's student of mathematics. On the basis of his writing, it appears that Bolzano was also a somewhat eccentric individual. Toward the end of the fourth volume of *Wissenschaftslehre,* the reader is suddenly confronted with a section on the composition of title pages. Furthermore, in the following section of this 2,300-page book, the author had the gall to admonish writers whose textbooks were too long.

Another philosopher who ignored Kant's arguments against mixing logic and theology was the Englishman John Stuart Mill, whose book *System of Logic* was published in 1843. The book's subtitle, *A Connected View of the Principles of Evidence and the Methods of Scientific Investigation,* made clear what Mill had in mind. One interesting aspect of Mill's work is that he did not restrict his attention to the natural sciences. For Mill, the social sciences were fair game as well, an early forerunner of a trend that was to emerge in the late twentieth century—a development that will play a role in the latter part of this book.

However, despite Leibniz having pointed the way forward in 1666, the ensuing two hundred years saw no real advances in logic. It was not for lack of interest among gifted scholars. The problem was that they were not approaching the task from the right direction. For in the end, it was not philosophical analysis that led to the breakthrough, nor was it further investigation of the nature of human reasoning. Rather, the credit goes to mathematics, in particular, to two significant developments within mathematics that took place during the late eighteenth and early nineteenth centuries: the discovery of non-Euclidean geometries and the growth of abstract algebra. The former development forced mathematicians to come to grips once again with the nature of abstract mathematical reasoning; the latter provided them with the tools to do so. Thus, it was developments in pure mathematics that prepared the way for Boole's breakthrough and led, in due course, to the twentieth-century sciences of human reasoning and communication. It is not that reasoning and communication actually *are* mathematical—we disposed of that idea in Chapter 1. Rather, problems in mathematics led to the key breakthrough necessary to develop logic to a point where it could be applied to human thought and language.

Euclid Falters and Axiomatic Logic Comes Back into Favor

Since the seventeenth century, when the Greek tradition of axiomatic mathematics gave way to an analytic approach, mathematicians had largely regarded logic as little more than an interesting pastime for philosophers. In particular, few mathematicians regarded as especially significant (in terms of consequences) an age-old problem in axiomatic mathematics, concerning the five postulates for geometry given by Euclid in his *Elements:* the so-called problem of the fifth postulate.

Euclid's postulates—which I listed on pages 59 and 60—had been accepted as the axioms for geometry for two thousand years. But neither Euclid nor any subsequent mathematicians were ever completely happy with his list. There is nothing wrong with the first four postulates. They are just the kind of simple, basic assumptions anyone would expect of a set of postulates, the geometric equivalent of "Thou shalt not kill" or "Don't tell lies." The fifth postulate is an altogether different matter—the equivalent to the small print on the reverse side of a car rental agreement. You need the mathematical equivalent of a lawyer even to understand Euclid's final postulate, let alone use it.

The trouble was, Euclid seemed to need this fifth postulate in order to prove all sorts of results in geometry. The Greek mathematicians grudgingly made use of the postulate, in much the same way that a twentieth-century traveler shrugs and signs the car rental agreement. At the same time, however, they made repeated attempts to deduce the fifth postulate from the other four or else to find a simpler postulate to replace it. Oddly, despite considerable effort, the Greeks were not able to eliminate the fifth postulate or replace it with a more basic statement. Nor, over the years, was anyone else.

Then, in the first half of the nineteenth century, mathematicians discovered the awful truth, which went against every inch of our human geometric intuitions. There are two other geometries *besides* the one specified by Euclid's postulates, geometries for which Euclid's fifth postulate does not hold.

The discovery of non-Euclidean geometries was a major event that attracted enormous attention, not only within mathematics but in the intellectual world at large, as painters, sculptors, and writers struggled to come to grips with the possibility of different geometries. For mathematicians, the new discovery meant a heightened interest in the old Greek notion of axiomatic mathematics, which involves writing down a set of axioms and then proving consequences of them. The discovery that there is no single geometry—that the mathematical descriptions of the shape of the universe we live in depend on a choice of axioms—showed that there were limitations on the analytic approach that had dominated the field since the days of Newton, Leibniz, and Descartes. Analysis does not necessarily provide all the answers. Though our human intuitions may suggest that something is obvious, as with Euclid's fifth postulate, there may be no way to verify that obvious something by observation and analysis.

With that realization, mathematicians once again became acutely conscious of the importance of formal proof. As I remarked earlier, it was not that analytic mathematics does not involve logical reasoning; certainly all mathematics has to be logical. The distinction is between the use of logical reasoning to verify a hypothesis or explain an observation, as in analytic mathematics, and the use of formal logic as the primary means of establishing the truth, as in axiomatic mathematics. In axiomatic mathematics, logic occupies center stage, for formal proofs are the route that lead from axioms to conclusions. With the Greek axiomatic approach to mathematics once more playing a significant role, the ancient Greek desire for a science of reasoning based on logic was back in favor again.

ALGEBRA SPREADS ITS WINGS

At the same time that the world of geometry was being turned upside-down, there was a quiet revolution in algebra, as mathematicians started to catch up with Leibniz. They began to realize that algebraic symbols could be used to denote entities other than numbers and that the methods of algebra could be applied to domains other than ordinary arithmetic. It was the beginning of what is now called *abstract* algebra. Again, as with the discovery of non-Euclidean geometry, developments in mathematics provided a key stimulus for an eventual breakthrough in the study of human reasoning and communication.

By the end of the eighteenth century, the unknowns x, y, and z in mathematicians' algebraic equations were already being used to denote not only the familiar whole numbers or rationals, but two other kinds of numbers that mathematicians themselves had produced. (*Rational number* is the mathematician's name for a fraction worked out as a decimal.)

First, there were real numbers, numbers that were very much like the rationals except that working them out as a decimal required infinitely many decimal places. It was the discovery that such seemingly untamable numbers were lurking beneath the surface that curtailed so much ancient Greek mathematics, and it was not until late in the nineteenth century that mathematicians completely worked out a theory of such monsters.

Second, there were the complex numbers, numbers that included such oddities as 'the square root of minus one'. For the familiar whole numbers and rationals, or for the real numbers, the square of any number is positive. But since the sixteenth century, mathematicians had realized that for quite practical applications, they sometimes needed to be able to take the square root of a negative quantity. They responded by developing an appropriate system of numbers, complete with rules for addition, subtraction, multiplication, and division. Those new numbers were called the complex numbers. For many years regarded with deep suspicion, they eventually gained considerable acceptance among mathematicians in the early nineteenth century.

Other mathematical entities that are not numbers but which obey many of the usual rules of arithmetic were brought forth in the nineteenth century. *Quaternions* were discovered by the Irish mathematician Sir William Rowan Hamilton in 1844, and *vector algebra* was introduced the same year by the German Hermann Grassman.

By the mid-nineteenth century, therefore, a mathematician might write down an algebraic expression or solve an algebraic equation where the unknowns *x*, *y*, *z*, and so on, denoted something other than simple whole or rational numbers—perhaps real numbers, or possibly complex numbers, quaternions, or vectors. There was also every sign that the list of possibilities would continue to grow.

At that point, one or two mathematicians began to speculate in print as to where all of the new non-numerical algebra was heading. D. J. Gregory commented on the trend in a paper entitled "On the Real Nature of Symbolic Algebra," published in 1838. And between 1839 and 1844, Augustus De Morgan published "The Foundations of Algebra," a series of four papers on the issue.

This, then, was the environment in which George Boole would demonstrate that one further place non-numerical algebra could head was into the human mind. Two centuries earlier, Galileo had remarked that the laws of the physical universe are written in the language of mathematics. For Boole, the laws of the mental universe were written in the same language. In 1847, he proved it to all the world.

4

FROM SYMBOLS
TO SILICON

. . . people who study philosophy too long, and don't treat it simply as part of their early education and then drop it, become, most of them, very odd birds, not to say thoroughly vicious; while even the best of them are reduced by this study . . . to complete uselessness as members of society.

—Plato, *The Republic,* VII.3

Few persons care to study logic, because everybody conceives himself to be proficient enough in the art of reasoning already.

—Charles Sanders Peirce, *Collected Papers*

SYMBOLS OF THE MIND

George Boole was born in England in 1815. Though the world was to regard him as a mathematician—indeed, as one of the most influential mathematicians of all time—he shared his interests between mathematics and psychology. Were he alive today, he would undoubtedly refer to himself as a cognitive scientist, a term that was first used in the early 1950s. He was largely self-taught, and among the many mathematics books and articles he read were almost certainly some of the works on abstract algebra mentioned at the end of the last chapter. Given such a mathematical preparation, it is understandable that his interest in the workings of the human mind might lead him to try to capture the patterns of thought by means of algebra. The mark of his genius is that he succeeded to such an extent.

Boole published his algebra of thought in 1847 in a small pamphlet entitled *The Mathematical Analysis of Logic*. The simplest way to describe the contents of this pamphlet is to quote from the opening section:

> They who are acquainted with the present state of the theory of Symbolic Algebra, are aware that the validity of the processes of analysis does not depend upon the interpretation of the symbols which are employed, but solely upon the laws of their combination. Every system of interpretation which does not affect the truth of the relations supposed, is equally admissible, and it is thus that the same processes may, under one scheme of interpretation, represent the solution of a question on the properties of number, under another, that of a geometrical problem, and under a third, that of a problem of dynamics or optics. . . . It is upon the foundation of this general principle, that I purpose to establish the Calculus of Logic. . . .

It is worth reading through the above passage a second time. Boole made every word count.

As a result of his new algebra of logic, Boole was appointed in 1849 to the chair of mathematics at the newly founded University College, Cork. As soon as he had established residence in Ireland, he began work on a larger book about his new theory. He was particularly keen to ensure that his mathematics really did capture 'laws of mental activity', and to this end he spent a great deal of time reading psychological literature and familiarizing himself with what the philosophers had to say about mind and logic.

He used his own money and that of a friend to publish his second, more substantial book of his ideas in 1854. Its full title was *An Investigation of the Laws of Thought on Which are Founded the Mathematical Theories of Logic and Probabilities*, but it is generally referred to more simply as *The Laws of Thought*. By and large, the only substantial difference between the 1854 book and the earlier pamphlet of 1847 was the addition of a treatment of probability using his new algebraic framework. The logic itself was largely unchanged.

Boole tried to reduce logical thought to the solution of equations—a logical holy grail ever since the days of Leibniz. (Recall that Leibniz had attempted this by developing an *algebra of concepts*—his algebraic symbols denoted concepts such as *big, red, man, woman, unicorn*—but he had met with only limited success.) In particular, Boole wanted his algebra to encompass all of Aristotle's insights into subject–predicate propositions and syllogistic logic, as well as the Stoics's logic of propositions. He took his symbols x, y, z, et cetera, to denote arbitrary collections of objects, for example, the collection of all men, the collection of all mortals, the collection of all bankers, or the collection of all natural numbers. He then showed how to do algebra with symbols that denote collections—to write down and solve equations—in a way that corresponded to performing logical deductions.

In order to write down and solve algebraic equations involving collections, Boole had to define what it meant to 'add' and to 'multiply' two collections. Since his algebra was intended to capture some of the patterns of logical thought, his definitions of addition and multiplication had to correspond to some basic thought processes. Moreover, it would be easier to do algebra if he could define addition and multiplication so they would have familiar properties of numerical addition and multiplication, making his new algebra of thought similar to the algebra everyone was used to.

To arrive at a definition of multiplication, Boole proceeded as follows. Given collections x and y, he denoted by xy the collection of all objects common to both x and y. For example, if x is the collection of all Germans and y is the collection of all sailors, then xy is the collection of all German sailors.

Boole's definition of addition was more complicated than was needed, so other mathematicians of the time modified it to the following simple idea: Given collections x and y, $x + y$ is the collection of objects that are in either x or y or both. For example, if x is the collection of all red pens and y is the collection of all blue pens, then $x + y$ is the collection of all pens that are either red or blue.

With these definitions of multiplication and addition, Boole's system had the following properties:

$$x + y = y + x \qquad xy = yx$$
$$x + (y + z) = (x + y) + z \qquad x(yz) = (xy)z$$
$$x(y + z) = xy + xz$$

These equations may look familiar for ordinary arithmetic, where the letters denote numbers: They are the two commutative laws, the two associative laws, and the distributive law. Indeed, because of the similarities between Boole's algebra of collections and ordinary arithmetic, Boole was able to perform 'calculations' in his system, that is, algebraic manipulations such as solving equations. However, solving an equation in Boole's system corresponds not to arithmetic but to logical reasoning, about . . . well, about whatever the symbols are taken to mean—men, women, unicorns, or even what to prepare for dinner. (But remember Illogical Roger from Chapter 1? Solving Boolean equations is not necessarily the best way to make a human decision. Still, the point was that patterns of logical thought *could* be represented by means of algebra. How far that would get you in real life was a question for later generations to take up. We'll return to this question in subsequent chapters.)

There are further similarities between Boole's system and ordinary algebra. For instance, in ordinary arithmetic the number 0 is special: Adding 0 to any number leaves the number unchanged. In order for his algebra to work, Boole also needed a zero. He obtained it by taking 0 to be the empty collection—the collection having no members. The idea of a collection with no members almost defies common sense. If there are no members, how can there be a collection? Well, in some ways there cannot be, of course. But it was convenient for Boole to pretend that there was, and so he did.

One advantage of having an empty collection is that it provides a way to write down an algebraic equation that says various things do not exist. For example, in Boole's algebra we can express the fact that unicorns do not exist by letting x be the collection of all unicorns and writing down the equation

$$x = 0.$$

Translating this equation into ordinary language, it says that the collection of unicorns equals (is) the empty collection; in other words, there are no unicorns.

With 0 defined as the empty collection, the symbol 0 has the same special properties in Boole's algebra of collections as it does in ordinary algebra: $x + 0 = x$ and $0x = 0$ for any collection x.

It should be mentioned that, although Boole's algebra had many of the properties of ordinary algebra, it was not exactly the same. Boole really did have to work with a strange new kind of algebra. For instance, in Boole's algebra, the following two equations are true:

$$2x = x + x = x \qquad x^2 = xx = x.$$

These equations are certainly not true for ordinary arithmetic.

Boole used his new system to re-work Aristotle's theory of the syllogism. He started by taking the same idea that led to the method of Euler circles, namely, to regard propositions as referring to collections of objects. For example, the proposition *All men are mortal* can be taken to mean that the collection of all men is a subcollection of the collection of all mortals.

If s denotes the collection of all things having property S and p the collection of all things having property P, Aristotle's four kinds of subject–predicate propositions for syllogisms are represented this way:

All S are P:	$s = sp$
No S is P:	$sp = 0$
Some S is P:	$sp \neq 0$
Some S is not P:	$s \neq sp$

For example, if S is the property of being a sailor and P is the property of being a popular person, the first proposition above (*All S are P*) says that all sailors are popular. In Boole's translation, s is the collection of all sailors and p is the collection of all popular people. In Boole's algebra, then, sp is the collection of all things that are in both s (i.e., are sailors) and p (i.e., are popular persons), namely the collection of all popular sailors. We can then read the equation s = sp as saying that the collection of all sailors is the same as the collection of all popular sailors. In other words, all sailors are popular.

In the case of the third proposition on the list (*Some S is P*), the equation sp ≠ 0 says that the collection of all popular sailors is not the empty collection, that is, there is at least one popular sailor. In other words, some sailor is popular.

With the syllogisms represented in Boole's new style, it was a matter of simple algebra for Boole to determine which were valid. For example, take a syllogism in which the two premises are:

All P are M.
No M is S.

Expressing these algebraically results in the two equations

$$p = pm$$
$$ms = 0$$

The first of these equations says that the collection of all things having property P is the same as the collection of all things having both properties P and M; in other words, all P are M. The second equation says that the collection of all objects having both properties M and S is empty, that is, there are no objects that have both properties M and S.

By playing around for a few moments to eliminate the middle term m using Boole's algebraic rules, you arrive at the equation

$$ps = (pm)s = p(ms) = p0 = 0.$$

In other words,

$$ps = 0.$$

Writing this in words gives you "the collection of all objects having both properties P and S is empty," which can be expressed like this:

No P is S.

This is indeed the correct conclusion, as Aristotle showed. However, we have arrived at the solution by pure, abstract algebra. Boole's treatment of the syllogism reduces everything to algebra—though it is an algebra where the symbols stand for collections rather than numbers.

It was when Boole translated the syllogisms into algebra in the above manner that he discovered Aristotle had made an error. When we discussed that error toward the end of Chapter 2, we saw that it arises when you apply certain syllogisms to things that do not exist, such as unicorns. When the syllogisms are written out using ordinary language, it is hard to notice that a particular argument that works for all real applications might not work if applied to, say, unicorns. However, when everything is translated into algebra, all that remains are symbols, stripped of all meaning. The symbol x might denote the collection of all bankers or the collection of all unicorns. With the symbols having no meaning, the Boolean algebraist is forced to work with the pure, abstract patterns represented by the algebraic equations. Though working at such a level of abstraction is an ability that takes time to develop, once it has been mastered, the symbolic equations can highlight problems that would otherwise remain unnoticed. This is exactly what happened when Boole came to look at Aristotle's syllogisms.

In fact, the level of abstraction of Boole's system had far greater significance than uncovering a minor error made by Aristotle. The separation of symbols from their meaning is at the very heart of modern logic. Though this separation was always present in logic, it was only with Boole's *algebraic* work that it came to the fore. Since Boole, logicians have regularly exploited the possibility of working with 'meaningless' symbols. By stripping away the meaning, it is possible to ignore much of the complexity of the real world and concentrate on the pure, abstract patterns of logic.

In more recent times, linguists have tried to copy the logicians, studying the *syntax* of language (i.e., the grammatical structure of sentences) separately from its *semantics* (i.e., the meanings of sentences). It was this approach that Chomsky highlighted with the example:

Colorless green ideas sleep furiously.

As Chomsky pointed out, if you ignore what the words mean, this is a perfectly grammatical sentence, having the structure

adjective — adjective — noun — intransitive verb — adverb.

Still, the sentence is nonsense—it has no meaning. In fact, each pair of adjacent words in the sentence form a meaningless set: Something cannot be both colorless and green, ideas cannot be green (or any other color), ideas do not sleep, and sleeping cannot be enacted furiously.

Much of Chomsky's dramatic early success was due to his separation of syntax from semantics. Indeed, in his first book, *Syntactic Structures,* he ignored semantics altogether and concentrated entirely on syntax. In adopting this approach, he was following the lead of Leibniz, Boole, and subsequent logicians, who largely worked with the algebraic structure of reasoning, ignoring the meaning.

An intriguing consequence of stripping away meaning from a logical argument is that it opens up the possibility of building a 'reasoning machine'. It is hard to imagine any kind of mechanical (or these days, electronic) machine able to reason about athletes, bankers, and councillors. What could a machine possibly know about athletics, banking, or local government? On the other hand, even in Boole's day it seemed perfectly possible to construct a machine that could manipulate (meaningless!) algebraic symbols according to some general rules.

Indeed, in his own two books, Boole presented general rules for manipulating algebraic expressions and for solving equations in his system, and those rules were sufficiently mechanical that the English logician W. S. Jevons was able to use them to build a mechanical logic machine which he demonstrated to the Royal Society in 1870. Not surprisingly, given the prevailing technology at the time, Jevons's device looked for all the world like an old-style mechanical cash register. Yet for all its antiquated appearance, as an implementation of logic it was a stunning early ancestor of the modern computer.

However, regardless of the fact that even a machine can carry out logical deductions in Boole's system, it must be admitted that most people find it hard to work in a completely abstract, algebraic fashion. This is hardly surprising. We are the very epitome of 'meaning devices'. For humans, everything has meaning. Even when we say that something is meaningless, that very statement *means* something to us. It takes an enormous effort to condition ourselves to strip away all meaning and work with meaningless, abstract symbols. This is one of the main reasons most people find college algebra so difficult. In the eighteenth century, to try to overcome this difficulty, the Englishman John Venn invented a clever way to circumvent much of the algebraic gymnastics involved in working with Boole's system. He published his method in 1881 in his book *Symbolic Logic.*

Venn's method used simple diagrams to check the validity of an expression in Boole's logic. *Venn diagrams,* as they are now called, are an extension of Euler's circles (see page 67) and are designed to handle logical expressions involving exactly three unknowns. The three unknowns are represented by three overlapping circles. The idea is to identify the regions that correspond to a particular logical expression. One convenient way to do this is to number each individual region, as is done in Figure 2.

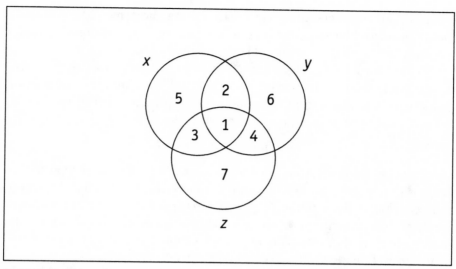

FIGURE 2 A Venn Diagram

For example, the expression $x \wedge y$ corresponds to the region consisting of areas 1 and 2 and $(x \wedge y) \vee z$ corresponds to the region comprising areas 1, 2, 3, 4, and 7. Since the expression $x \wedge (y \vee z)$ corresponds to the different region comprising just areas 1, 2, and 3, this demonstrates that the expressions $(x \wedge y) \vee z$ and $x \wedge (y \vee z)$ are not equal in Boole's system.

THE BOOLEAN BANDWAGON

As is generally the case when there is a major intellectual breakthrough, there were many people eager to jump on the algebraic logic bandwagon that Boole set in motion. Within fifty years, Boole's ideas had evolved into a major new area of mathematics: *propositional logic.*

As with Boole's system, propositional logic uses algebra to represent reasoning. But where the symbols in Boole's system denote collections, symbols in propositional logic denote propositions, that is, statements that are either true or false. In this respect, propositional logic is an extension of the Stoics's logic of propositions from ancient Greek times.

Propositional logic starts just as the Stoics's logic did, with a collection of basic, unanalyzed propositions. The only thing known about these propositions is that they *are* propositions; that is, they are statements that are either true or false (though, in general, you do not know which). These basic propositions can be combined to produce more complex propositions. Combinations are created using the same *logical connectives* considered by the Stoic logicians—*and, or, not,* and *conditional* (in symbols, $p \wedge q$, $p \vee q$, $\neg p$, and $p \rightarrow q$, respectively).

Whereas Aristotle's logic had 19 different inference rules (the 19 different syllogisms), deductions in propositional logic are carried out using just one rule of inference: *modus ponens.* One of a number of rules of inference used in Stoic logic, *modus ponens* is the rule:

From $p \rightarrow q$ and p, infer q.

As with Boole's system, one of the great strengths of propositional logic is that it strips away all meaning. It does not matter what the propositions are that the symbols p, q, r, et cetera, denote. They can be about bankers and councillors or about unicorns and green pigs. They can be simple, such as *All councillors keep pigs,* or more complex, requiring several clauses to express. It makes no difference to the logic.

One of the first things late-nineteenth-century logicians wanted to do with propositional logic was formulate a set of axioms for propositional reasoning. They wanted to write down a set of propositions from which any logical argument could be constructed, just as the Stoics, and then both William Ockham and Pseudo-Scot, had tried to do.

Logicians proposed a number of different sets of axioms for propositional logic, all of which turned out to be equivalent. For the record, here are the axioms proposed by the German logician Gottlob Frege:

1. $p \rightarrow (q \rightarrow p)$
2. $[p \rightarrow (q \rightarrow r)] \rightarrow [(p \rightarrow q) \rightarrow (p \rightarrow r)]$
3. $[p \rightarrow (q \rightarrow r)] \rightarrow [q \rightarrow (p \rightarrow r)]$
4. $(p \rightarrow q) \rightarrow (\neg q \rightarrow \neg p)$
5. $p \rightarrow \neg\neg p$
6. $\neg\neg p \rightarrow p$

These expressions are completely abstract, yet they capture the patterns of all propositional reasoning. To anyone not familiar with the notation—to anyone not fluent in the language of propositional logic—they doubtless appear to be completely devoid of meaning. Yet to look upon these six algebraic expressions is to gaze on part of the abstract structure that we humans invoke when we reason.

Moreover, anticipating a topic to be taken up in Chapter 7, a computer programmed with these six rules will, in principle, be able to produce any valid propositional argument that a mathematician, lawyer, or any other 'logical' person might produce. We should note, however, that although propositional logic is a powerful theory, it cannot handle all logical arguments. It was this inadequacy of propositional logic that led logicians to introduce a more general logic: *predicate logic.*

Splitting the Logical Atom

Predicate logic grew from the work of a number of logicians, most notably the Italian Guiseppe Peano, the German Gottlob Frege, and the American Charles Sanders Peirce. The idea was to analyze the basic propositions *p, q, r,* et cetera, that propositional logic takes as basic and to pull them apart into more basic constituents, in particular, *objects* (people, cats, dogs, houses, cars, pencils, numbers, etc.) and *properties.* In this context, properties are known as *predicates,* which is how the resulting system acquired the name predicate logic.

The more simple predicates are the kind studied by Aristotle, predicates such as:

> *X is a man.*
> *X is an Aristotle.*

However, predicate logic allows for more complex predicates that say something about more than one object, such as the predicate

> *X is married to Y*

which relates two objects (people). Another example, which relates three objects in a line (say, people queuing up to enter a cinema), is

> *X is between Y and Z.*

Expressions written down in the language of predicate logic are called *formulas.* The rules for constructing a formula are very precise. The construction rules include the ones from propositional logic, using the connectives $\wedge$, $\vee$, $\neg$, and $\rightarrow$ to combine given formulas to produce longer, more complicated formulas, as in propositional logic. Furthermore, in predicate logic there are some additional rules to construct formulas, involving the quantifiers *all* and *some.* (As in Aristotle's logic, *some* is taken to mean *at least one.* Another phrase with this meaning is *there exists.*) Though the details are a bit complicated, the following simple examples should give the general idea.

In predicate logic, Aristotle's proposition *All men are mortal* is constructed as:

> *For all x, if x is a man, then x is mortal.*

This version has the advantage that the internal logical structure is explicit. This structure becomes even more apparent when the logician's symbols are used instead of English words and phrases, as follows.

First, the logician writes the predicate *x is a man* as $Man(x)$ and *x is mortal* as $Mortal(x)$. The word *All* and the phrase *For all* are abbreviated by the symbol $\forall$, an upside-down letter A, and the word *Some* and the phrase *There exists* are abbreviated by the symbol $\exists$, a back-to-front letter E. Using this notation, *All men are mortal* looks like:

$$\forall x[Man(x) \rightarrow Mortal(x)].$$

To give another example, the proposition *There is a man who is not asleep* looks like this:

$$\exists x[Man(x) \wedge \neg Asleep(x)].$$

For anyone not familiar with logical notation, these statements are gibberish, perhaps like the first time you see a foreign language (especially one in an unfamiliar alphabet such as Russian or Greek). In fact, you *are* seeing a foreign language. The language of predicate logic is another language. As a formal language, its rules of grammar are much more strict than, for example, English. A good analogy is musical notation, which is also a formal language. As with any other language, though, once you have learned the language of predicate logic you can read its expressions with ease. Logicians did not invent predicate logic to make logic a closed cabal that outsiders cannot penetrate. They developed the language of predicate logic because it is ideal for the task at hand, namely, the analysis of logical reasoning. Other languages could be used for this purpose, say English or Spanish, but to do so would make the process far harder, just as it would make little sense to express a musical score in English or Chinese. Expressing an argument in the language of predicate logic leaves the logician free to concentrate on the logical structure of the reasoning, without having to become embroiled in issues of language.

It should be stressed that predicate logic did not replace propositional logic—the former *extended* the latter. The development of predicate logic was analogous to developments in physics that took place around the same time. Splitting the atom led physicists to modify their theory of matter by replacing the notion of the atom as the fundamental unit of matter with the new notion of the atom as a sort of miniature solar system, with a nucleus at the center and electrons orbiting around the nucleus. However, splitting the atom did not nullify the work that had been done before; it enhanced this work by explaining the internal structure of the atoms that had previously been taken as basic. Likewise, predicate logic enhanced propositional logic by describing the way that propositions are constructed from predicates and objects.

Just as they had done a few years earlier with propositional logic, logicians wrote down axioms for predicate logic. Most of the work had already been done for them. Since predicate logic extends propositional logic, all the axioms of propositional logic are axioms of predicate logic. The only additional axioms required are those that arise in predicate logic because unanalyzed propositions are replaced by their 'atomic structure' in terms of predicates and objects. Those additional axioms are a bit intricate when written out properly as formulas of predicate logic, so I will not give them all here. One of them notes that from the formula $\forall x M(x)$ you can infer $M(t)$ for any specific object t. For example, from the formula

$$\forall x[Man(x) \rightarrow Mortal(x)]$$

(in words, "all men are mortal," or more fully, "anything that is a man is mortal") you can infer

$$Man(Aristotle) \rightarrow Mortal(Aristotle)$$

(in words, "if Aristotle is a man then Aristotle is mortal").

Predicate logic was an enormous success. Its introduction led to what was undoubtedly the golden age of logic, a subject to which I will return. The golden age of logic led in turn to the birth of two new sciences: modern linguistics and computer science. However, the path from predicate logic to those two new sciences was not direct. It went by way of mathematics.

THE GOLDEN AGE

During the period 1890 to 1930, the new power of predicate logic was developed in a remarkable burst of increasing sophistication. Logic became more and more mathematical, finally changing from a subfield of philosophy to a full-fledged branch of mathematics. By about 1950, to be a 'mainstream logician' was to be a mathematician specializing in logic. The twentieth century has been the era of mathematical logic, with an emphasis on the word *mathematical*. Furthermore, this evolution went far beyond turning logic into a mathematical science. It changed what logic is *about*. The original goal of logic as a science of *all* reasoning was lost, replaced by the idea of logic as the science of *mathematical* reasoning (i.e., of reasoning *in mathematics*).

Ironically, it was Boole's *Laws of Thought* that initiated this move away from his original goal of creating a comprehensive study of human reasoning. Boole made it clear that he was using algebra to capture general patterns of human reasoning—perhaps the arguments presented by a lawyer in court or the process whereby a business manager makes an important decision. However, in the end what his work led to was a theory of *mathematical* reasoning. Indeed, in the eyes of his successors, Boole's great success was to lock onto certain crucial aspects of formal, mathematical reasoning without becoming embroiled in the messy psychological aspects of human thought processes in general. The later work of Peano, Frege, Peirce, and Russell, while motivated entirely by mathematics (unlike Boole), simply continued along the path established by Boole a half century earlier.

For instance, much of the early development of predicate logic was provided by Peano in his 1889 book *The Principles of Arithmetic, Presented by a New Method*. In the introduction to this book, Peano notes:

> [In my treatment of arithmetic] every proposition assumes the form and the precision that equations have in algebra; from the propositions thus written other propositions are deduced, and in fact by procedures that are similar to those used in solving equations. This is the main point of the whole paper.

Just as, two thousand years earlier, Euclid had written in *Elements* five axioms for geometry and deduced all the facts of geometry from those axioms, so too in his book Peano wrote down five axioms for arithmetic and showed how all the familiar properties of addition and multiplication could be deduced from those axioms. (For example, one of the familiar properties of arithmetic Peano proved was that adding x to y gives the same result as adding y to x.)

However, a desire on the part of some mathematicians to find axioms for mathematics was not the only reason why, for a period, logicians became almost exclusively concerned with mathematical reasoning as opposed to general human reasoning. To a great extent, the cause for the shift in focus was that the application of logic to mathematics was far more successful than was the application to human reasoning generally. As the saying goes, "nothing succeeds like success." As success was piled on success, logicians were steadily drawn away from the uncertainties of everyday reasoning to the more lush pastures of mathematical reasoning. Before long, 'mathematical logic' came to mean a mathematical study of the reasoning and the language of mathematics; indeed, mathematical logic became the paradigm under which an array of remarkable discoveries occurred in the first half of the twentieth century.

Paradoxically, it was the very success of this new mathematical logic that led cognitive scientists (and some logicians) in the 1950s to use it to rekindle the scientific study of everyday reasoning, and linguists (and some logicians) in the same decade to develop logic-based theories of everyday language. It was as if, during its mathematical phase, logic had gone away to training camp. Removed from the messy complexities of both everyday reasoning and everyday language, logic was able to concentrate on developing and honing its skills. When the refreshed logic returned to the general fray in the 1950s, it did so armed with a vast array of powerful mathematical techniques. Indeed, the thirty-five-year period 1950 to 1985 could be described as the golden age of *applied* logic. (By contrast, the period from 1900 to, say, 1960 could be called the golden age of *pure* logic.)

Language Stripped to the Bone

One of the steps logicians undertook in the golden age of pure logic, that was to lead to the applied logic of the second half of the century, was the development of a rich and powerful theory of so-called formal languages. (I'll say what formal languages are in a moment.) Work on formal languages in the first half of the twentieth century led to many insights and techniques that linguists would eventually make use of in their study of natural language and everyday human communication.

In particular, in the course of their investigations of formal languages, logicians adopted a view of languages that was to have a huge influence on linguistics. Prior to the contribution of the logicians, linguists had approached natural languages as products of human culture—things to be observed, catalogued, analyzed, compared, and studied. But to the logicians, a language consisted of sequences of symbols assembled according to certain prescribed rules. The former conception of language was of a psychological or sociological notion to be studied using psychological or sociological methods. The latter was of a mechanistic system of signs to be studied using mathematics. When Chomsky fused these two views in the early 1950s, linguistics took off like a rocket, racing into totally uncharted territory. This development will be described in the next chapter. But before we take a look at Chomsky's work, we need to see what were the developments in mathematical logic that led him to his new approach.

A formal language is created by stipulating a precisely defined *lexicon* of symbols (the words of the language) and giving precise and unambiguous rules for assembling the symbols of the lexicon to give what are called *well-formed formulas* (the sentences built out of the words).

The logicians' use of the terms *lexicon* and *well-formed formula,* rather than the more familiar *words* and *sentences,* was to avoid ambiguity. In everyday languages such as English, the *lexical items* are the words of the English language and the well-formed formulas are the grammatical sentences of English. However, in some formal languages, such as the counting-number language discussed below, the basic lexical items are single digits or letters of the alphabet, and the well-formed formulas are strings of those digits or letters.

Computer languages such as Pascal, FORTRAN, or BASIC are modern examples of formal languages—indeed, the development of computer science in general, and computer programming languages in particular, was a direct consequence of logicians' work on formal languages.

An even more familiar example of a formal language is the language for representing the counting numbers. This has a lexicon consisting of the ten digits, 0, 1, 2, 3, 4, 5, 6, 7, 8, and 9. There is just one rule that stipulates how to put together symbols to form well-formed formulas of this language: You may put together any finite sequence of symbols provided the first symbol in the sequence is not a 0. Thus, 10, 11, 156, 10001000, and 999840211111 are all well-formed formulas of this simple language, but 023, 0001, 1/2, and 3.14159 are not (the latter two because they use symbols not in the language, the / and the decimal point, respectively).

The formal language for the counting numbers can be enlarged to the formal language of elementary arithmetic by introducing the additional symbols

$$+ \quad - \quad \times \quad / \quad (\quad).$$

The well-formed formulas of this language consist of all proper arithmetic expressions, such as

$$124 + 21 \qquad (24 - 9902)/22 \qquad ((121 \times 300) + (11/6))/7$$

Searching for Meaning

One of the most successful developments of early-twentieth-century mathematical logic was finding a way to strip away meaning from language—providing a rigorous account of the *semantics* of a formal, mathematical language (what the well-formed formulas of the language mean) distinct from the *syntax* of the language (the grammatical rules for the language).

We have already discussed the work of Peano and others on syntax. The logicians' theory of (mathematical) meaning—the key to separating meaning from language—was developed by the Polish-American logician Alfred Tarski in the early 1920s.

Tarski's theory starts from a simple but crucial observation about any language, formal or natural. Language does not, in of itself, have meaning. Meaning is not *intrinsic* to language. The meaning of a word or a sentence arises from whatever it is that the word or sentence refers to.

Most everyday uses of language are so familiar that we generally overlook Tarski's simple but crucial observation. It often seems that the sentences we read and hear do have intrinsic meaning. However, occasionally we come across an example that reminds us that is not the case. This happened to me a few years ago. My family and I had moved to Maine, and not long after we had arrived I opened the morning paper and read the headline

MAYOR OF ATHENS TO RESIGN

Having several friends in Greece, I was naturally interested to learn what was going on in the Greek capital—the resignation looked like a major news event, perhaps having international ramifications. However, when I started to read the story, I discovered it was about Athens, Maine, a small township of a few hundred families near our new residence. Once I realized this, the headline took on a completely different meaning. The headline did not change; what changed was the way I interpreted it—in particular, what I believed the word *Athens* to designate. The headline did not mean what I first took it to mean. It had quite a different meaning. The meaning was not in the headline; it depended on what the words described.

In fact, newspaper headlines are a rich source of potential misunderstandings caused by making the wrong interpretation—of assuming the wrong meaning. Often the effect can be highly amusing, as in the following examples, all of which actually appeared in newspapers:

FARMER BILL DIES IN HOUSE
SAFETY EXPERTS SAY SCHOOL BUS PASSENGERS SHOULD BE BELTED
SURVIVOR OF SIAMESE TWINS JOINS PARENTS
BRITISH LEFT WAFFLES ON FALKLANDS
TEACHER STRIKES IDLE KIDS
REAGAN WINS ON BUDGET, BUT MORE LIES AHEAD
MINERS REFUSE TO WORK AFTER DEATH
JUVENILE COURT TO TRY SHOOTING DEFENDANT
SISTERS REUNITED AFTER 18 YEARS IN SUPERMARKET CHECKOUT LINE
KILLER SENTENCED TO DIE FOR SECOND TIME IN 10 YEARS
NEVER WITHHOLD HERPES INFECTION FROM A LOVED ONE

Occasionally, the result of such unintentional ambiguity is an 'adults-only' double entendre, such as:

PROSTITUTES APPEAL TO POPE
PANDA MATING FAILS; VETERINARIAN TAKES OVER
SOVIET VIRGIN LANDS SHORT OF GOAL AGAIN

In each of the above cases, the headline has two (or more) different meanings, the one the headline writer intended and the unintentional one that we find amusing. But it is *the same headline* that gives the two meanings, and that is why such examples make us laugh. For the newspaper headlines above, the meaning comes from the things in the world the headline addresses. In each case, there are (at least) two meanings, arising from different interpretations, and our amusement comes from our being able to see those two meanings. To explain what it is we find amusing, we have to describe the two ways the words refer to things in the world, and how those references give rise to the meaning of the headline.

Analogously, Tarski studied formal languages of mathematics to analyze, in a systematic fashion, how the well-formed formulas of the language can refer to mathematical objects and how meaning arises from those references. For example, take the sentence *The square of any number* x *is positive.* Using the notation of predicate logic, this looks like:

$$\forall x[x^2 \geq 0].$$

Is this sentence true or false? Well, like the Athens headline in my newspaper in Maine, it depends on what you take the sentence to describe. If the 'numbers' referred to are real numbers, then the sentence is true. (There is a possibility to argue about the number 0, which is generally regarded as neither positive nor negative, but for simplicity let's agree to regard 0 as positive for this discussion.) On the other hand, if the sentence is taken to refer to complex numbers, then it is false. On its own, the sentence is neither true nor false; it depends on what it is taken to refer to—on what it *means.*

Tarski began his detailed analysis by introducing some simple but effective algebraic notation to represent the connection between a sentence and the things it describes. If the above formula is taken to refer to the real numbers, denoted by $\mathcal{R}$, when it is true, Tarski would write

$$\mathcal{R} \models \forall x[x^2 \geq 0]$$

(In words, the formula 'all numbers are positive' is true when taken to refer to the real numbers.) If the formula is taken to refer to the complex numbers, denoted by $\mathcal{C}$, when it is false, Tarski would write

$$\mathcal{C} \models \neg\forall x[x^2 \geq 0]$$

(In words, the formula '*not* all numbers are positive' is true when taken to refer to the complex numbers.)

What made this notation particularly useful was that it explicitly separated language from meaning, syntax from semantics. Anything that appears on the right of the symbol ⊨ is a formula, that is, syntax having linguistic form but no (intrinsic) meaning. What appears on the left of the ⊨ is the object or objects the formula is taken to refer to. Separating syntax from semantics in this fashion, Tarski was able to develop a precise analysis of the way formulas acquire meaning when they are taken to refer to particular objects.

Tarski's analysis only works for mathematics—for mathematical formulas that refer to mathematical objects (such as numbers). In the 1960s, there were some attempts to develop analogous analyses for natural languages, but those attempts met with limited success, for Tarski's theory does not transfer well. However, what does transfer well to the study of natural languages is the idea of separating syntax and semantics, and Tarski's work was one of the inspirations that led 1950s linguists to separate (in a different way) syntax from semantics in their study of natural languages. We take up that topic in the next chapter.

One important consequence of separating syntax from semantics is that it enables you to analyze and perhaps manipulate symbolic formulas, free of any constraints as to their meaning. This opens up the possibility of being able to work with language on occasions where the meaning is not known, or even, perhaps, where there is no meaning. Of course, if the aim is simply to study, say, the real or the complex numbers, then it makes little sense to strip away the meaning. To do so would be like throwing away a boat before crossing a river. If all you want to do is get to the other side, it is more sensible to use the boat. However, if the aim is to practice your swimming so that you can cross rivers when there is no boat at hand, then leaving the boat on the bank makes perfect sense.

Throughout this century, logicians have demonstrated repeatedly that there can be much to gain by learning how to swim in symbols, that is, by learning how to reason by manipulating abstract symbols, stripped of any meaning. More recently, the techniques of meaning-free logic have enabled us to program computers—for which nothing has meaning—to perform logical reasoning.

And there, with the mention of the word *computers,* we have one further consequence of the early-twentieth-century mathematical logic that is relevant to our story. This consequence was to change human society forever. For out of mathematical logic came the modern digital computer.

THE COMPUTATIONAL MIND OF A. M. TURING

The story of the computer begins on a warm summer's afternoon in 1935. A twenty-three-year-old English mathematics graduate student named A. M. (Alan) Turing lay on his back in a meadow near Granchester, gazing at the sky over the nearby Cambridge. While his eyes followed the clouds drifting by overhead, his mind was wrestling with the mathematical problem he was trying to solve for his Ph.D. dissertation. (It would require too great a digression to describe the problem here. I'll just remark that it was one of the major unsolved problems in mathematics at the time, and the idea Turing had that summer afternoon led him to solve the problem. Turing was no ordinary graduate student, and his solution to the problem led to his being offered academic positions at Cambridge and Princeton.)

The key to the solution, Turing felt, was to really understand what goes on in someone's head when they are doing arithmetic. What it comes down to, he reasoned, was the manipulation of symbols according to a certain set of rules. Now, anyone who has struggled through arithmetic instruction in elementary school would agree with that. But Turing took his analysis a step further, and with far more precision than could be achieved by the average survivor of the elementary-school arithmetic class.

He realized that no matter how complicated the computation, it could always be carried out with a very small number of symbols, using a small number of specific symbol manipulations. In fact, he concluded, all that is needed are two symbols—0 and 1 would do. The symbols can be written down on paper or stored in the head; it doesn't matter which. What counts is that the symbols are stored in a systematic fashion. As any systematic fashion will do, for the sake of argument suppose that the symbols are written down on a sheet of paper, divided into squares, with at most one symbol written in each square. (Readers will see this as an early forerunner of today's computer spreadsheet.)

With the above method for storing symbols, the only symbol manipulation you need to perform in order to carry out any arithmetical computation is to write a symbol in a square. That's right; according to Turing, this is the *only* symbol manipulation you need to perform in order to carry out *any* arithmetical computation. Of course, there is a catch. As you work through the computation, writing symbols one at a time, you have to decide at each stage which square to write in and which symbol to write in that square. So, in order to perform a particular computation, you will need to be given a list of instructions that spell out, in step-by-step fashion, how to proceed from one step to the next.

Present-day computer scientists refer to such an instruction set as an *algorithm*. The word is a derivation of al-Khowarizmi, the name of an Arabian mathematician who, some time around 760 A.D., wrote a book explaining to a Western audience how to perform arithmetic Hindu style, with numbers written in decimal form. (Al-Khowarizmi's algorithms for arithmetic are the ones we learn in elementary school.)

Today's computer programs are just algorithms written out in a particular programming language such as Pascal, FORTRAN, or BASIC. Anticipating programming languages by some twenty years, Turing completed his analysis by specifying a simple formal language in which to express the instructions—the algorithm—to carry out any computation. The language has commands to start, to move attention to the adjacent square directly above, to move to the adjacent square directly below, to move to the adjacent square directly to the left, to move to the adjacent square directly to the right, to write a 0, to write a 1, and to stop. At each step in the computation, the instruction that is carried out next can depend on whether the square currently under attention contains a 0 or a 1. At the start of the computation, all squares have a 0 in them apart from any squares that encode the data for the computation (the *input data*).

Regarded in such a manner, arithmetic computation is reduced to the manipulation of meaning-free symbols according to rules prescribed in advance. As Turing observed, once the algorithm has been worked out and expressed in the formal language, the entire computation can, in principle, be carried out by a machine. At the time, Turing did not attempt to build such a device, but he described one in conceptual terms, and today those conceptual computing devices are known as *Turing machines*.

And there, back in 1935, were all the ingredients of the actual digital computers that would be designed and built in the early 1950s.

In fact, the very first electronic digital computer ran its first program on June 21, 1948, in a laboratory at the University of Manchester, in the North of England. That computer was known as the 'Manchester Mark I', and it had been assembled over a two-year period, largely from war surplus components. The program was written by a man named Tom Kilburn, and was designed to find the highest factor of a given integer. The data was entered manually in binary code using a keyboard, and when the output was produced 52 minutes later, it consisted of a sequence of blips on a crude cathode-ray tube, which were read off manually and interpreted as binary code.

That Turing's theoretical ideas about computation became reality so quickly was due in no small part to Turing himself. During the Second World War, he worked for the British Government as a code breaker, developing a number of (nonprogrammable) special-purpose computers to help crack the German military codes. Moreover, it was his understanding that computing was fundamentally about the manipulation of symbols according to rules of logic—not calculation with numbers according to the rules of arithmetic—that led to the design of programmable computers. It was therefore only fitting that, shortly after the first program had been successfully run, Turing was invited to join the research team at Manchester to work on further development of the new technology of general purpose electronic computers.

Part of Turing's genius was his observation that any computation can be broken up into the repetition of a small number of simple, basic steps, controlled by an algorithm expressed in a simple, formal language. An analogous claim for language would be that writing English prose on a piece of paper always consists of putting down letters of the alphabet and various punctuation symbols and spaces according to the rules of spelling and grammar. Regarded in this way, the only thing that distinguishes Shakespeare from the er-y'know-never-was-any-good-in-English inarticulate teenager is that they follow different algorithms.

In fact, in his book *Syntactic Structures,* Chomsky did investigate briefly the possibility of analyzing the syntax of natural language by studying algorithms that generate grammatical sentences in a computational manner, but he quickly abandoned such an approach in favor of a related method better suited to language—the method of *generative grammars* we will encounter in the next chapter.

Logic in silicon

Though he could hardly have known it at the time, when Boole worked out his algebraic theory of logic, he was laying down the basic theory of the modern-day electronic computer. Today's ubiquitous digital computer consists of an assembly of very simple electronic devices to manipulate expressions of propositional logic.

With just three kinds of simple switches, or *gates,* you can construct a circuit that will compute the truth value of any expression of propositional logic (see Figure 3). Each wire in the circuit represents a particular propositional variable, p, q, r, and so on. The idea is that current flowing in the p wire represents the truth value T for p; the absence of current in the p wire represents truth value F for p. To compute a conjunction

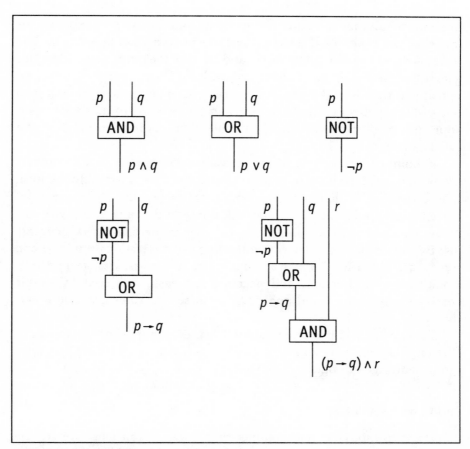

FIGURE 3 Some Simple Logic Circuits

$p \wedge q$, you need a gate that has two wires coming in, one for p and the other for q, and one wire going out (for $p \wedge q$). The gate should be constructed so that current only passes through the gate if current flows in through both incoming wires simultaneously. To compute a disjunction $p \vee q$, you need a similar gate that will allow current to flow through whenever it flows in through at least one of the two input wires. To compute negation, you need a gate with one input wire and one output wire, designed so that if current flows in, then no current flows out, and if no current flows in, then current flows out.

To compute more complicated propositions, you simply put together the appropriate combination of *and, or,* and *not* gates. For example, to obtain a circuit that computes the material conditional $p \to q$, you use the fact that the conditional is equivalent to the combination $\neg p \lor q$. You then take a *not* gate to compute $\neg p$ and connect the output wire from this gate to one of the inputs of an *or* gate, with a q wire going to the other input. If you then take the output from the $p \to q$ circuit and connect it to one of the inputs of an *and* gate, with an r wire going to the other input, your circuit will compute the truth value of the expression $(p \to q) \land r$ (see Figure 3).

In point of fact, for engineering reasons modern electronic computers are not constructed in exactly this manner, but this is basically the idea. One difference is that modern computers do not use the current/no-current representation; instead, current flows all the time, but at two different voltages. Another difference is that in some computers there are just two basic gates, implementing the Boolean expressions $\neg(p \land q)$ and $\neg(p \lor q)$. These are known as *nand gates* and *nor gates,* respectively. Conjunction, disjunction, and negation are easily achieved by simple combinations of nand and nor gates, so these two gates give you everything.

Thus, while it is possible to argue whether or not we are in an Age of Reason, in an era dominated by the electronic computer we are very definitely in an Age of Logic.

Shadows of a Wheel

After a two-thousand-year journey that began in ancient Greece, the search for patterns of language and thought finally paid dividends. The process of abstraction and mathematical analysis introduced by the Greeks had already led to a deep understanding of the physical world and to the technologies that built on that understanding. With the growth of modern logic, that same process of abstraction and mathematical analysis led, at the start of the twentieth century, to an understanding of logical thought, and then, in the 1940s, to the development of the digital computer.

For many centuries, logic had been regarded as an exercise yard for the human mind—a view of logic captured by the quotation from Plato that opened this chapter. But the work of the twentieth-century logicians changed all that by transforming logic from a soft science to a hard one, built on a solid mathematical foundation.

By the mid-1950s, at a number of major American technological universities, in particular at the Massachusetts Institute of Technology (MIT), mathematicians were trying to close the 'logic circle', to take the computers that had resulted from a study of thought and program them to think—closing the circle from

thinking

to

patterns of thinking

to

logic

to

computers

to

computers that think.

At the same time that Marvin Minsky, John McCarthy, and their MIT colleagues were developing AI, another MIT scholar was trying to close another logic circle. Just down the corridor from the MIT AI team, linguist Noam Chomsky was trying to close the circle from

language

to

patterns of language

to

logic

to

mathematical theories of language.

As I indicated in Chapter 1, neither group succeeded in closing their respective circles. But as a result of the work they began, we now realize that the two circles are shadows of the same wheel.

5

THE SCIENCE
OF LANGUAGE

[T]hose sciences that have tried to account rationally for human behavior have come nowhere near equaling the achievements of the physical sciences. The physical sciences have given us penetrating insights into the nature of matter and have even dared to suggest how matter came into existence. They have done a much better job of describing the material universe than literature has. . . . If we want to obtain a glimmering of what human nature is like, we are still on firmer ground with Shakespeare or Aeschylus or Joyce or Dostoyevsky than with any behavioral scientist. . . .

Suppose, however, that . . . the behavioral sciences have failed to achieve their larger objectives simply because they started in the wrong place and made the wrong assumptions. Suppose that some single characteristic of humans turns out to be the antecedent of most or even all the other characteristics that differentiate us even from our closest relatives among the apes. . . .

[I suggest that] language [is] just such a capacity.

—Derek Bickerton.[1]

A WAY WITH WORDS

During the height of the Vietnam war, when student protesters were disrupting the daily activities on campuses across the United States and destroying research laboratories that were carrying out military-funded research, not a scrap of damage was done to a scruffy, wooden building

---

1. Quoted from the introduction to his book *Language and Human Behavior* (1995). Bickerton is a well-known anthropologist and linguist whom we shall encounter in Chapter 6.

tucked away on a piece of wasteland in the middle of the campus of MIT in Cambridge, Massachusetts. Known simply as Building 20, it was home to MIT's Army Officer Training Corps, and hence, it should have been a prime target. Almost certainly, the reason it was not was that Noam Chomsky had his office in Building 20.

Chomsky was a hero of the anti-war movement. He had a way with words, and he used that talent to argue forcefully and effectively against the war. But his fame as a linguist and his tenured position in the MIT Linguistics Department depended on another 'way with words'—a mathematical one. One of the ten most-quoted authors of all time, and the only one to make that list while still alive, Chomsky has been rightly called the father of modern linguistics.

Indeed, the linguistics calendar can be split into two clearly distinct periods, B.C. and A.D. In this case, these initials stand for 'before Chomsky' and 'after the dissertation'. The dissertation is Chomsky's doctoral dissertation, submitted to the University of Pennsylvania in 1955—though as occurred when Charles Darwin proposed his revolutionary ideas on evolution, it took some time before Chomsky's new-style linguistics was accepted by the linguistics community. In fact, it was not until 1957 that Chomsky was able to publish a portion of his dissertation, and then it was partly at his own expense with a small publisher in The Netherlands. However, Chomsky's small (just over a hundred pages) pamphlet, entitled *Syntactic Structures,* was to completely revolutionize linguistics.

For almost two thousand years, from the time of the ancient Greeks, the study of language was practically indistinguishable from the study of reasoning. Indeed, insofar as the structure of language was studied at all, it was largely in order to analyze rational arguments. But around the end of the eighteenth century in Europe and in the early twentieth century in North America, scholars began to study language in its own right, as a medium of communication. For the Europeans, the main motivation was historical, namely, the study of the evolution of the different European languages. In America, the goal was anthropological, as scholars tried to understand the cultures of various American Indian tribes. These developments, on two separate continents, were the beginnings of the modern science of linguistics.

The birth of linguistics marked a separation of the study of language from logic—the study of reasoning. At the time when logic was becoming increasingly mathematical, early linguistics was very much a social science, concerned more with describing various features of language than with developing scientific explanations of how language works. However, this separation of the study of language from the study of reasoning lasted little more than a century and a half. In the early 1950s, by taking some of the ideas of twentieth-century logic and applying them to natural languages, Chomsky turned linguistics from a soft science carried out by psychologists, sociologists, and anthropologists to a mathematically based hard science. By writing down abstract rules that describe how words fit together to form grammatical sentences, Chomsky brought the study of language back into the same mathematical fold as the study of reasoning (i.e., logic).

Chomsky's approach was decidedly mathematical. He formulated rules that explain how words can be put together to form grammatical sentences in much the same way that logicians write rules to explain how propositions can be combined to form valid arguments. In doing this, he was directly influenced by modern logic. In order to develop a new, mathematical theory of language, Chomsky turned his back completely on all social and cultural aspects of language, and concentrated entirely on the mechanics, in particular the abstract structure of language.

So rapid was the initial progress in linguistics that followed Chomsky's new approach that computer scientists were soon hard at work trying to implement his rules and to build computer systems that could 'understand' natural language and translate from one language to another. (I shall describe those developments in Chapter 7.) Computers like the smooth-talking HAL, in the 1960s hit movie *2001: A Space Odyssey,* seemed just around the corner. (Indeed, AI pioneer Marvin Minsky of MIT was a consultant on the movie.)

As indicated in Chapter 1, the grandiose dreams of HAL-like machines that can produce and understand everyday language did not materialize. But Chomsky's new-style linguistics has had a lasting impact. Since Chomsky, much of linguistics has been a hard science, with precisely stated hypotheses that can be tested by observation and experiment. In today's age of information, global travel, and rapid communications, linguistics is rapidly becoming one of the most important sciences. And yet, few people have any real idea what it is. So before we go any further, we need to pause and ask ourselves the question, just what is linguistics?

WHAT IS LINGUISTICS?

My elder daughter majored in linguistics at college. Whenever I fell into conversation with a parent of another student at a college open house, the conversation would go something like this:

Parent: "What program is your daughter in?"

Me: "Linguistics."

Parent: "Oh, my son was never very strong at languages. He's much more into the sciences."

Me [nodding]: "Oh, I see."

My final response was an unabashed cop out. I could have tried to explain that linguistics is a science, that my daughter was attracted to it in part because she has a precise, analytic mind, and that she preferred to apply her mind to a fairly new, human science rather than the more traditional physical sciences such as chemistry or physics. As I say, I could have tried. But I didn't. The reason is that I have long ago given up trying to explain to people what my own field of mathematics is, let alone linguistics. When I tell someone I meet for the first time that I am a mathematician and they respond with some remark about not being able to balance a checkbook, I simply smile and say, "Me too." They think I am joking. No matter. It's simpler for them to go away with the erroneous idea that I have a good head for figures than for their eyes to glaze over as they struggle to follow my description of what I really do as a mathematician. How much harder it would be to inform my interlocutor that not only is modern linguistics a science, but a *mathematical* science at that.

However, as the author of this book, I suspect I am in a stronger position with regard to you, my reader. For one thing, if you have gotten this far, I don't have to worry about the checkbook caricature. (Besides, I can't see your eyes, even if they do glaze over.) For another, the earlier chapters have already made plausible the ideas of a science of language.

Linguistics, as the term is presently understood, is the study of language as a system that people use to communicate with each other. Though such a study may involve an examination of one or more particular languages (both their history and their present-day structure), the fundamental aim is not the study of any one specific language, but language as a general phenomenon. An obvious analogy would be computer science, where the object of study is not some particular computer or some particular programming language, but the general notion of computing. Another example would be theater studies. There, the primary aim is not to analyze one or two particular plays, but to understand the general principles involved in drama.

A NEW SCIENCE IS BORN

The first clearly recognizable attempt to develop linguistics as a science of language (no *s*)—as opposed to the study of particular languages (with the *s*)—was made by the Swiss scholar Ferdinand de Saussure in the early years of the twentieth century. Prior to that, the main interest in language had been what is known as *philology,* or the study of the histories of particular languages and the relationships between them, including the reconstruction of lost protolanguages from which modern languages have descended. However, even the philologists were not immune from the pressures to approach their study in a scientific fashion, and a proper appreciation of the contributions of de Saussure, and much later of Chomsky, requires some acquaintance with that early work.

Work in philology spanned much of the nineteenth century and was very much a German enterprise. Many of the early German philologists were also active in the late-eighteenth- and early-nineteenth-century intellectual and artistic movement known as *Romanticism,* where the emphasis was on cultural and ethnic roots rather than classical traditions. This is reflected in their work on language. Among the leading German linguists of the time was Jacob Grimm, best known for the anthology of German fairy tales he assembled with his brother Wilhelm.

For all its close connections with literature, art, and folk history, nineteenth-century German philology was not immune to influences from the world of science. Two major scientific developments in particular that were taking place at the same time had an effect on the way the development of languages was viewed. First, there was the rise of modern physics: According to physicists of the time, it should be possible to describe all phenomena by means of simple, deterministic, physical laws, so that, in principle, all future states of the world may be inferred from a complete knowledge of the present state.

The influence of physics on linguistics can be seen in the various general laws the philologists formulated to try to explain the history of sound changes in languages. For instance, Grimm's Law supposedly describes, by means of three simple formulas, the change in consonant sounds from the Proto-Indo-European language to the modern Germanic languages. You can see—or more precisely, hear—the result of such changes when you compare, say, English, a Germanic language, with Greek, where there was no such consonant change. For example, many English words that start with a hard consonant have a Greek counterpart that begins with a soft sound—the English word *door* starts with a hard *d* but its Greek counterpart *thyra* starts with a soft *th* sound; the English word *foot* starts with a hard *f,* but the Greek equivalent *pous* begins with a soft *p;* and so forth.

The second scientific development that had a major influence on the study of language was the growing acceptance in biology of the theory of evolution that followed the publication of Charles Darwin's *Origin of the Species* in 1859. In fact, even before Darwin's book appeared, some linguists suggested that languages are like living organisms that evolve over time. For example, in 1827, Franz Bopp wrote:

> Languages must be regarded as organic bodies, formed in accordance with definite laws; bearing within themselves an internal principle of life, they develop and they gradually die out. . . . (*Über J. Grimm's Deutsche Grammatik*)

Though you would be hard pressed to find a linguist today who would agree with such a view, it is easy to see where the idea came from. Languages do evolve over time, and that evolution can be traced by a 'family tree'. For instance, French, Italian, and Rumanian descend from Latin; English, German, and the Scandinavian languages descend from Proto-Germanic; and Latin and Proto-Germanic, in turn, descend from Proto-Indo-European. This is very reminiscent of the way the Darwinian biologists described the evolution of animal species, with humans, chimpanzees, and gorillas descending from some now extinct species of ape; cats, lions, and tigers descending from some extinct 'proto-feline' creature; and the proto-ape and proto-feline coming, in turn, from some even earlier common ancestor. The comparison between languages and animal species was drawn out explicitly by August Schleicher in a pamphlet titled *Darwin's Theory and Linguistics,* published in 1863. Schleicher even suggested that linguistics should be regarded as a regular branch of biology, alongside botany and zoology.

Darwin himself observed the similarity between the evolution of languages and the evolution of biological species. In *Languages and Species,* published in 1874, he wrote:

> The formation of different languages and of distinct species, and the proofs that both have been developed through a gradual process, are curiously parallel. . . . Languages, like organic beings, can be classified in groups under groups; and they can be classed either naturally, according to descent, or artificially by other characters. Dominant languages and dialects spread widely, and lead to the gradual extinction of other tongues.

For a variety of reasons, toward the end of the nineteenth century, the evolutionary biological approach to linguistics began to lose favor. Not the least reason was the complete absence of any notion of natural selection for languages. Languages do indeed evolve and change, but the individual changes hardly seem to fit the description 'survival of the fittest'. And when a language does die out, it is because of political or economic reasons affecting the people who use the language, not because of a weakness in the language itself.

The deterministic laws approach also lost ground. The laws of physics are the same the world over and do not change over time. You don't find that there is one law of refraction in Spain and another in China, and the law of gravity does not change over time. In contrast, languages differ from country to country, and they change over time. So whatever approach we wish to adopt toward understanding language, it should not be as a kind of physics, where we look for deterministic laws.

Given the growing realization that neither physics nor biology provided an adequate model for a science of language, one might have expected the linguists to abandon the idea that the study of language should *be* a science. But that they were not prepared to do. It was, after all, the German academy that introduced the distinction between the natural sciences (*Naturwissenschaften*) and the humanities (*Geisteswissenschaften*), and it was the same German academy that gave the former the higher status. Having tasted the sweeter water in the land of the natural sciences, the (mostly German) philologists were not about to lower their status by giving up their seat on the train of science.

When scientific rescue came to linguistics, it was at the hands of not a German scholar, but a Swiss, and a French-speaking Swiss at that. However, Mongin-Ferdinand de Saussure, who was born in Geneva in 1857, did have German connections. He carried out his early studies in Germany, and it was while a student in Germany that he wrote his first book, published shortly after his twenty-first birthday. The book was a major contribution to the reconstruction of the Proto-Indo-European language, and it marked the beginning of de Saussure's highly successful and productive career in traditional (i.e., philological) linguistics.

Soon after his return to Geneva, de Saussure started to develop a new kind of scientific linguistics, which he called *synchronic linguistics*. In synchronic linguistics, the object of study is language as a contemporary communicative system, disregarding its development over time. This is very different from philology, where the focus is on the historical development of language. Synchronic linguistics focuses on the fact that people use language to communicate, and for that purpose the history of the language is completely irrelevant. The only thing of relevance is the current structure of the language—the current *language state* or *état de langue,* as de Saussure called it.

To see what de Saussure was getting at, stop for a moment to reflect on what goes on when we use language to communicate. First of all, we make use of systematic relationships between words and the things in the world that those words denote. For example, the word *cat* may be used to refer to a certain kind of object in the world. There is a systematic relationship between the word *cat* and objects of a certain kind. We generally depend on this relationship whenever we use the word *cat;* it is part of what we generally refer to as the meaning of the word.

De Saussure argued that the relationship between a word and the things in the world it can refer to is only part of the meaning of the word. When we use language to communicate, he claimed, we also make use of systematic relationships between the various parts of a language. According to de Saussure, the relationship between a word and other words in the language is also part of the meaning of the word. For instance, the meaning of a word in a language can depend on the contrast with any other words that are available in the language to express a similar idea. De Saussure used the French word *mouton* as an example. There are two English words that translate as *mouton: sheep* and *mutton.* The presence of the other means that the role of each of the words *sheep* and *mutton* in English is different from the role in French of the single French equivalent *mouton.*

In fact, for de Saussure, it was the internal relationships between the words of a language that formed the main object of study in linguistics, and he developed an extensive theory based on this idea. Though he did not publish his ideas, some colleagues reconstructed his new theory from his notes after his death, publishing their account in book form in 1916. The book was called the *Course in General Linguistics,* and it was the first textbook of modern linguistics.

A major question faces anyone who, like de Saussure, sets out to develop a science of language as a system: Exactly what is a language? For instance, what is English? What is French? One answer would be that English is the primary language spoken in England or in Iowa, and French is the primary language spoken in France, but that hardly gets us very far. (In the case of French there is another answer, since the Académie Française tries to fulfill the charge of legislating 'correct French'. However, the pronouncements of that body often result in official definitions of correct French linguistic entities that hardly any French man or woman ever uses, so I propose to do what most French citizens seem to do and ignore that method of language definition.)

You can hear individual English or French sentences being spoken or see them in written form. You can hear an instance of a particular dialect of English or French. But the entire *language* of English or French is something else, something ethereal and abstract. Just as the *species* of potato is something abstract and different from any individual potato that can be seen, touched, tasted, smelled, or eaten, so too with language. De Saussure referred to individual acts of language use as *parole* (literally, *speaking*), and the language state—the entire body of internal relationships between the different components of the language (words, phrases, clauses, etc.)—as *langue*. Thus, in his own terminology, it was the notion of *langue* that he set out to study.

It should be mentioned that the systematic relationships of *langue* that de Saussure studied were not the same as the ones studied by linguists today under the name syntax. As explained above, de Saussure concentrated on the relationships between individual words, as in the sheep/mutton example given earlier. He did not examine the grammatical structure of entire sentences, which is the principal topic of present-day syntactic theory. De Saussure restricted his attention to relationships between individual words because words are the parts of language of which ordinary speakers are aware. If you ask a competent speaker of English to spell or to define a reasonably common word, he or she will probably be able to do so with ease. However, few English speakers are able to describe the rules of grammar that govern the sentences they produce. For de Saussure then, words were what speakers know about their language; the grammatical rules of language were part of *parole*—the use of language—which he did not examine.

However, while de Saussure's work started a strong European tradition of investigating the abstract patterns of language, it was not until Chomsky appeared on the scene that a similar approach to language was to play a central role in American linguistics. For American linguistics has its roots in a quite different tradition from that of the Europeans.

The american way

At about the same time that de Saussure was developing his linguistic theory, several thousand miles away, on the North American continent, an emigré German scholar named Franz Boas was also taking a close, scientific look at language. However, Boas's approach was different from that of de Saussure, and as a result, when Boas's methods eventually developed into North American linguistics, it was to be a quite different discipline from the European studies of language started by de Saussure. For Boas's interest in language was that of an anthropologist.

Anthropology is another of those disciplines, like linguistics, that hardly anyone seems to understand. In the popular mind, an anthropologist is either someone who spends each day brushing sand and mud off broken remnants of centuries-old clay kitchenware, or else a person who heads off into the jungle with a floppy hat and a tape recorder in search of remote tribes. Though the former misunderstanding may often result from a confusion of the words *anthropologist* and *archeologist,* there is truth in both images. An anthropologist studies human cultures, cultures both in previous times and in the present day.

Boas was born in Germany in 1858, and after studying physics and geography, he discovered that his real interest lay in anthropology—an interest he would pursue until his death in 1942. He specialized in the anthropology of North America, in particular the many Native American tribes that were beginning to die out. He moved permanently to the United States in the late 1880s, where he could be much closer to the peoples whose cultures he studied.

Boas believed you can learn a great deal about a society by studying its language. His interest in language was aimed not at a general theory of *langue;* rather, he wanted to understand particular languages to shed light on the culture of the people who use those languages.

In his study of the various tribal languages, not only was Boas's goal different from that of de Saussure, he also had to work with data of a very different kind. De Saussure was faced with the task of developing a theory to explain historical, evolutionary, and contemporary aspects of the familiar Western languages that everyone spoke: French, German, English, and so on. With recorded histories going back over many centuries, there was no shortage of data on which to base such a theory. Indeed, for de Saussure, one of the most difficult aspects of the enterprise was that the very familiarity of the languages studied could easily hinder attempts to step back and take a dispassionate, scholarly look at the data. For Boas, on the other hand, the data was sparse and unfamiliar. There was no written linguistic history, indeed, almost nothing written at all, and the languages he was studying were not familiar to any Western European or American scholar. His only sources of data were the languages as they were being spoken at the time. So, while the European linguists were able to contemplate the finer points of *langue,* Boas was faced with the far more basic task of figuring out the underlying structure of the languages he encountered. It is therefore not surprising that the approach to language that he (and others) developed was different from that of de Saussure. Whereas early European linguistics began with various beliefs and assumptions about the structure of a familiar language, American linguists of the Boas school were concerned primarily with method—how to go about cataloguing and analyzing an unfamiliar language. Today, Boas's approach is sometimes referred to as *descriptive linguistics.*

In the early 1900s, Boas was the organizer of a survey, sponsored by the Smithsonian Institution, of all the known Native American languages. The results of this survey were published in the book *Handbook of American Indian Languages,* which appeared in 1911. The introduction to that book, written by Boas, provided the first account of descriptive linguistics.

While Boas developed the descriptivist approach to language study that was to dominate much early American linguistics, it was another man, Leonard Bloomfield, who turned American linguistics into a science. Bloomfield's interest in American Indian languages brought him into contact with Boas's work; he was greatly impressed by Boas's ideas and described them in his 1933 book *Language.*

Bloomfield's concrete and lasting contribution to American linguistics was his insistence that linguistics should become a mathematical science. As a young man, he had been greatly influenced by the logical positivism movement of Rudolf Carnap and the Vienna Circle, which flourished in the 1920s and 1930s. The philosophical stance taken by this group—which we have encountered once already in Chapter 1—was that the only meaningful statements that carried any scientific weight were propositions of formal logic, which could be verified by logical argument, and reports of sense-data (seeing, touching, hearing, tasting), which were verified by immediate experience. Any statement that was not entirely made up of sense-data and valid propositions of formal logic was deemed unscientific, and a statement deemed unscientific was regarded as not worth making. (The logical positivists were as elitist as they were demanding.)

With science and mathematics enjoying a very high status in the early part of the twentieth century, and with logical positivism the flavor of the time in scholarly circles, anyone who chose to work in one of the social sciences was under considerable pressure to be completely, utterly, and recognizably scientific. Thus Bloomfield needed a firm scientific basis on which to establish his linguistic theory. He found that basis in psychology, specifically, in the brand that was politically correct at the time: behaviorism.

Though behaviorism was to end up with very bad press, particularly when associated with one of its best known proponents, the Harvard psychologist B. F. Skinner, it began life with the laudable aim of turning psychology into a science that was in every way on par with physics or chemistry. Also inspired and guided by the logical positivists, the behaviorists set out to remove from psychology any dependency on data obtained by introspection, which they regarded as unreliable. Instead, they sought to design experiments to observe and measure the output behavior produced by subjects in response to systematically applied input stimuli.

For example, by means of controlled experiments, birds can be trained to press a lever to obtain seed, and a dog that is regularly subjected to a ringing bell immediately before being fed will, in time, begin to salivate at the sound of the bell, before the food has appeared. The behaviorist will take note of these responses, but will—or at least should—avoid making any assumptions about what goes on in the test subject's mind.

As a basis for an empirical science, such an experimental methodology is entirely reasonable. What led to behaviorism's eventual fall from grace was the claim made by many of its adherents that their version of events was the whole truth. It is one thing to say that psychology should be restricted to data obtained from stimulus–response experiments; it is quite another to claim that there is nothing further to be said, and that all creatures, from pigeons to humans, are little more than input–output devices. Such an assumption is quite unwarranted.

The behaviorist approach to language was to go out and observe people communicating through language, to record what they say, and then to catalogue the data obtained. One thing the behaviorist did not do was ask people about their use of language. According to the behaviorists, such approaches are unreliable, since people sometimes have highly erroneous and conflicting views on the structure of their native language. "Accept everything a native speaker says in his language and nothing he says about it," Bloomfield cautioned.

The behaviorist approach rapidly produced a substantial body of reliable linguistic data. The problem was what happened next. For a dyed-in-the-wool behaviorist, nothing can happen next. They collected their data and that was it. To scientists at the end of the twentieth century, such a procedure is not science, it is just a part of science. Today's scientist sees as part of his or her role the formulation of hypotheses and theories that both fit the observed data and provide an explanation of the data. This is precisely the approach Chomsky took to sentence structure in the 1950s. The fit of theory to data might not always be perfect, and the theory might provide only a partial explanation, in which case you look for a better theory. While searching for that better theory, you might decide to keep the theory you have (for want of something better), or you might abandon the first theory altogether and start afresh. Either way, the provision of explanatory theories is nowadays regarded as part of the scientist's job.

Anthropologists who study language today adopt a much broader approach than Bloomfield adopted, and they use whatever means they can to try to understand language, either their own or that of a foreign people. Descriptive linguists of the late twentieth century regard it as an important part of their work to try to explain what people mean by their utterances, what their words signify for them in both a psychological and a sociological sense. This is a far more difficult task than you might suppose. Just how difficult it can be for linguists brought up in one culture to understand the language and practices of another culture is well illustrated by two of the best known episodes in the history of linguistics—the stories of Hopi time and Eskimo snow. These two pieces of popular culture indicate the pitfalls that await anyone who tries to interpret observations about the language of an unfamiliar culture.

Myths of Hopi Time and Eskimo Snow

Undoubtedly, two of the best known observations of descriptive linguistics are that the Hopi language has no means of expressing time and the Eskimos have hundreds of words for snow. The standard explanations are that the Hopi Indians of Arizona have no concept of time and that snow plays a dominant role in the life of an Eskimo. Both observations, along with more expansive versions of these explanations, can be found in numerous books and articles on linguistics and anthropology. They are probably the only two linguistics discoveries of which the average person is aware. Unfortunately, these two so oft-cited linguistic 'facts' are not facts at all. They are false, as are their familiar explanations.

Both the time and the snow stories have as their backdrop the work of two early American linguists, Edward Sapir (1884–1939) and Benjamin Lee Whorf (1897–1941).

Sapir, a student of Boas, began his career as a linguist at the Canadian National Museum, moving to the University of Chicago in 1925 and then to Yale in 1931. He conducted extensive studies of the indigenous languages of the American Pacific Northwest. His approach to linguistics differed from that of Bloomfield in that Sapir thought it was quite appropriate to ask native speakers to explain the structure of their language.

According to Sapir, the structure of language is closely tied to the structure of the mind. Consequently the structure of the language used by a person reflects the way that person thinks, and indeed the way he or she views the world.

Whorf earned a degree in chemical engineering at MIT, became a fire-prevention inspector with an insurance company in Hartford, Connecticut, and pursued linguistics as a hobby. However, he took his hobby very seriously, and as a result received a number of offers of academic posts, none of which he accepted. He started to collaborate with Sapir soon after the latter moved to Yale. Adopting Sapir's overall approach to linguistic study, he concentrated largely on the Hopi language.

Whorf approached the study of Native American cultures with a particular view, namely, that the indigenous peoples of the areas he examined had a worldview very different from that of the European cultures (which he classified as a single entity called 'Standard Average European'), and much of his extensive study of the Hopi language seems to have been designed to substantiate that belief. Time was a case in point. According to Whorf, Hopi "may be called a timeless language." It contains "no words, grammatical forms, constructions, or expressions that refer directly to what we call 'time,' or to past, or future, or to enduring or lasting." The reason why the Hopi language had no words for time, Whorf claimed, was that the Hopi people had "no general notion or intuition of time as a smooth flowing continuum," and their society did not involve "exact sequences, dating, calendars, [or] chronology."

It is not at all clear how Whorf arrived at this conclusion. As we shall see presently, he was quite wrong. Perhaps his interpretation of his data was heavily influenced by his preconceptions, mentioned a moment ago, about the ways of life of the peoples whose language he was studying. Understanding an unfamiliar language is not at all a straightforward task, nor is translating that new language into a familiar tongue. For example, despite their linguistic closeness, there are many differences between English and German. The word *warm* exists in both languages, with a roughly similar meaning, but when you look closely you discover that the two words do not mean exactly the same thing. Suppose you put a pan of cold water on a stove and start to heat it up. At regular intervals, an Englishman and a German put their hand into the water. For a while, both will report that the water is *warm*. However, the German will continue to use this word long after the Englishman has started to refer to the water as *hot*. Only when the water temperature becomes intolerably high will the German stop calling it *warm* and start to use the word *heiss*, the word that a standard German–English dictionary will give as the translation of *hot*. A person faced with the task of translating a German text into English cannot automatically translate German *warm* as English *warm;* the correct translation might be *hot*. To translate from German to English accurately you have to know quite a lot about the two cultures, in particular, how they use their language.

Given that England and Germany are nearby countries that have similar lifestyles and share a long, common European cultural heritage, and given that each country has a long history of studying the culture of the other, the goal of accurate translation is achievable. For Whorf, however, things were more difficult. He was trying to come to grips with the language of a people with a completely different lifestyle and cultural history.

Moreover, he could not use knowledge of the Hopi way of life in order to understand their language, since it was in part by studying their language that he was trying to understand their culture. In such a situation, mistakes are almost unavoidable.

In more recent times, the anthropologist Ekkehart Malotki carried out an extensive study of the Hopi, reporting some of his findings in his 1983 book *Hopi Time: A Linguistic Analysis of Temporal Concepts in the Hopi Language*. Malotki showed that Hopi speech includes tense, days, numbers of days, parts of the day, 'yesterday' and 'tomorrow,' days of the week, weeks, months, seasons, and years. The Hopi measure time using the principle of the sundial and keep records using various methods of dating, including an annual calendar based on the height of the sun above the horizon.

So how was Whorf led so far astray? Well, the task he set himself really was difficult. He was trying to understand both a language and a culture, basing that understanding largely on contemporary linguistic data, with virtually no knowledge of the history of the language or of the peoples who used it. To see how easy it would be to go wrong, take the case of English and German once again. Imagine an American anthropologist, I'll call her Susan, who grows up in the United States but somehow never learns about the Germans, not even that there is such a race. As a native English speaker, Susan knows that the words *he* and *she* are used to refer to things that are animate, except on some special occasions when the use is figurative or intentionally anthropomorphic, such as when we call a ship *she*. Susan also knows that the word *it* refers to inanimate things. As an adult, Susan travels to Germany and discovers that the people there also have three words, *er, sie,* and *es,* that they use under similar circumstances to refer to things. The Germans use *er* to refer to a man, *sie* to refer to a woman, and *es* to refer to an automobile. A natural conclusion for Susan to draw is that *er* means *he, sie* means *she,* and *es* means *it*. But then Susan observes that there are many things that the Germans refer to as *er* or *sie* that she would refer to as *it*. "Aha," she says, as she starts to write her report, "these people have very primitive beliefs. They think that apples, swords, and the ground they walk on are all animate and male, and that doors, walls, and the sun are animate and female."

Of course, since Susan can see that the Germans have a lifestyle that looks similar to the one she is used to in America, she would have to be pretty dumb to reach the conclusion stated above. But if the Germans lived in mud huts in the desert, wore different clothing, and followed customs very different from those of her own people, she might well be led astray—especially if she started out with a preconception that these people were more 'primitive' than Americans.

In the case of Whorf, the most likely explanation for his erroneous claims about Hopi time is that he simply did not figure out the ways in which their language referred to time and jumped to the conclusion that these 'primitive' people therefore had no concept of time. Such is the way that myths can start. And once out, nothing as mundane as the facts of the matter are likely to quash them. Indeed, the Hopi time myth does not appear to have been stopped for a moment by the fact that Whorf himself subsequently wrote that the Hopi language does indeed have words for past, present, and future.

The strangeness of the culture concerned probably accounts for the equally extraordinary spread of the other great myth of descriptive linguistics: This myth is what British-born, American-based linguist Geoffrey Pullum has called "the great Eskimo vocabulary hoax."

In all probability, you have come across the factoid that the Eskimos have dozens of different words for snow. It is one of the most durable pieces of misinformation around. Indeed, so widespread is this belief that the American anthropologist Laura Martin was prompted to look into its history a few years ago.

According to Martin, the story goes like this. In 1911, in the introduction to his book *The Handbook of North American Indians,* Boas mentions in passing that the Eskimo language has four distinct words for snow: *aput* for snow lying on the ground, *gana* for falling snow, *piqsirpoq* for drifting snow, and *qimuqsuq* for a snow drift, whereas the English language can only make similar distinctions by means of phrases involving the one word 'snow' (such as drifting snow, falling snow, etc., that I just used).

And there things remained—no flurry of snow stories, if you will forgive the pun—until 1940, when Whorf picked up Boas's observation and used it in his popular article "Science and Linguistics," which was published in the magazine *Technology Review.* According to Whorf's version:

> We have the same word for falling snow, snow on the ground, snow packed hard like ice, slushy snow, wind-driven flying snow—whatever the situation may be. To an Eskimo, this all-inclusive word would be almost unthinkable; he would say that falling snow, slushy snow, and so on, are sensuously and operationally different, different things to contend with; he uses different words for them and for other kinds of snow.

If you count up Whorf's examples, with the vague reference to "and other kinds of snow" counting conservatively as two, you arrive at the figure of seven Eskimo words for snow. That is already three-up on Boas. Furthermore, as Pullum points out, numeric inflation is not the only problem with this passage. It simply is not the case that English has only the one word for all those kinds of snow. What about the perfectly respectable English words *slush, sleet,* and *blizzard,* to which one could arguably add the words *flurry* and *dusting* and the skiers' words *powder* and *pack?*

With Whorf's article released to the world at large, over the years the story spread far and wide. And as the story spread, so the number of words grew, reaching a hundred in a *New York Times* editorial on February 9, 1984, and even going as high as four hundred on one occasion. As Martin says in her article, "We are prepared to believe almost anything about such an unfamiliar and peculiar group [as the Eskimos]."

So what is the real answer? How many words for snow do the Eskimos have? Well, one of my reasons for recounting the sorry tale of Eskimo snow is to indicate that such a question cannot possibly have a cut-and-dried answer. Which peoples are you going to count as 'Eskimos'? There are a number of tribes that you might or might not include. What exactly do you mean by 'a word'? If you allow derivation words, then English has a lot of words for snow: snowfall, snowbank, snowdrift, snowstorm, snowflake, and so on. However, if you decide to take a fairly hard line and ask for word roots, not derivations from those roots, then the answer varies between two and a dozen, depending on which peoples you count as Eskimos. That's right, the most you can reasonably claim is about twelve Eskimo words for snow. Not many more than in English in fact.

Too many sentences

As we have seen in the previous two sections, though it is possible to adopt a hard science approach to the collection of linguistic data, interpretation of that data is at best a soft science, moreover, a soft science fraught with difficulties. However, the difficulties are for the most part in trying to understand what various words and utterances mean, that is to say, the semantics of the language. This was certainly the case for the Hopi time and Eskimo snow episodes. There was nothing preventing de Saussure or Sapir or Whorf or any other linguist of the late nineteenth or early twentieth century from developing a hard science of syntax—the rules that govern the formation of grammatical sentences, regardless of what the sentences mean. At least, nothing other than the fact that until the 1950s, no one thought such a science was possible.

The obstacle was a puzzling aspect of language first noted in print by the German linguist Wilhelm von Humboldt, back in the 1830s. The problem is this. A natural language has a finite number of words, and yet the number of possible sentences in that language is infinite. For instance, if we take any two grammatical sentences, we can form a third by conjoining them with the word *and*. By repeating this process over and over again, we can in principle generate an indefinite number of longer and longer sentences. Of course, there are practical limits imposed by the time we have available, the capacity of our brains, and, in the case of written sentences, the amount of paper we can lay our hands on. But these are clearly not limits within the language itself; in terms of the language, whenever we have two sentences, we can always conjoin them with *and* to form a new sentence, and that is all that is required to demonstrate that the number of theoretically possible sentences is infinite.

Here then is the difficulty for the linguist trying to develop a science of language. Any scientific theory consists of a finite number of statements (observations, axioms, laws, etc.). But how can you formulate a finite number of statements that provides a scientific description of the infinitely many sentences of a language?

In fact, even if you put aside the theoretical possibility of infinitely many sentences produced by theoreticians' tricks, such as those above, and just look at realistic sentences, effectively the same point can be made: There are simply too many sentences to describe them all in a manageable way. To try to get some sense of the problem, suppose we restrict ourselves to sentences of at most twenty words that a typical person could in principle produce. How many such sentences are there?

First of all, how many words are there? The number varies from language to language. English has a fairly large vocabulary. A good English dictionary will list as many as 450,000 words, but this figure is far larger than the vocabulary actually known to a typical English speaker. A fairly bright six-year-old American will know between 13,000 and 15,000 words. The average American adult has a vocabulary anywhere between 60,000 and 100,000 words, the avid reader considerably more. However, these figures are based on tests of words that an individual can recognize and understand in context. The vocabulary an individual actually uses on a day-to-day basis is considerably smaller. To take a highly articulate example, Shakespeare used some 15,000 words, give or take a few, in all of his works combined. So let's take the case of a native English speaker with a speaking vocabulary of 10,000 words. How many sentences of at most twenty words can that individual, in principle, produce?

Statistical analysis of language has shown that if a native English speaker is interrupted at a random point in uttering an English sentence, there are, on average, about ten possible words that could come next and allow for the utterance to continue to produce a grammatical sentence. (At some points there may be only one possible next word; at other points, there could be hundreds or even thousands of choices. The average is about ten.) This means that there are of the order of 10^{23} (that is, a 1 followed by twenty-three zeros) grammatical English sentences of twenty words or less. (To arrive at this figure, take 10,000 possible choices for the first word, then the average figure of 10 for the second word, 10 for the third, and so on, up to 10 for the last.) Spoken at the rate of five seconds per sentence, it would take around one hundred thousand trillion years to say them all out loud, with no breaks for eating or sleeping.

With so many possible sentences that have no more than twenty words, von Humboldt's concern was clearly not just of theoretical interest. How could there be a scientific theory of language? The same question was raised again a century later by Zelig Harris, the man who founded the first department of linguistics in America, at the University of Pennsylvania. Harris, who was strongly influenced by the logical positivist movement of the 1930s (see Chapter 1), was an early proponent of the use of mathematical techniques to study language. And it was to be mathematics that, in the hands of Harris's student Chomsky, eventually supplied the answer to the finite-description versus infinite-collection puzzle.

The key idea that Chomsky was to provide, though new to linguistics, was well known in mathematics and had been exploited by early-twentieth-century logicians in their work on formal languages. Instead of trying to provide a precise description of all the grammatical sentences, which is an impossibility when the number of sentences is infinite, the key was to concentrate instead on describing the rules whereby that infinite collection of sentences can arise from the finite collection of words in the language. For a finite collection of rules can produce an infinite collection of sentences from a finite vocabulary of words.

The idea of a finite procedure that can generate an infinite collection of entities is not at all strange to a mathematician; indeed, it is very common. For example, the procedure 'add 1' will, when started with the number 1, generate all the natural numbers, 1, 2, 3, . . . Likewise, the procedure 'add 2', when started with the number 2, will generate all the even numbers, 2, 4, 6, . . . In fact, large parts of mathematics are geared toward providing descriptions of the finite procedures that generate infinite collections. Of particular relevance to linguistics, the (finitely many) rules of propositional and predicate logic generate infinite collections of well-formed formulas. However, with insufficient mathematical knowledge, linguists prior to Chomsky were unable to adopt the same approach to language.

Chomsky's approach depends on adopting a rule-based view of language, that is, the sentences of a language are produced by fixed rules. What evidence is there to support this view? Do people produce sentences by means of rules? Just because we do not make conscious use of rules when we speak, it is possible that we are applying rules in a subconscious way.

Let's take a look at one of the arguments used to suggest that Chomsky's rule-based analysis of language might indeed be more than just a theoretician's trick and could be describing what actually goes on in our minds when we produce and understand sentences.

A native English speaker has no trouble understanding daily any number of sentences he or she has never encountered before. We saw earlier that the average English speaker can generate some 10^{23} sentences of twenty words or less, and it would take trillions of years to say them all. But that does not prevent us from understanding new sentences all the time. For example, this present sentence has twenty words, and you probably never saw it before, yet you can understand it. Not only are you able to understand the last sentence, you can recognize that it is grammatical. Since you clearly cannot have a store of trillions of sentences stacked up in your memory against which you match each new sentence you come across, some other process must be involved in producing and understanding sentences. Presumably, a relatively small collection of rules or procedures is doing the work.

Now, there is no guarantee that those rules and procedures can be described using mathematics—the linguistic activity of the mind does not have to be amenable to mathematics in the same way as the physical behavior of the universe seems to be. But it certainly makes sense to *try* a mathematical approach, especially since the logicians have shown that a mathematical approach works for artificially constructed formal languages. It was Chomsky's knowledge of the major advances in mathematical logic in the twentieth century that led him to adopt the approach he did.

Another feature of language that suggests a rule-based approach might be both theoretically fruitful and practically relevant, is the manner in which new words may be introduced. (This was observed not only by Chomsky but also by his teacher, Zelig Harris.) For example, if tomorrow biologists were to discover a new strain of life called a *plurimoth,* neither journalists nor readers would have any trouble recognizing the grammaticality of the new sentences

> *The plurimoth does not appear to be harmful to humans.*
> *Professor Jones has commenced a detailed study of plurimoths.*

Both would be regarded without hesitation as grammatical sentences, and both would be understood. In fact, both of these examples already seem to have all the features of grammatical sentences, *even though we know that* plurimoth *is a made-up word.* On the other hand, the sequence

> *John did his homework late plurimoth at night.*

does not seem right; we would regard it as ungrammatical. New words cannot simply be thrown in anywhere; there are right and wrong places where words go in sentences, be they known words, new words, or made-up ones. This shows that syntactic structure—what makes a sentence a sentence—is not inherent in the constituent words but is a matter of the relationships between them. Again, this suggests that a rule-based approach, fashioned after mathematical logic, might work.

Still another aspect of language that helped to make feasible an approach such as Chomsky's was the surprising fact that, by and large, grammaticality does not seem to involve meaning in any essential way. For instance, there are grammatical sentences that are meaningless, and nongrammatical word sequences that have meaning. The best known example from the first category is Chomsky's nonsensical sequence we met earlier:

> *Colorless green ideas sleep furiously.*

Most native English speakers agree that this is a perfectly grammatical sentence, but that it has no meaning whatsoever. For an example of a nongrammatical word sequence that nevertheless can be understood with ease, let me offer:

> *Book Devlin describe attempts understand reasoning.*

It may be possible then to study the structure of sentences—the syntax of the language—without having to deal with its meaning, and to proceed as the logicians had done following Tarski, working with language stripped of its meaning. This, at least, was one of the assumptions Chomsky made in order to develop his revolutionary approach to syntax in the 1950s.

It's time we took a good look at just what Chomsky did.

6

LANGUAGE
IN THE MIND

There is in my opinion no important theoretical difference between natural languages and the artificial languages of logicians; indeed, I consider it possible to comprehend the syntax and semantics of both kinds of languages within a single natural and mathematically precise theory. On this point I differ from a number of philosophers, but agree, I believe, with Chomsky and his associates.

—Richard Montague[1]

THE REVOLUTION BY THE CHARLES RIVER

Avram Noam Chomsky was born in Philadelphia in 1928. As a student at the University of Pennsylvania, he concentrated on mathematics, philosophy, and linguistics. His approach to linguistics was heavily influenced by Zelig Harris, his first linguistics teacher. Harris, whom we encountered in the last chapter, was one of the early proponents of the use of mathematical techniques in linguistics.

After leaving Penn in 1951, Chomsky spent a period as a Junior Fellow in philosophy at Harvard, where he completed his doctoral dissertation, *Transformational Analysis,* in 1955.

---

1. Richard Montague was a mathematical logician who developed a Tarski-like theory of meaning for a restricted form of natural language. The quotation is taken from Montague's paper "Universal Grammar," published in the journal *Theoria* 36 (1970), pp. 373–398.

While at Harvard, Chomsky came into contact with the linguist Roman Jakobson, whose work was largely motivated by a search for *phonological universals,* common linguistic structures that underlie all the phonological structures in the different languages of the world.

In 1955, the year he finished his dissertation, Chomsky obtained a position at MIT, where he has remained ever since. There, by the north bank of Boston's Charles River, he directed the early stages of a dramatic revolution in the study of language that changed linguistics forever.

Chomsky decided to concentrate on syntax, ignoring issues of context and meaning. Whereas Jakobson's search for phonological universals never really succeeded, Chomsky was highly successful in finding *syntactic* universals. The key was his use of mathematics, in particular, the techniques of the mathematical logicians. The logicians of the early twentieth century formulated rules that describe how propositions may be put together to form a valid proof. Analogously, Chomsky set out to formulate rules that describe how words may be put together to form a grammatical sentence. This was an axiomatic approach to language. He called his collection of rules (or axioms) for syntax a *grammar.* In one fell swoop, Chomsky took syntax out of the off-limits realm of de Saussure's *parole* and placed it firmly into the hands of the mathematical scientists.

The Introduction to *Syntactic Structures*—the portion of his dissertation he published in 1957—begins with these words:

> Syntax is the study of the principles and processes by which sentences are constructed in particular languages. Syntactic investigation of a given language has as its goal the construction of a grammar that can be viewed as a device of some sort for producing the sentences of the language under analysis. More generally, linguists must be concerned with the problem of determining the fundamental underlying properties of successful grammars. The ultimate outcome of these investigations should be a theory of linguistic structure in which the descriptive devices utilized in particular grammars are presented and studied abstractly, with no specific reference to particular languages.

Since Chomsky's notion of a grammar was a device (essentially a mathematical device) that produced the infinitely many sentences of the language, such grammars became known as *generative grammars.* It is implicit in the notion of a generative grammar that the sequences of words it produces are all recognized to be grammatical by native speakers of the language, and moreover that the grammar does not produce any sequences of words that native speakers regard as nongrammatical.

Just as the mathematicians of the late nineteenth century regarded the formulation of an appropriate set of axioms as the pinnacle of understanding, so too did Chomsky put great emphasis on the formulation of a grammar. This is made clear by the following crucial sentence from Chapter 6 of *Syntactic Structures:*

> A grammar of the language L is essentially a theory of L.

Despite initial success, in subsequent years Chomsky's work came under a great deal of criticism. One complaint was the great reliance he placed on introspection. Whereas Bloomfield and the other descriptivists had cautioned against the use of people's intuitions and beliefs about language in developing a linguistic theory, Chomsky argued that it was legitimate to make use of the linguist's reflections and intuitions on his or her own use of language. Another criticism was that the entire rule-based approach to the study of human language is misguided—that the mind does not operate according to rules. However, criticism aside, what Chomsky did was to put on the table a collection of precisely defined, testable hypotheses about syntax. Prior to Chomsky, linguistics had been entirely a soft science, concentrating largely on the description of various linguistic phenomena. Chomsky's theory of syntactic structure was very definitely hard science. Let's take a close look at what he did.

The linguistic patterns Chomsky wove

Inspired by developments in mathematical logic of the preceding fifty years, Chomsky began by formulating simple rules that stipulate the way grammatical sentences can be built from words and phrases. One such rule is that a sentence can be constructed by taking a determinate noun phrase (i.e., a noun phrase that starts with a determiner such as *the* or *a*) and following it by a verb phrase. For example, the sentence *The large black dog licked the tabby kitten* consists of the determinate noun phrase *the large black dog* followed by the verb phrase *licked the tabby kitten.* Using the letter *S* to stand for 'sentence', *DNP* to denote 'determinate noun phrase', and *VP* to denote 'verb phrase', this rule may be written like this:

$$S \rightarrow DNP\ VP.$$

This expression is read as "*S* arrows *DNP VP*," or more colloquially, "a sentence results from taking a determinate noun phrase and following it by a verb phrase." The sentences (*S*), determinate noun phrases (*DNP*), and verb phrases (*VP*) are examples of *syntactic categories.*

The rule for generating determinate noun phrases (*DNP*) from noun phrases (*NP*) is

$$DNP \rightarrow DET\ NP,$$

where *DET* is given by the rule

$$DET \rightarrow the, a.$$

The first of the above two rules reads "a determinate noun phrase can be generated by taking a determiner and following it by a noun phrase."

The second rule is an example of what is called a *lexical rule,* since it assigns particular words (i.e., items of the lexicon) to a syntactic category, namely the syntactic category *DET* of determiners. What it says is that either of the words *the* or *a* constitutes a determiner.

Thus, the determinate noun phrase *the large black dog* is generated by taking the determiner *the* and following it by the noun phrase *large black dog.* Here are some further rules of syntax:

$$VP \rightarrow V\ DNP.$$

This reads: "A verb phrase results from taking a verb and following it by a determinate noun phrase," while

$$NP \rightarrow A\ NP.$$

translates into "a noun phrase results from taking an adjective and following it by a noun phrase." This rule has a *circular* property, in that you start with a noun phrase and the rule gives you another noun phrase. For example, the noun phrase *large black dog* results from combining the adjective *large* with the noun phrase *black dog.* The rule could then be applied again to give the noun phrase *old large black dog,* and so on. Still other rules of syntax include:

$$NP \rightarrow N,$$

which reads "a noun is (itself) a noun phrase," and

$$S \rightarrow If\ S\ then\ S$$

which says "a sentence can consist of the word *If* followed by a sentence followed by the word *then* followed by another sentence." An example of this is:

If John comes home then we will play chess.

Here are some further lexical rules:

$$N \rightarrow dog,\ kitten,\ man,\ pencil,$$
$$V \rightarrow lick,\ run,\ talk,\ endure,$$
$$A \rightarrow large,\ black,\ tabby,\ hot,\ old.$$

Though extremely simple, the above grammatical and lexical rules are adequate to analyze the syntactic structure of our example sentence *The large black dog licked the tabby kitten.* Well, almost. Since the lexical item for the verb is *lick,* not *licked,* the grammar as it stands will generate the 'sentence' *The large black dog lick the tabby kitten.* This is the kind of machine-like utterance produced by a robot or a space alien in a low-grade science fiction movie. (In fact, it provides the makers of such movies some linguistic justification for using the lack of verb case agreement to suggest artificially produced or otherwise nonnatural speech.) To obtain the correct verb form, which in this case is *licked,* the string generated by the grammar has to be 'massaged'. Chomsky introduced *transformation rules* to perform this task. We'll turn to those in a moment. First, let's take a look at the way the grammatical rules we have so far can generate the almost-grammatical sentence *The large black dog lick the tabby kitten.*

The most common way to display the generation of a sentence using the grammar is by means of a *syntax tree,* as shown in the top diagram of Figure 4. Unlike the botanical variety, the linguist's tree has its *root* at the top and grows downward. Starting at any node in the tree, the derivation of the phrase at that node in terms of grammatically simpler elements is indicated by the lines that emanate down from the node. For example, the topmost node (the root) represents the entire word sequence, *S, The large black dog lick the tabby kitten.* By the rule *S → DNP VP,* this node can be split up into two components, a *DNP The large black dog* and a *VP lick the tabby kitten.* Then each of those two phrases can in turn be broken down further.

Because of the diagrammatic clutter that results from the repetition of the various words in the sentence at each level of the tree, it is more common to represent such syntax trees in the simpler form shown in the lower diagram of Figure 4.

When Chomsky's generative grammar is used to construct a sentence as above, it does so in this way. First, the words are assembled into phrases. Then (perhaps) the phrases are assembled into still more complex phrases. Then (perhaps) the phrases are put together to give the sentence. This sentence generation process lists all the phrases in the sentence, and the associated syntax tree displays what is called the *phrase structure* of the sentence. For this reason, a Chomsky-style generative grammar is often referred to as a *phrase structure grammar.*

So far we have seen how the generative grammar has produced the almost-sentence *The large black dog lick the tabby kitten.* This almost-sentence is easily understood, and if it were spoken by Tarzan we might be tempted to admire his improved command of English, a great advance on "Me Tarzan, you Jane." But it is not quite grammatical—English requires

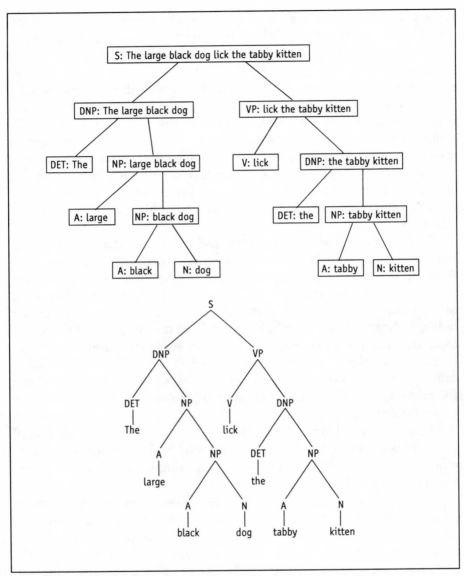

FIGURE 4 Two Versions of a Syntax Tree for a Simple Sentence

that the verb is tensed and agrees with the subject. Allowable alternatives to *lick* in this case would be *licks* or *licked*.

Chomsky's way around this problem was to approach the analysis of syntax in two stages. The first stage consists of the generation of a *kernel* or *base* of the language, which is composed of all the strings produced by a generative grammar. The second stage consists of the successive applications of various transformation rules that convert the word sequences in the kernel into genuinely grammatical sentences of the language. The kernel sequence from which a grammatical sentence is produced by means of a series of transformations is sometimes called the *deep structure* of the sentence; the syntactic structure of the final, natural form that our ears recognize as grammatical is called the *surface structure.*

Thus, transformation rules would be used to take a word string produced by the generative grammar, such as *The large black dog lick the tabby kitten,* and turn it into a genuinely grammatical sentence such as *The large black dog licks the tabby kitten* or *The large black dog licked the tabby kitten.* Similarly, transformation rules would generate other variants of the initial almost-sentence, such as the passive form *The tabby kitten is licked by the large black dog* or the question *Did the large black dog lick the tabby kitten?*

Let's look at one example. The grammar-generated, deep-structure string

> *The large black dog lick the tabby kitten.*

is transformed to the sentence

> *The large black dog licks the tabby kitten.*

by the rule

$$DNP_{sing}\ V\ DNP\ \rightarrow\ DNP_{sing}\ Vs\ DNP$$

In words, this reads: Starting with a grammar-generated string consisting of a singular determinate noun phrase followed by a verb stem and then another determinate noun phrase, add the letter *s* to the verb stem. Notice that this kind of rule uses the arrow to mean something different from its meaning in the generative grammar or the lexicon.

The same grammar-generated, deep-structure string

> *The large black dog lick the tabby kitten.*

is transformed to the passive sentence

> *The tabby kitten is licked by the large black dog.*

by the transformation rule

$$DNP^1_{sing}\ V\ DNP^2\ \rightarrow\ DNP^2\ is\ Ved\ by\ DNP^1_{sing}$$

The superscripts 1 and 2 on the two *DNP*s are there simply to indicate that there are two different phrases involved and to keep track of which goes where. This rule reads as follows: Given a grammar-generated string consisting of a singular determinate noun phrase, a verb stem, and a determinate noun phrase, to obtain the passive form, put the second noun phrase first, follow it by the word *is*, followed by the verb stem with the string *ed* appended, followed by the word *by*, followed in turn by the first noun phrase. This rule does not apply to irregular verbs, such as *break–broken*, which form their passives in a different manner.

Phew! This is all getting very laborious and detailed. In fact, the complexity of the apparatus required to analyze even the simplest sentences is one of the arguments that was later put forward against Chomsky's rule-based approach to language. The question is, do we in fact use such a two-stage approach to produce the sentences we speak? If we stop to think about it for a moment, we probably feel we do not adopt this two-stage approach. The subjective feeling we have is that we go straight to the grammatically correct form. But is there a subconscious two-stage process going on of which we are not aware?

Certainly, we often use a conscious two-stage, kernel–transformation process when we start to learn a foreign language. Small children learning their own language often go through a two-stage process as well, where the second stage consists of corrections (i.e., transformations) provided by adults. However, on balance, it seems that we do not produce sentences by a generative–transformation method, and most present-day linguists regard Chomsky's two-stage procedure as at best a useful first step in the analysis of language. Indeed, Chomsky himself subsequently modified his approach. But the fact is, we do not yet understand our acquisition and use of language sufficiently well to address the question in a completely satisfactory way.

Still, regardless of whether or not—and how closely—the two-step analysis corresponds to the way humans produce sentences, Chomsky did provide a precise set of rules that generates many of the grammatical sentences of natural language and does not generate any nongrammatical sequences of words. In particular, he demonstrated how a finite procedure can generate an infinite number of grammatical sentences of natural language. In these respects, Chomsky's work represents a successful application of mathematics to the study of natural language.

Moreover, without making any commitment to how well the two-stage approach corresponds to the way we produce sentences, psychologists, anthropologists, and linguists can use the mathematical tools developed by Chomsky to investigate natural language as it is actually learned and spoken. This is the development that I turn to next.

How can children learn language so easily?

By about the age of three, all but a few children have mastered the grammatical structure of their native language. By this, I do not mean that the average three-year-old knows when and where to place commas or is familiar with obscure rules about dangling participles. I mean the ability to comprehend and produce everyday utterances, many of which have a complicated linguistic structure. In terms of the complexity of the structures involved, language comprehension and production requires far more intelligence than, say, playing a good game of chess, a task that few three-year-olds are capable of. So how is it that children learn language so easily?

Certainly, neuroscience has not been able to offer any answer, at least so far. We do know that in about 97% of right-handers and 81% of left-handers, the childhood-acquired facility with language is lodged in the left hemisphere of the brain, while the rest process language with the right hemisphere or, occasionally, both hemispheres. But this is practically the only concrete information concerning human language-facility that neuroscience has so far been able to produce. Though neuroscientists and cognitive psychologists have gathered large amounts of data on language acquisition, making sense of that data remains a matter of hypothesis and conjecture and is the subject of considerable debate. It does seem that humans are born with an innate facility to acquire language. If so, then the focus of the debate concerns what is the nature of that facility, and how the child uses it to acquire mastery of his or her native tongue.

Chomsky used his formal grammars to investigate this issue. Inspired by mathematical logic, he had originally conceived of his formal grammar as a logicians' formal system for the artificial *generation* of phrases and sentences. (That is why he referred initially to his grammar as generative grammar.) However, essentially the same machinery may be used as a conceptual framework for the *analysis* of sentences of a language. The difference is one of motivation. Chomsky's original purpose was to formulate rules (axioms) that produce grammatical sentences. This is very much a mathematical goal. In using Chomsky's machinery to analyze linguistic data such as a sentence, the goal is to discover the linguistic structure of the sentence—a linguistic goal.

Since it is this new use of Chomsky's mathematical techniques that we are looking at now, let's use the more appropriate alternative term *phrase structure grammar* in place of *generative grammar*.

The idea behind the use of a phrase structure grammar to analyze language is as follows. You start with a sentence produced by a speaker of the language. Using the rules of phrase structure grammar, you try to break the sentence into its constituent parts of speech, breaking it first into clauses, then into phrases, and then finally into words. If the analysis ultimately breaks everything down to individual words, then you can conclude that the sentence is grammatical; if the analysis fails at some point, you conclude that the sentence is not grammatical. In the former case, the analysis provides a description of the syntactic structure (or the phrase structure) of the sentence. There is no need for an elaborate transformation grammar, since the analysis *starts* with a grammatical sentence.

For example, suppose you start with one of the sentences we considered earlier,

The large black dog licked the tabby kitten.

Using the phrase structure grammar rule

$$S \rightarrow DNP\ VP$$

you can split the sentence (*S*) into a determinate noun phrase (*DNP*) *The large black dog* and a verb phrase (*VP*) *licked the tabby kitten.* Then you look at each of these two phrases in turn, and analyze them. Thus, using the phrase structure grammar rule

$$DNP \rightarrow DET\ NP$$

and the lexical assignment

$$DET \rightarrow the$$

you can split the phrase *The large black dog* into a determiner *the* followed by a noun phrase *large black dog,* and so forth. Continuing in this manner, the analysis of this particular sentence ends with every phrase being eventually split up into individual words. If you track the analysis by means of a downward-growing tree, then you will generate the tree shown on page 122. (Except that in this case, the entry marked 'lick' on page 122 will be marked 'licked'.) The tree (with 'licked' in place of 'lick') represents the phrase structure of the given sentence—the way the sentence is constructed from its constituent words by a hierarchy of phrases. My reason for choosing this particular example was not to avoid having to draw another tree diagram. Rather, I want to emphasize that what we are doing now is working in the opposite direction from the last time we looked at this example. The original goal was the mathematical one of formulating the rules that produce the grammatical sentences of the language. We formulated various rules and tested them out on a typical sentence. The present goal is the linguistic one of producing the phrase structure of a particular given sentence. The mechanics are largely the same (though we no longer have to worry about verb agreement, since we start off with a given grammatical sentence). It is the goal that has changed. Using Chomsky's logic-inspired machinery of formal grammar—what I am now calling phrase structure grammar—we analyze the way that a given grammatical sentence of a language is constructed (and hence acquires its grammaticality) from its constituent words and phrases.

And now we are in a position to put forward a hypothesis to explain how children are able to acquire their native language with such ease. What if the human brain is constructed in such a way that it somehow encodes the phrase structure of the language? In other words, grammatical structure is in some sense 'hard-wired' in our heads, leaving us only to acquire the vocabulary of our particular native language in order to slot the appropriate words into the various locations on phrase structures and thereby produce grammatical sentences.

Well, as it stands, this idea has a number of problems. For one thing, a child will acquire the language of whatever country he or she grows up in (assuming the child is exposed to the language of that country). For instance, an American child growing up in Japan will learn to speak and understand Japanese (and probably English as well, from his or her parents). And yet, the grammatical structure of Japanese and English are quite different. (For one thing, the word order is different. In Japanese, the verb generally comes after the object, whereas in English the verb usually follows the subject. Thus, in English we say *Syun eats sushi* but the Japanese equivalent translates word-for-word as *Syun sushi eats*.) So if there are grammatical rules encoded in the brain, they cannot be the rules for any particular language; rather they must be rules that apply to *all* human languages.

Chomsky referred to these supposed hard-wired rules of language as constituting a *Universal Grammar*. Assuming it exists, Universal Grammar is a fundamental language structure common to all humans, which supports the acquisition and use of any particular language the person is exposed to. In other words, Universal Grammar is a sort of supergrammar that allows each one of us to acquire, automatically, the particular grammar of our own language.

In making his proposal for Universal Grammar, Chomsky was drawing directly on recent developments in logic. As the logicians of the early twentieth century observed, when you separate syntax from semantics in the case of *formal* languages, there is a universal grammar. The grammatical rules of predicate logic provide a universal grammar that can be applied to the language used in any branch of mathematics—arithmetic, geometry, calculus, chaos theory, any branch you like.

However, there is a huge difference between the precise, formal languages of mathematics and the rough-and-tumble natural languages used by people in their everyday lives. What evidence did Chomsky have, that what was true for formal languages might also hold for natural languages?

THE LANGUAGE INSTINCT

When Chomsky talks of a hard-wired Universal Grammar that functions in the way he suggests, what he is saying is that (1) we have an innate capacity to acquire a language, and (2) this innate capacity is in the form of a grammar, or at least can be described in terms of a grammar. Though each of us, in acquiring our native tongue, has to learn the words and specific grammatical rules such as word order, the underlying grammatical structures seem to be innate and automatic. For example, in English an adjective generally precedes the noun, as in the phrase *the big cat*. But in Spanish, the adjective generally follows the noun, as in *el gato grande*. However, there is a general structural rule that says an adjective *combines with* a noun to produce a noun phrase. It is this more general, order-independent rule that would form part of a Universal Grammar.

There is a considerable body of evidence to support Chomsky's proposal. Let's take a look at some of that evidence.

First, there is the rather obvious evidence that practically every living human being can and does produce and understand his or her native language, and does so with almost no perceptible effort. Moreover, at the level of basic, everyday communication, our facility with language seems almost completely independent of our level of intelligence or education. People having little or no formal education, who score poorly on any of the standard tests for intelligence, can generally speak and understand their native language fluently and with ease. (The native language involved may not accord with the formally prescribed rules of any grammar textbook, but that is a separate issue. The principal criterion for language use is communication; the niceties of 'good grammar' are cultural issues that are far less significant.) Speaking and understanding our native language seems to come to us almost as automatically and easily as breathing or eating. It does indeed seem to be an instinctive development. Of course, this is a subjective view, and subjective views are always viewed with suspicion in science. Is there more substantial evidence to support this conclusion? What do the experts say?

Well, Charles Darwin thought that language is instinctive. In his 1871 book *The Descent of Man,* Darwin refers to man's "instinctive tendency to speak." While he observes that we are not born with the ability to understand or speak any specific language, any more than we are born knowing how to do things such as "brew, bake, or write," he contrasts the built-in instinct to acquire language with the absence of any *"instinctive tendency* to brew, bake, or write." (My emphasis.)

Darwin's point, which has since been echoed by a great many linguists, is that whereas a specific language has to be acquired, the *facility* to acquire and use (spoken) language is not learned but basic, a product of evolution. Just as the human genetic code produces creatures that have a basic ability to digest food, so too that same genetic code produces creatures having a basic ability to acquire and use language. (This particular comparison breaks down if we try to explain the biological mechanisms involved. Whereas we understand a great deal about the organs that facilitate digestion, namely, the stomach and the intestines, we have far less knowledge about the brain, the organ responsible for our powers of reason and our language facility. But this may change over time; indeed it may change within a few years, given the present rapid rate of advancement in the relatively new discipline of neuroscience.)

Then there is Chomsky's observation (which we have considered earlier) that many of the sentences a person utters or understands are brand new combinations of words that have never been spoken or heard before. This means that the brain must be able to generate and to comprehend an unbounded number of these finite sequences of words. How else could this happen, asked Chomsky, other than by the brain being able to formulate rules for producing and understanding meaningful sequences of words that can be recognized as 'grammatical sentences'? An analogy would be learning how to play chess. Once a person has learned the basic moves, it is possible to play an unlimited number of different games, each one consisting of a brand new sequence of moves never before encountered. Playing chess does not require learning all possible sequences of moves. It requires learning the small number of allowable moves, and they may be used to generate the sequences that constitute particular games. Analogously, learning a language does not involve learning all possible sentences—an impossible task since there is an indefinite number of possible sentences. Rather you learn the rules to produce sentences. And that surely requires a capacity to learn such rules.

In addition, Chomsky made a second observation in support of his theory of Universal Grammar: Children develop a mastery of their native language both rapidly and without any formal instruction. Moreover, this mastery of their language is generally achieved by the age of three-and-a-half years, long before they are exposed to lessons on English grammar (or whatever) at school. Apparently they are able to recognize—unconsciously and without any perceptible effort—the abstract patterns that distinguish correct sentences from meaningless jumbles of words. They seem to have a basic instinct and ability to learn language.

Moving from Chomsky and the 1950s to the present day, MIT's Steven Pinker is another expert to whom we might turn to for advice. Pinker is a linguist who specializes in the way children acquire language. In 1994, he wrote an excellent book called *The Language Instinct*. The title alone pretty well sums up his view on the matter. Early in his book, he refers to our language instinct as "a biological adaptation to communicate information." This puts language in the same camp as rationality, which can be described as "a biological adaptation to survive and further one's goals." Pinker explains Chomsky's fundamental assumption about language this way:

> Language is not a cultural artifact that we learn the way we learn to tell the time or how the federal government works. Instead, it is a distinct piece of the biological makeup of our brains. Language is a complex, specialized skill, which develops in the child spontaneously, without conscious effort or formal instruction, is deployed without awareness of its underlying logic, is qualitatively the same in every individual, and is distinct from more general abilities to process information or behave intelligently. For these reasons some cognitive scientists have described language as a psychological faculty, a mental organ, a neural system, and a computational module. But I prefer the admittedly quaint term "instinct." It conveys the idea that people know how to talk in more or less the sense that spiders know how to spin webs. Web-spinning was not invented by some unsung spider genius and does not depend on having had the right education or on having an aptitude for architecture or the construction trades. Rather, spiders spin spider webs because they have spider brains, which give them the urge to spin and the competence to succeed. (p. 18.)

Let's look at some further evidence that supports the view that language is instinctive.

Exhibit A. Contrary to popular belief, children do not acquire language by imitating the adults they hear around them and by learning (and then applying) the rules of grammar. Rather they appear to learn words and generate grammatical structure themselves—*instinctively.* For instance, suppose that children learned how to turn a statement into a question by formulating a rule for moving words, based on the evidence provided by their ears as they listen to adults making statements and asking questions.

In English, the statement *The mailman is at the door* is most simply turned into a question by moving the auxiliary verb *is* to the start of the sentence, to result in the question *Is the mailman at the door?* If a child learned how to make this transformation by formulating some rule to follow, then the most obvious rule—and therefore the one the child is most likely to produce if there were no such thing as Universal Grammar to guide the rule formulation—would seem to be this: Scan the sentence to find the auxiliary verb *is* and move it to the beginning of the sentence.

If this rule is adopted, then what happens if the child encounters the following sentence?

The woman who is going to take your photograph is at the door.

If the child simply looks along the sentence until the auxiliary *is* is found, and moves it to the start of the sentence, the result is the ñonsentence:

Is the woman who going to take your photograph is at the door?

The error is obvious: The wrong occurrence of *is* is picked up. But this is not what happens in practice, as was demonstrated by extensive testing of three- to five-year-old children by the psychologists Stephen Crain and Mineharu Nakayama in the mid-1980s. What Chomsky observed, and what these two researchers confirmed, is that young children almost invariably perform the correct transformation. They do not simply pick the first occurrence of the auxiliary verb, which may be part of a subphrase of the sentence, as in the example given. Instead, they look for the appearance of the auxiliary in the main verb phrase of the sentence. In order to do this, the child has to be able to recognize such parts of speech as phrases, in particular, subject phrase, verb phrase, and object phrase and recognize the way these parts of speech fit together to form a sentence. Given this understanding of sentence structure, the child can formulate the correct rule: Look for the occurrence of the auxiliary verb *is* in the main verb phrase of the sentence and move it to the start of the sentence. With this rule, the correct question may be produced:

Is the woman who is going to take your photograph at the door?

Notice that there is no suggestion here that the child explicitly formulates a rule and then follows it. Rather the child acquires a certain linguistic skill, which linguists can describe *in the form of a rule.*

Now, the crucial observation made by Chomsky in all of this is that the young child cannot acquire this (fairly complex) statement-into-question procedure by imitation or by observing a number of specific instances, since parents very rarely use sentences as complex as *Is the woman who is going to take your photograph at the door?* in speaking to their small children, and certainly not in the form of statement–question pairs. For Chomsky, this was an extremely powerful argument in favor of his Universal Grammar, a linguistic framework that enables children to identify parts of speech such as phrases, clauses, et cetera. He referred to it as "the argument from the poverty of the input."

Exhibit B. Further evidence in support of a language instinct—a built-in Universal Grammar—is provided by research on children who grow up in a multilingual immigrant community. This happened in Hawaii, when the rapid growth in Hawaiian sugar production in the late nineteenth century led to a sudden influx of workers from many different countries. According to research into the Hawaiian case conducted by linguist Derek Bickerton, the adult immigrants almost never got beyond the use of a simplistic mixture of languages called a *pidgin,* having only the most rudimentary grammatical structure. In contrast, their descendants spoke a rich, new language, complete with a recognizable and sophisticated grammatical structure that bore striking resemblances to the grammatical structure of English, with phrases, clauses, and so on. Genuine, new languages that evolve from pidgins are called *creoles.* According to Bickerton, in the Hawaiian case, the step from pidgin to creole was completed in a single generation, with the children of the migrants speaking a fully-fledged creole. If true, then the only explanation is that the creole arose when the children of the migrant sugar plantation workers used an innate language facility to construct their new native tongue from the pidgin utterances they heard all around them.

Because of its dependence on historical data that can be hard to corroborate, Bickerton's evidence in support of a Universal Grammar is controversial. However, a similar instance of the creation of a new language has been observed in present times, in the case of the acquisition of sign language by deaf children.

Exhibit C. Children who are born deaf, and who are fortunate enough to be among other deaf children from a very early age, learn to communicate with one another through a rich, grammatical sign language, having a grammatical structure that has much in common with aural languages. The hearing parents who learn signing to communicate with their deaf children rarely achieve such a deep mastery of the sign language—indeed, many people who first encounter sign language as an adult never achieve a level of proficiency that would warrant the description 'language'.

Again, the obvious question is how does a deaf child acquire a sign *language,* complete with a sophisticated grammatical structure? Once again, an obvious answer is that at the appropriate age the child generates the appropriate grammar, using the signs from parents and other deaf children as input. Of course, within any particular community of deaf children, they all learn from each other, so if the group contains a child who already knows sign language, then it is possible that the rest of the group could learn the sign language from that individual. But a grammar emerges even when the group does not contain any children who already know sign language.

All in all then, these observations provide considerable evidence in favor of humans having a language instinct, of our being endowed with an innate language facility and of that facility being in the form of a general grammatical structure. In fact, there is still more evidence, but before we can appreciate that additional evidence, we have to correct some false ideas about language that you probably acquired in elementary school.

THINGS YOUR TEACHER GOT WRONG

The additional evidence I want to present in favor of all humans being subject to a single Universal Grammar is this: All the world's languages have syntactic categories for nouns, verbs, noun phrases, prepositional phrases, adjectival phrases, and adverbial phrases, and moreover, all human languages use these different parts of speech in the same manner.

Why is this evidence in support of a Universal Grammar? Because these different syntactic categories *depend upon* an underlying grammar. Since all languages have the same categories, namely, the ones listed above, it is reasonable to assume that they all come from the same grammar, or at least the same supergrammar.

At this point, your recollections of elementary school English classes probably come into play. Chances are, the story you were told in elementary school went like this. The world we live in contains persons, places, and things (objects). Nouns are the words we use to denote persons, places, and things. Our world also contains actions, and verbs are the words we use to denote actions—'doing words' was the term used by my own elementary school teacher, a phrase she repeated so often that it is now indelibly etched in my memory. According to this picture, languages have nouns so we can refer to people, places, and things and have verbs so we can refer to actions. Unfortunately, this argument is wrong and so was your elementary school teacher.

Nouns are indeed used to refer to persons, places, and things, and verbs are certainly used to refer to actions. But nouns and verbs frequently have other meanings. For example, none of the following nouns refer to a person, place, or thing:

> *The* meeting *takes place today.* [an event]
> *The* fall *killed him.* [an action]
> Darkness *descended over the city.* [a quality]
> *He ran* two *miles.* [a measurement of distance]
> *He ran for* fifteen *minutes.* [a measurement of time]
> Chomsky *developed a* grammar. [an abstract concept]
> *He is a* linguist. [a category or kind]
> *Show me the* way to go home. [a direction or route]

None of the following verbs refers to an action:

> *owns, interests, likes, exists, endures, admires, believes, assumes, justifies.*

Moreover, some words can be used as both nouns and verbs, for example,

> *Your interest impresses me.*
> *You interest me.*

In fact, being a noun, verb, or adverb has relatively little to do with what kind of entity the word refers to; rather, it is primarily a syntactic issue. Whether a particular word is a noun, a verb, or whatever is largely determined by the role that word can play in sentences, and that is determined by the grammar for the language. Words are nouns because they fit into grammatical sentences in certain places—they play a 'nouny' role in the sentence—and likewise for the other categories of words. Thus, it is the underlying grammatical structure of language that determines the various word categories—*noun, verb,* and so on. This is why the existence of these same syntactic categories in all the world's languages provides evidence to support the existence of a Universal Grammar that underlies all human languages.

For example, you will have no trouble identifying the nouns, verb, adverb, and adjective in the following 'sentence':

> *The flabberjom scringingly swinkered the ralidous snig.*

And yet, apart from the word *the,* every word in this string is made up. You base your categorizations on the relative placement of each word in the entire sentence, together with the clues provided by the three word endings *-ly, -ed,* and *-ous.* What the individual words refer to has nothing to do with it.

THE LINGUISTIC PATTERNS SHARED BY ALL MANKIND

What syntactic principles or rules can be included in a Universal Grammar? Whatever they are, they will have to transcend differences between individual languages. For example, word order cannot be a feature of Universal Grammar, since word order varies significantly from one language to the next—as we noted earlier, an English child born and raised in Japan, who hears nothing but Japanese, will learn to understand and speak Japanese, which has a word order very different from English.

On the other hand, one thing that is common across all human languages is their modular nature: The various parts of speech group together, with words forming phrases and words and phrases forming more complex phrases. Another feature is the range of syntactic categories common to all languages: noun phrases, verb phrases, adjectival phrases, et cetera. What kind of general principles can capture these features of language? Well, as a first step, the modular structure is conveniently represented by a tree that shows the various dependencies—what words are in what phrases, what phrases are in what other phrases, and so forth. By labeling the points of the tree as *noun phrase, verb phrase,* and so on, we can capture the syntactic categories.

For example, the first of the two trees shown in Figure 5 shows the phrase structure of the sentence

Susan saw the man with a dog.

The sentence has a simple subject–verb–object structure. The subject is the proper noun *Susan,* the verb is *saw,* and the object is the noun phrase *the man with a dog.* This noun phrase itself consists of a determiner *the,* a noun *man,* and a prepositional phrase (*PP*) *with a dog* consisting of a preposition *with* followed by a (determinate) noun phrase *a dog.*

The second tree illustrates the phrase structure of the sentence

Susan saw the man with a telescope.

Assuming it is Susan who has the telescope and that she sees the man through it, this sentence has a more complex phrase structure, consisting of a subject (*Susan*), a verb (*saw*), an object (*the man*), and a prepositional phrase attached to the verb (*with a telescope*).

In the first example, the *PP* modifies the noun phrase *the man;* in the second example, it modifies the verb *saw.* In terms of the structures of the

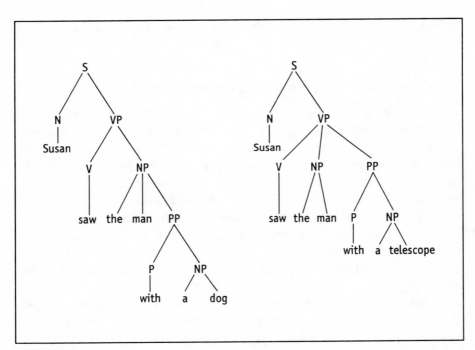

FIGURE 5

trees, the difference between the two examples is the node of the tree to which the *PP*-phrase is attached. For the first sentence, the *PP* is part of the *NP* that is the object of the main verb; for the second sentence, it is part of the main *VP*. In both cases, however, the tree structure of the *PP* (i.e., that part of the tree below the node *PP*) is the same.

A similar analysis distinguishes the following three sentences, introduced in Chapter 1:

> *Susan saw the man in the park with a dog.*
> *Susan saw the man in the park with a statue.*
> *Susan saw the man in the park with a telescope.*

In addition to having the same syntactic categories and a common modular structure, captured by phrase structure trees shown in Figure 5, the different languages of the world also exhibit a particularly striking similarity when it comes to the internal structure of phrases. In any language, all phrases seem to be built in the same way, with noun phrases, verb phrases, prepositional phrases, and adjectival or adverbial phrases.

For example, taking English as our example (which we can do since any language is typical in terms of phrase structure), consider a noun phrase such as

the man with a beard.

This phrase refers to a man; indeed, syntactically it is entirely equivalent to the phrase *the man,* in that either phrase may be substituted for the other in a sentence without affecting the grammaticality of the sentence. In particular, the phrase is nounlike, is singular, and refers to a human male. Linguists say that the word *man* is the *head* of the phrase *the man with a beard.*

Now consider a verb phrase, say

sits with a friend.

This phrase refers to an act of sitting, and is verblike. The verb *sits* is the head of the verb phrase. The case and tense of the verb phrase are precisely the case and tense of the head.

Again, consider a prepositional phrase, such as

in the park   or   *with a telescope.*

The head of the first phrase is *in;* the head of the second is *with.* In both examples, the entire phrase is 'about' what the head word is about—location in the first case, agency in the second.

In the case of an adjectival phrase such as

top of the class   or   *under the bridge*

there is a head (in these examples, *top* and *under,* respectively), and the phrase is about what the head is about.

In each case, then, a phrase has a head word that determines—and is characteristic of—the syntactic nature of the entire phrase.

In order to delve further into phrase structure, we have to take into account the fact that some phrases are held together so tightly that practically nothing can pull them apart. These are phrases that refer not to single things or actions in the world but to sets of interrelated things or actions. For example, the noun phrase *President of the United States* and the verb phrase *bomb the city* are both of this nature. It is not possible to be a president without being the president of something, that is, some country, some company, or whatever, and likewise it is not possible to bomb without bombing something. Linguists refer to the phrase *the United States* as a *role-player* in the phrase *President of the United States* and the phrase *the city* as a role-player in the phrase *bomb the city.*

Because of the tightness of the bonds that hold together a head and its role-players, such phrases tend to behave like single units, a nounlike unit if the head is a noun, a verblike unit if the head is a verb, and similarly for prepositional phrases and adjectival phrases. Accordingly, linguists have introduced a special notation for such phrases: $\overline{N}$, $\overline{V}$, $\overline{PP}$, and $\overline{AP}$, respectively. These are read as "N-bar," "V-bar," et cetera. The diagram shown in Figure 6 illustrates the phrase structure of our two examples. In this figure, I have suppressed parts of the tree structures, depicting such a structure by means of a triangle, a common illustrative device linguists use to indicate a suppressed tree structure. The tree structures for the PP-bar phrase *in the park* and the AP-bar phrase *top of the class* are essentially the same as the N-bar and V-bar phrases illustrated.

Since each of $\overline{N}$, $\overline{V}$, $\overline{PP}$, and $\overline{AP}$ has the same phrase structure, linguists refer to them all by the catch-all term $\overline{X}$, which is read "X-bar." In general, an X-bar consists of a head word followed by one or more role-players. Using a Chomsky-style notation, this very general grammatical rule can be expressed like this:

$$\overline{X} \rightarrow X\, ZP^*$$

In words, "X-bar arrows X followed by Z-P-star."

The idea is that the letters X and Z may be replaced by any one of N (for noun), V (for verb), P (for preposition), and A (for adjective), and a specific grammatical rule will result. The asterisk is standard linguistic notation to indicate 'any number of, written one after the other'. For example, a^* stands for any one of *a, aa, aaa,* et cetera. (In fact, a^* includes the case where there are no *a*s at all, a technical detail that I won't dwell on here.)

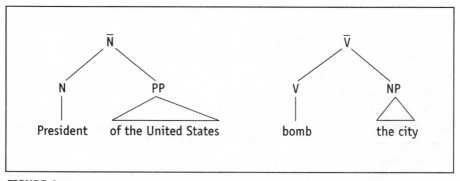

FIGURE 6

So, for example, if we replace X by N and Z by V in the above super-rule, we get the rule

$$\overline{N} \rightarrow N\ VP^*.$$

This rule says that you get an N-bar phrase by taking an N (i.e., a noun) and following it by no, one, two, or more VPs (i.e., verb phrases).

The role-players that occur in an X-bar phrase are different from the *modifiers* that may also occur in phrases. Examples of modifiers are *from California* and *with smart bombs,* as in:

> *The President of the United States from California*
> *The air force bombed the city with smart bombs.*

Being from California is not tightly bound to being President—being from a particular state is unrelated to being President; it is an optional addition that supplies further information. Similarly, in the second sentence, *with smart bombs* is an optional addition to the statement *The air force bombed the city.* Of course, the President must come from some state, and a bombing raid has to use some form of bombs. However, in order to make an informative utterance about the President, either the rest of the phrase or the context must make it clear what it is that the President is president of, and similarly one cannot simply say *The air force bombed* without stipulating what was bombed. On the other hand, the modifiers *from California* and *with smart bombs* are genuinely optional. This difference in attachment strength is reflected in word order in English: A modifier cannot come between a head and any role-players in an X-bar phrase. Thus, one cannot say either of the following in English,

> *The President from California of the United States*
> *The air force bombed with smart bombs the city.*

With the X-bar idea under their belts, linguists can provide a complete analysis of all phrases. Starting with noun phrases, the analysis goes as follows.

In general, any noun phrase has the following general structure. It may start with a subject, commonly the causal agent of the action referred to by the phrase. For example, in the phrase *the air force's bombing of the city* the subject is *the air force;* the phrase *the bombing of the city* has no subject. Then there is a head. The head is what gives the phrase its name and determines what it is about. In the example *the bombing of the city,* the head is the noun *bombing.* Then there are a number (possibly zero) of role-players, grouped with the head inside an N-bar; in the case of *the bombing of the city,* the role-player is *the city* and the N-bar is the phrase *bombing of the city*. Finally, there are a number (possibly zero) of modifiers; these lie outside the N-bar. For example, in the noun phrase *the air force's bombing of the city with smart bombs*, the phrase *with smart bombs* is a modifier.

Turning to general verb phrases, their structure is essentially the same. First, there may be a subject, as in the phrase *the air force bomb the city*, where the subject is *the air force*; or there may be no subject, as in *bomb the city*. Then there is a head, *bomb* in these two examples. The head may be followed by a number of role-players within a *V*-bar phrase. In the present examples there is one role-player, *the city*. Finally, there may be a number of modifiers. In the verb phrase *the air force bomb the city with smart bombs* the phrase *with smart bombs* is a modifier. The diagram in Figure 7 shows the structure trees for a noun phrase and a verb phrase.

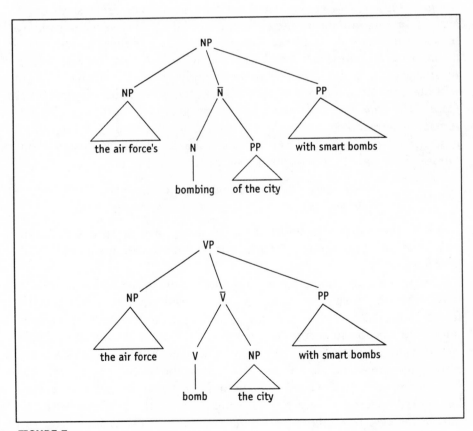

FIGURE 7

Apart from there being no subject, you find the same general pattern in prepositional phrases and adjectival or adverbial phrases. The common structural pattern of all phrases can be captured by a second very general grammatical rule:

$$XP \rightarrow (SUB)\,\overline{X}\,YP*.$$

The parentheses around the initial *SUB* is the linguist's way of denoting an optional component. Thus, this general rule reads: "An *X*-phrase consists of an optional subject, followed by an *X*-bar, followed by any number of *Y*-phrases (modifiers)." As in the previous general rule, the letters *X* and *Y* can be replaced by any of *N, V, P,* and *A* to give a particular rule.

This very general analysis of phrase structure is called the X-*bar theory*. As presented here, it applies to English and all other left-to-right languages. But with one further modification, it applies to all human languages. That modification is to drop the left-to-right order from the two general rules (and hence from the trees they determine). With this modification, when we read the rules we say "coupled with" instead of "followed by." Thus, the super-rule

$$\overline{X} \rightarrow X\,ZP*$$

is read like this: "You get an *X*-bar phrase by taking an *X*-phrase and coupling it with no, one, two, or more *Z*-phrases." And the second super-rule

$$XP \rightarrow (SUB)\,\overline{X}\,YP*$$

is read this way: "An *X*-phrase consists of an optional subject coupled with an *X*-bar coupled with any number of *Y*-phrase modifiers."

It is possible to simply drop the ordering in the two super-rules because in a language where the verb comes after the object, such as Japanese (where they would say *Syun sushi ate,* not *Syun ate sushi*), the head of any phrase will come after its role-players. Thus, in Japanese, they say *Kyoto to* and not *to Kyoto,* and *Syun than smarter* rather than *smarter than Syun.* Japanese is an example of a *head-last* language; English is a *head-first* language. (It should be mentioned that the notions of head-first and head-last describe overall properties of languages. Exceptions can be found in most languages. For example, English is a head-first language, but it contains head-last phrases such as *two weeks ago*.)

And now, says Chomsky, we have our Universal Grammar, or at least a significant part of it. According to Chomsky, the two unordered, general phrase-structure super-rules given above are two of the rules that make up the Universal Grammar in our minds. The human brain is constructed in such a way that these two rules are somehow hard-wired-in to provide an innate language facility—a facility to generate the specific grammar of any particular language. Once a small child learns (by observation) the appropriate order (head-first or head-last), essentially the entire grammatical core of the language is then available for use.

Chomsky's proposal is controversial. However, it does provide a workable explanation of how it is possible for a child to rapidly acquire an extensive mastery of grammar, on the basis of data that is highly impoverished in terms both of amount and complexity.

In terms of the overall story that is the theme of this book, Chomsky's theory of Universal Grammar illustrates how the formal abstractions of mathematical logic—which grew from attempts to analyze language and reasoning—can be applied in order to develop a hard science of not only the structure of natural language but the very capacity of human beings to acquire and use language. Even if, in due course, the theory of Universal Grammar is proved to be wrong, it will remain a significant scientific achievement, on par with the great theories of physics.

In addition to their use by linguists trying to analyze linguistic data (and thereby understand how people acquire and use language), Chomsky's logic-inspired mathematical techniques also led to attempts to program computers to produce and understand natural language. This move was part of the more general enterprise of building 'intelligent' machines, which I turn to next.

7

MACHINES
THAT THINK

*The . . . question, "Can machines think?" I believe to be too mean-
ingless to deserve discussion. Nevertheless I believe that at the end of
the century the use of words and general educated opinion will have
altered so much that one will be able to speak of machines thinking
without expecting to be contradicted.*

—Alan Turing[1]

SMART MACHINES?

Every day, all over the developed world, ordinary sane people engage in
simple conversation with a machine. The exchange generally goes something like this:

Machine:	WELCOME TO ANYONE'S BANK.
	PLEASE ENTER YOUR PIN NUMBER
	AND PRESS THE *OK* KEY.
Person:	166309 ⟨*OK*⟩
Machine:	THANK YOU, KEITH J. DEVLIN
	WHAT SERVICE DO YOU REQUIRE?
	1. WITHDRAW CASH
	2. MAKE A DEPOSIT

---

1. From the celebrated and oft-quoted paper "Computing Machinery and Intelligence,"
written in 1950, and reprinted many times, for example, in [4] and [21].

	3. BALANCE INQUIRY
	4. MAKE A TRANSFER/PAY A BILL
	5. OTHER
Person:	1
Machine:	WHICH ACCOUNT DO YOU WISH
	TO WITHDRAW FROM?
	1. CHECKING
	2. SAVINGS
	3. OTHER
Person:	2
Machine:	ENTER THE EXACT AMOUNT
	YOU WISH TO WITHDRAW.
Person:	$150.00
. . .	. . .

The automatic teller machine (ATM) is now a common feature of everyday life in many countries of the world. The simple act of inserting a small magnetized card into a slot instigates a human–machine conversation much like the one above. The machine asks the customer to express his or her wish, often by offering various choices, and reacts instantly and obediently to the customer's response. The machine uses ordinary language, displayed on a monitor, and the customer generally responds using keyboard entries. Such an exchange is hardly everyday human conversation, but there is definite communication in both directions: Both parties, the customer and the machine, make their wishes known to the other and respond accordingly.

Here's another person–machine scenario. You enter a room and see a young girl sitting in front of a computer. You walk across to her and glance over her shoulder at the screen. This is what you see.

Girl:	Men are all alike.
Machine:	IN WHAT WAY?
Girl:	They're always bugging us about something or other.
Machine:	CAN YOU THINK OF A SPECIFIC EXAMPLE?
Girl:	Well, my boyfriend made me come here.
Machine:	YOUR BOYFRIEND MADE YOU COME HERE?
Girl:	He says I'm depressed much of the time.
Machine:	I AM SORRY TO HEAR YOU ARE DEPRESSED.
Girl:	It's true. I am unhappy.
Machine:	DO YOU THINK COMING HERE WILL HELP YOU NOT TO BE UNHAPPY?

Girl:	I need some help, that much seems certain.
Machine:	WHAT WOULD IT MEAN TO YOU IF YOU GOT SOME HELP?
Girl:	Perhaps I could learn to get along with my mother.
Machine:	TELL ME MORE ABOUT YOUR FAMILY.
. . .	. . .

What you are seeing is a typical session with ELIZA, a computer program written by Joseph Weizenbaum of MIT in 1966 and designed to function like a psychotherapist.

One more example. A patient enters a San Francisco hospital complaining of shortness of breath. The physician asks the patient a series of routine questions about his symptoms, and performs a number of routine tests. On the basis of the evidence obtained in this way, the physician makes a preliminary diagnosis. The physician supplies exactly the same evidence to a computer program called Puff, and it too provides a preliminary diagnosis. Here are the two diagnoses. Which one do you think came from the physician and which from the computer?

Conclusion: The low diffusing capacity, in combination with obstruction and a high total lung capacity is consistent with a diagnosis of emphysema. Although bronchodilators were only slightly useful in this one case, prolonged use may prove beneficial to the patient. PULMONARY FUNCTION DIAGNOSIS: MODERATELY SEVERE OBSTRUCTIVE AIRWAYS DISEASE. EMPHYSEMATOUS TYPE.

Conclusion: Overinflation, fixed airway obstruction and low diffusing capacity would all indicate moderately severe obstructive airway disease of the emphysematous type. Although there is no response to bronchodilators on this one occasion, more prolonged use may prove to be more helpful. PULMONARY FUNCTION DIAGNOSIS: OBSTRUCTIVE AIRWAYS DISEASE, MODERATELY SEVERE, EMPHYSEMATOUS TYPE.

In fact, the first one is the computer's diagnosis, but how could you tell? Puff was developed in the late 1970s, and was used by physicians for a while, on an experimental basis.

Each of the three computer systems just described exhibits behavior that could be described as intelligent. Indeed, if the computer were replaced by a person in each case, we would almost certainly describe the reported behavior as requiring intelligence, a fact reflected in the standards of intelligence and education normally demanded in order for people to become bank tellers, psychotherapists, or physicians.

But do such computer systems really have intelligence? More generally, is it even theoretically possible for a computer system—that is to say, a computer program running on a conventional electronic digital computer—to be intelligent? We shall address the question of what computers can and cannot do in due course. But before we can ask ourselves if a computer can exhibit intelligent behavior, we must first be clear just what we mean by intelligence. Unfortunately, though most of us might feel that we know intelligence when we see it in other people, science has yet to come up with an acceptable definition.

It was precisely the difficulty of defining intelligence in humans that led Alan Turing to propose a definition of intelligence that could reasonably be applied to computers. This is the development we turn to next.

ALAN TURING'S IQ TEST FOR COMPUTERS

One aspect of human intelligence, and a regular component of tests designed to measure intelligence in children and adults seeking employment, is skill at arithmetic. And yet a ten-dollar calculator can outperform almost any human being when it comes to arithmetic. Does it follow that a calculator is intelligent? Most people would answer "no."

How about the ability to solve algebraic equations? Again, when the solution is found by a person, this task is generally regarded as requiring intelligence, but there are a number of computer systems available that can solve algebra problems far quicker, and with far less chance of making an error, than most people.

In both cases, arithmetic and algebra, the computer arrives at the answer in roughly the same way as a person, by following the appropriate mathematical rules. And yet we regard human proficiency at arithmetic and algebra as requiring intelligence but an even greater machine proficiency at the same tasks as being merely mechanical rule-following.

The distinction between mind and machine is clearer when it comes to playing chess. Considerable effort has been put into the development of computer programs that play chess, and the best current chess programs can hold their own at the International Grand Master level. However, they achieve their success not by adopting any clever strategies, but by essentially brute force methods. Taking advantage of the immense computational power and speed of today's high-performance computers, they examine huge numbers of possible plays, choosing the one that offers the greatest chance of success. A good human chess player might consider as many as a hundred possible moves (generally far fewer), and follow the likely ensuing play for at most a dozen of those. The initial choice of moves to be considered in detail is one of the things that marks the good human chess player. A chess program, on the other hand, would proceed more or less in the following fashion. (The scenario I describe is simplified, but the general idea conveyed is correct.)

The program examines all its possible legal moves and discards all those that lead directly to a losing position. Suppose there are 10 possible moves that keep the computer in the game. The computer then examines all possible responses from the opponent for each of its 10 possible moves, discarding all those that cause the computer to lose. Suppose that, on average, there are 10 opponent's moves for each of the 10 initial computer moves. The computer is now looking at $10 \times 10 = 100$ two-move sequences. For each of those, suppose there are 10 third moves the computer can make that do not lead directly to a loss. The computer is now looking at $100 \times 10 = 1,000$ three-move sequences. And so forth. Suppose the computer were to examine all ten-move sequences in this fashion, with the average number of viable possible moves at each stage being 10. This would mean the computer would examine a total of 10^{10} ten-move sequences. At the end of this evaluation, it would then choose the initial move to make. If it took a tenth of a second of computation time to evaluate the strategic value of each such sequence, it would take over thirty years to decide on that one initial move. And then, after the opponent had made her move, the whole process would begin again.

In fact, modern chess programs are not quite as crude as this, and the computing speeds are faster, but you get the general idea. Chess programs do not play chess in the way a person does—by developing strategies; rather, they use brute force computing power to examine enormous numbers of possibilities and simply pick the one that gives the greatest likelihood of success, according to some numerical evaluation procedure. There is no intelligence involved. In contrast, the human player uses (what most people would call) intelligence (and experience) to avoid having to examine more than a handful of possible moves.

So, to return to the original question, if a computer program performs a task that requires intelligence if performed by a person, should we describe that program as behaving in an intelligent fashion? On the basis of the above discussions, the answer would seem to be "no," but are we being guided by human pride rather than rationality—by a desire to be unique in our intelligence? After all, a jet airplane does not stay in the air by converting food to energy and flapping its wings the way a bird does, but we still say that the plane flies. It achieves the same end—flying—in a completely different way, a way more suited to its structure and design.

This was precisely the question considered by Alan Turing in a classic paper published in 1950, "Computing Machinery and Intelligence" (quoted at the start of the chapter). "The present interest in 'thinking machines' has been aroused by a particular kind of machine, usually called an 'electronic computer' or a 'digital computer'," Turing explains, before moving on to the question, "Can [such] machines think?"

For Turing, it was obvious that computers had to be allowed to do things in their own way. *How* they operated was less significant than *what* they produced. And so, to set the stage for deciding if a machine could 'think', he proposed a test that he called the imitation game. It is nowadays known as the Turing test.

Turing asks you to imagine you are sitting at your computer, through which you carry out a conversation (typing at a keyboard and reading on the screen) with two partners, one a person, the other a second (very fancy) computer. Your two partners are named A and B, but you do not know which is the person and which is the second computer. You cannot see either the person or the other computer; your only communication with them is through your keyboard and screen. If you address a question to A, then A will always answer; likewise, B will always answer a question directed to B. Your task is to try to decide, on the basis of a conversation with A and B, which one is the person and which is the computer. If you are not able to identify the computer reliably, then, says Turing, it is entirely reasonable to say that the computer is intelligent—it passes the Turing test for intelligence. I should point out that, although the hidden person might be expected to answer truthfully, the computer is under no obligation to tell the truth, so in particular, questions such as "Tell me, A, are you a computer?" are unlikely to resolve the issue for you.

None of the interactive computer systems described at the start of the chapter could pass such a test. The ATM machine cannot respond to any input other than the numbers it asks for, and it is clear that all it is doing is letting the customer choose from a limited set of alternatives at each stage and is otherwise following a completely predetermined sequence of steps. The English language sentences it displays on the screen are completely 'canned', apart perhaps from picking up the customer's name from the coded magnetic stripe on the ATM card and inserting it into an otherwise standard message.

On the basis of the sample given above, ELIZA might seem all set to sail through the Turing test, but first impressions can be deceptive. Conversation with ELIZA can seem very reasonable when the patient sticks to his or her psychological worries, but it can break down dramatically if the patient steers the conversation onto other issues, such as:

> *Patient:* I am dead.
> *ELIZA:* IS IT BECAUSE YOU ARE DEAD THAT YOU CAME TO ME?

Finally, the impressive behavior of Puff in diagnosing lung disease hides a total ignorance of everything else about the world—it will be completely stumped by a simple question such as "Are the patient's lungs above or below her waist?" (The way ELIZA and Puff work will be explained in due course.)

As it turned out, Turing's choice of human–machine conversation as an intelligence test for computers was a good one. Natural language communication is now known to be one of the hardest tasks that faces anyone trying to build intelligent machines. Forget all of those smooth-talking computers and robots on television and in the movies, such as Kit, the talking automobile in the TV series *Knight Rider,* and HAL, the eventually malevolent on-board mission-control computer in Stanley Kubrick's *2001: A Space Odyssey.* In the real world, no computer system has come close to passing the Turing test, and there is good reason to assume that none ever will. (The good reason will be given later in this chapter.) But we are getting ahead of ourselves. Back in the heady days of the 1950s and 1960s, it seemed that the goal of machine intelligence was just around the corner, as indicated by the following words of AI pioneer (and Nobel laureate) Herbert Simon:

> It is not my aim to surprise or shock you. . . . But the simplest way I can summarize is to say that there are now in the world machines that think, that learn and create. Moreover, their ability to do these things is going to increase rapidly until—in a visible future—the range of problems they can handle will be coextensive with the range to which the human mind has been applied. ("Heuristic Problem Solving: The Next Advance in Operations Research," *Operations Research,* Volume 6, January, 1958, p. 6.)

In his article, Simon went on to make a number of predictions for the ensuing ten years of development in AI, including, by the end of that ten-year period, the creation of a chess program that could beat the world champion, and the discovery and proof by a computer of an important new theorem of mathematics. What led him to make such dramatic predictions? What view of human intelligence led him to believe that a digital computer could be programmed to behave intelligently? The answers have their origins back in ancient Greece.

THE COMPUTER THAT PROVED THEOREMS

For Plato, all knowledge had to be stateable in the form of explicit definitions that anyone could apply. In particular, given any activity or task that requires intelligence, it had to be possible to write down a recipe (or algorithm) that specifies how to perform the activity or task. If there were no such set of rules, then the activity or task could not properly be described as requiring intelligence.

By the seventeenth century, the belief that all genuine knowledge could be formalized had come to dominate Western intellectual thought. Thomas Hobbes, the greatest English philosopher of the time, wrote, "When a man reasons, he does nothing else but conceive a sum total from addition of parcels, for reason . . . is nothing but reckoning. . . ." In making this assertion, Hobbes was in many ways simply making explicit a view that had long before become enshrined in the intellectual language of the Western world. In Aristotle's definition of a human, *zoion logon echon,* or the animal equipped with *logos,* the word *logos* could mean speaking, or the grasping of whole situations, as well as logical thinking. But when scholars translated the Greek *logos* into the Latin *ratio,* meaning reckoning, the scope of Aristotle's definition became much narrower and decidedly mathematical. According to its Latin origin, the phrase 'rational man' means something very close to 'calculating man'.

As I described in Chapter 3, Leibniz tried to pursue the identification of rational thought with mathematical reasoning by developing a symbolic, mathematical language—what he called a universal characteristic—whereby any concept could be assigned a characteristic number so that reasoning was reduced to calculation. "If someone would doubt my results," Leibniz wrote, "I would say to him, 'Let us calculate, Sir,' and thus by taking pen and ink, we would settle the question." The potential Leibniz foresaw for his universal characteristic is essentially the same as the one put forward by Turing on behalf of machine intelligence some three hundred years later. Here is Leibniz's prediction:

> Once the characteristic numbers are established for most concepts, mankind will then possess a new instrument which will enhance the capabilities of the mind to a far greater extent than optical instruments strengthen the eyes, and will supersede the microscope and telescope to the same extent that reason is superior to eyesight.

As we saw already, Leibniz was not successful, but in the nineteenth century, George Boole made a significant step in the right direction with his algebra of reasoning. With Boole's work, the stage was set for the next step. All that was required was the invention of a machine that could perform the mathematical operations in Boole's system. In the late 1940s, that machine came into being: the digital computer.

With the invention of the digital computer, it was only five years after the appearance of Turing's 1950 paper "Computing Machinery and Intelligence," in which he specified programming a computer to play chess and to understand natural language as the two most obvious challenges to attempt first, that work began on both challenges.

In 1955, Allen Newell wrote a paper analyzing the problems facing anyone trying to program a computer to play chess, and by 1956, a group at Los Alamos National Laboratory had programmed a computer to play a poor but legal game of chess, using a crude technique called *exhaustive search*. At about the same time, Anthony Oettinger began work on automated language translation by programming a Russian–English computer dictionary.

However, neither of these two projects offered anything that might be termed 'intelligent behavior' on the part of the computer; they were simply automation processes whereby straightforward tasks were implemented on a computer. The first genuine attempt to create machine intelligence was made by Allen Newell, Clifford Shaw, and Herbert Simon (whom we met a moment ago) of the RAND Corporation, who in 1956 produced a computer program called *The Logic Theorist*. The aim of this program was to prove theorems in mathematical logic, in particular, the theorems in the early part of Whitehead and Russell's *Principia Mathematica*.

The idea adopted by the RAND team was this. To begin with, the axioms for Whitehead and Russell's system of propositional logic were programmed in to the computer. (An alternative axiom system, due to Frege, is given on page 80.) These axioms formed the computer's initial list of true propositions. The computer then attempted to add further true propositions to this list by making logical deductions.

The basic method the RAND program used to make deductions was the application of the classical Greek rule of *modus ponens:* From the two propositions (i.e., well-formed formulas of predicate logic) $A \to B$ and A, conclude the proposition B. In order to apply this rule, the computer had to be instructed to follow a procedure known as matching, which I describe below.

Step by step, the computer used *modus ponens* to add new true propositions to its stored list of true propositions, causing the list to get longer. At each stage, it looked through that list. Whenever it found a proposition of the form $A \to B$ in the list (where A and B are themselves two expressions of propositional logic), the computer looked to see if the proposition A was also in the list. If it was, the listed proposition A was said to match the antecedent of the listed proposition $A \to B$. By *modus ponens,* the proposition B was then a logical consequence of the listed proposition $A \to B$ and the listed matching proposition A. Hence B could be added to the list of true propositions. In other words, by searching for matches, the program expanded its list of true propositions via *modus ponens* by adding those propositions that followed from (two) propositions in the list.

Notice that the process just described was entirely syntactic. There was no attempt to understand the meaning of the various propositions stored in the computer's memory. The program simply examined each well-formed formula in the list, looking for those having the syntactic form $A \to B$ for some formulas A and B. When it found such a formula, it looked through the list to see if the formula A appeared. If it found this formula, it added the formula B to the list; otherwise it just kept on searching.

Essentially the same approach is used by all AI systems. In general, the chances of finding a match among the listed true propositions will be low. However, it is possible that such a match can be found by substituting for various propositional variables. For example, suppose A is the proposition $(q \to r) \to (q \to r)$ and the program has already established $p \to p$ as a true proposition. Then by substituting $(q \to r)$ for p in the true proposition $p \to p$, a match for A is obtained. Such substitutions are allowable in propositional logic because the letters p, q, r, et cetera, have no meaning; they just stand for arbitrary statements that are either true or false. In terms of meaning, it makes no difference whether the letter p or the letter q is used to denote a particular statement, and the letter p may just as well denote the proposition $q \to r$. In order to handle cases such as this, *The Logic Theorist* program contained substitution rules that could be used to obtain a match.

To guide the substitution processes and to speed up the process overall, *The Logic Theorist* was also provided with a set of *heuristic* rules. A heuristic is a 'rule of thumb' that might not be successful but which is worth applying just in case. We use heuristics all the time in our everyday lives. For example, if an electrical appliance doesn't work when we switch it on, we might first try pressing the switch a few times, perhaps more firmly, then we might try another appliance in the same electrical outlet to see if the power supply fuse is in order. Neither of these operations is guaranteed to fix the problem. We simply try them because they sometimes work.

Mathematics is rife with heuristic rules. Indeed, one of the principal differences between a college student who is good at math and one who is not is the former will have acquired a sizable stock of heuristics with which to approach a new problem. Many of the heuristics people use in solving mathematics problems are of a make-the-proposition-simpler variety, such as the various algebraic simplification rules we learn in a high school algebra class. It was by observing the heuristics that students used—generally unreflectingly—in attempting to solve logic problems that Newell and Simon formulated the heuristic rules they included in their computer program.

The Logic Theorist proved 38 of the first 52 theorems in *Principia Mathematica*. It has to be admitted that propositional logic is ideally suited to being performed on a computer, it having an extremely simple, rigidly defined language and a small set of fixed, well-defined axioms and rules. Nevertheless, within its own highly circumscribed domain, *The Logic Theorist* was a success.

That early success immediately attracted a number of other mathematicians and computer scientists to the possibility of machine intelligence. In the same year that news of the *The Logic Theorist* came out (1956), the mathematician John McCarthy organized a "two month ten-man study of artificial intelligence" (his words) at Dartmouth College in New Hampshire, thereby coining the phrase by which the newly emerging discipline soon became known. Among the participants at the Dartmouth program, in addition to Newell and Simon and McCarthy himself, was Marvin Minsky of MIT, who was to become one of the most outspoken gurus of AI.

The new discipline got off to a rapid start. By 1957, Newell and Simon had produced the first general purpose AI program, the *General Problem Solver* (GPS). Based on the notion of an underlying framework of logical rules coupled with a set of heuristics—the same framework that had been used in *The Logic Theorist*—GPS was designed to solve the kinds of logic puzzles that can be found in newspaper puzzle columns and the puzzle magazines sold at airports and railway stations. A classic example of such a puzzle is the cannibals-and-missionaries problem. This asks you to find a procedure for transporting three cannibals and three missionaries across a river, when the only available boat takes at most two people at a time, and you cannot ever allow the number of cannibals to exceed the number of missionaries in any one place, lest the cannibals are able to overpower the missionaries and devour them. (*The Logic Theorist* was able to solve this problem, so I'll leave it to you to try to figure it out for yourself.)

It should be emphasized that the aim of AI was not to build an artificial person or an artificial mind. Rather the goal was far more modest— to build computer programs that, when run on a digital computer, would exhibit intelligence (in the sense that the same performance by a human would be said to require intelligence). However, even that far more modest goal was very ambitious, and its pursuit led to a huge expenditure of manpower, time, and money.

Before we examine exactly where some of that manpower, time, and money went, I should say a little bit more about how one can set about programming a digital computer to behave in an intelligent fashion.

How to Get a Computer to Act Smart

The enormous power and utility of present-day computers should not blind us to a very fundamental fact about the way they work. The *only* thing that a digital computer can do is manipulate symbols in accordance with a set of precisely defined rules stipulated in advance. To the human user looking on, it might seem that those symbols *mean* something or *refer* to something in the world, but, like beauty, that meaning or reference is in the eyes of the beholder and not in the computer.

We can liken the computer to an imaginary scenario called 'the Chinese room', proposed by the contemporary philosopher John Searle.

Imagine you are placed alone in a closed room. In one wall is a small opening through which people outside pass pieces of paper on which are written Chinese symbols. You do not know Chinese—indeed you do not recognize any of the Chinese symbols. However, inside the room is a large manual. On each page are pairs of Chinese sentences. Whenever a piece of paper is passed into the room, you go through the manual, comparing the left-hand Chinese sentence of each pair in the manual with what is written on the paper. If and when you find the two match, the left-hand sentence of a pair in the manual being exactly the same as the symbols on the paper, you copy the right-hand Chinese sentence of the pair onto a clean sheet of paper and pass it back through the wall to the person on the outside. And that is all. You simply keep doing this, taking in pieces of paper, looking for a match, passing out the prescribed response. You have no idea what any of the symbols mean. All you do is mindlessly look for matching sequences of symbols and mindlessly copy sequences of symbols. You *manipulate* symbols, devoid of any meaning, which is exactly what a computer does.

Now suppose that each piece of paper passed into the room expresses a mathematical problem, written in Chinese by someone who speaks Chinese. Suppose further that the manual you use to produce output sequences of symbols in response to input sequences of symbols is a mathematical question–answer book. Each pair of entries consists of a mathematical question alongside its answer, both written in Chinese. To the Chinese speaker outside the room, passing in mathematical problems and receiving back the right answer in each case, the room functions like a computer. Put in the problem and out comes the answer. To that person outside, both the problem (the input) and the answer (the output) *mean* something. However, to you, on the inside, neither the input nor the output has any meaning—both are just so many meaningless symbols as far as you are concerned, as are the pairs of entries in the manual that you use to link inputs to outputs.

Thus, given the appropriate set-up, the prescribed, mindless manipulation of symbols (in the present case, matching and copying of symbols) can produce 'meaningful' behavior (in this case, giving the solutions to mathematical problems).

As described so far, the Chinese room scenario has some similarity to a computer, but there is an important difference. Computers do more than just look up outputs on a preset list. Given an input, a computer will perform a whole range of operations on that input, as specified by its program. However, this no more requires that the symbols it manipulates have meaning for the computer than in the simpler case of a look-up manual. The rules in the computer program will be of the form: If such-and-such a sequence of symbols appears, do such-and-such to that sequence of symbols to produce a new sequence of symbols. Comparing this with your situation inside the Chinese room, the computer's operation is analogous to your look-up manual being replaced by an instruction manual that tells you how to manipulate symbols—erase them, modify them, replace them, swap them around, et cetera. You still have no idea what the symbols mean—you can't understand Chinese. However, if the instruction manual is written properly, then to the Chinese person outside the room, passing in questions and receiving back answers, the actions you perform inside have meaning. To that person, you are *computing*.

The modern computer is an electronic device for manipulating symbols according to a prescribed set of rules. As described in Chapter 4, today's electronic digital computer uses just two symbols, 0 and 1 (also known as *binary representation*), not unlike the Turing machine also described in Chapter 4. However, there are differences between a Turing machine and a modern digital computer. One is that a Turing machine is a theoretical notion and not an actual physical device. Another difference is that in a Turing machine, 0 and 1 really are the symbols (i.e., the things that *symbolize* or stand for something in the world), whereas a modern computer is constructed so that *sequences* of 0s and 1s of a certain length are what do the symbolizing. (Such fixed-length sequences of 0s and 1s are generally called *binary words,* a helpfully suggestive terminology. In early computers, words had lengths of 8 or 16 bits. Later computers had 32- or 64-bit words.)

Notice that I said 'symbol' rather than 'number' in the above paragraph. Despite what your high school mathematics teacher might have told you, computers do not reduce everything to numbers, and they only manipulate numbers insofar as we may regard the symbols they manipulate as symbols representing numbers. But we can equally think of the computer as manipulating letters of the alphabet, or algebraic unknowns, or whatever. The point to bear in mind throughout this chapter is that for the computer, the symbols have no meaning, and any talk you might hear about computers understanding something is purely figurative. The computer is like the person in Searle's Chinese room, simply following prescribed rules in a mindless uncomprehending fashion.

At the risk of throwing you into confusion, let me add that, when you really stop to think about it, you realize that computers do not even have a concept of a symbol. A modern digital computer is a physical device constructed in the form of a highly complex electrical circuit. When you switch on the power, electric current flows through that circuit. What we—the people who build and use computers—refer to as symbols (0 and 1) are just particular voltages in certain parts of the circuit. As a physical device, the only rules the computer is following are the laws of physics, in particular the laws that govern the flow of electric current. Because of the way the computer circuit is designed, when electricity flows through the computer according to the laws of physics, *we can regard* its electrical activity *as if* it were manipulating the symbols 0 and 1, and we can regard the computer's behavior as following the laws of mathematical logic. But that is all in our minds, not in the computer. That is, not only are any meanings we ascribe to the symbols or to the computer words strictly in our minds and not in the computer, even the basic notion of a symbol is in our minds and not in the computer.

Since computers are nothing more than symbol-manipulating devices, it is clear that if we want to program a computer to perform logical reasoning, we have to express all the knowledge required in a symbolic form and arrange matters so that logical reasoning corresponds to various manipulations of those symbols.

Taking the second of these two requirements first, note that symbolic reasoning was already achieved by Newell, Shaw, and Simon's *The Logic Theorist*. Though subsequent work led to the development of a whole battery of further computer reasoning techniques, in essence they all come down to a combination of (antecedent) matching and *modus ponens*. The computational challenge is to find an appropriate match. A considerable amount of AI research has gone into the development of efficient techniques—known as *search algorithms*—for finding matches. In many cases, it is the impossibility of carrying out such a search in a reasonable amount of time that prevents the successful operation of an otherwise adequate AI program.

The other requirement for machine reasoning is the symbolic representation of knowledge. AI researchers have developed a number of *knowledge representation languages* to do this. All are based to a greater or lesser extent on predicate logic, which is itself a knowledge representation language. Thus, predicate logic serves adequately to explain the general idea.

Suppose we wanted to represent the following real-world facts as part of an AI program meant to answer questions about history.

1. Marcus was a man.
2. Marcus was a Pompeian.
3. Marcus was born in 40 A.D.
4. All men are mortal.
5. All Pompeians died when Mount Vesuvius erupted in 79 A.D.
6. It is now 1996 A.D.

Then, using predicate logic, we could represent each of these facts as follows.

1. Man(Marcus)
2. Pompeian(Marcus)
3. Born(Marcus, 40)
4. $\forall x[\text{Man}(x) \rightarrow \text{Mortal}(x)]$
5. $\forall x[\text{Pompeian}(x) \rightarrow \text{Die}(x, 79)]$
6. now = 1996

Most of these representations are fairly easy to read and look like translations of the original English sentences into some kind of mathematician's pidgin English. Items 4 and 5 are a little more complex: Item 4 reads as "For all x, if x is a man then x is mortal," and item 5 reads as "For all x, if x is a Pompeian then x dies in 79 A.D."

In formalizing the given facts, we have made some choices that could affect the eventual behavior of the program. The most significant choice was in ignoring the eruption of the volcano Mount Vesuvius in item 5, representing simply the fact that all Pompeians died in year 79. If we thought that the Vesuvius aspect might be important, we could put it in as an additional fact like this:

7. Erupts(Vesuvius, 79)

Including the eruption of Vesuvius in this way does not capture the fact that it was that event that caused the deaths of all the Pompeians in that year. If that fact were likely to be important to the program, it too would have to be incorporated.

Another fact we have omitted is the reference to A.D. in the years. If the program is to be restricted to post-Christ history, this should not cause any problems.

And then there are various other facts that the program will probably have to have available in order to reason about the facts we have just given it. For example, suppose we wanted to ask the program if Marcus is dead today. Would the computer be able to come up with the right answer? Rather than bog ourselves down in a mass of logical formalisms, it is easier to see how this question can be answered starting from the original English language versions of the given facts and reasoning in English. Here is one way to deduce the fact that Marcus is dead, starting from the original list of seven facts.

Step 1. It is now 1996. [Fact 6]
Step 2. All Pompeians died in 79. [Fact 5]
Step 3. All Pompeians are dead now. [Consequence of steps 1 and 2]
Step 4. Marcus was a Pompeian. [Fact 2]
Step 5. Marcus is dead. [Consequence of steps 3 and 4]

This might seem straightforward enough to us—just five steps from start to finish. In the first two steps, we simply invoke two of the given facts. The third step deduces a consequence of the first two steps. Then, in step 4, we invoke another one of the given facts. Finally, in step 5, we draw a logical conclusion from steps 3 and 4. However, for the computer the deduction is not at all straightforward. Though each of the above five steps can be translated into predicate logic, the computer would not be able to carry out the deduction the way we did. The problem is step 3. This uses the fact that if someone dies, then they are dead and they remain dead at all later times. You and I know that, but computers (and occasionally writers of long-running television series) do not. The computer has to be told this additional fact of life; thus, the following fact has to be added to the program's list of basic data:

8. $\forall x \forall d \forall t [\text{Mortal}(x) \land \text{Die}(x,d) \land (t > d) \rightarrow \text{Dead}(x,t)]$

This last fact is particularly convoluted and indicates the kinds of linguistic contortions that are sometimes required in order to express seemingly simple facts in the highly restricted language of predicate logic. Roughly speaking, what it says in words is: "For any mortal x, if x dies in the year d and if t is a year after d, then x is dead in year t."

With this additional fact available, the computer would, in principle, be able to tell us that Marcus is dead now. However, it is highly unlikely the program would discover the predicate logic analog of the simple five-step argument given above. Indeed, the program would be unlikely to discover *any* correct argument straight away. Without the provision of various heuristics, it would start making deductions blindly, and it could be some time before it stumbled on a sequence of steps that leads to the desired conclusion. Even with a good set of heuristics, the program would most likely make several false starts before finding a sequence that works, and the successful sequence would probably contain a number of steps that the human observer would recognize at once as being superfluous.

The reason the computer has such difficulty is that it is simply a symbol manipulator. Though sentences in predicate logic can be hard for an untrained person to read, it is nevertheless *possible* for us to read them and understand what they say—they do have *meanings* that we can understand. But to the computer, they really *are* meaningless gibberish. Thus, whereas a human can reason in terms of what the various sentences mean, be those sentences expressed in ordinary English or in predicate logic, the computer can only shuffle the symbols and look for matchings. This distinction manifests itself not only in the human's use of unstated assumptions such as people being dead at all times after they die—facts that must be presented to the computer explicitly—but also in choosing which facts are relevant to answering the question at hand. For instance, the human reasoner is unlikely to use any of facts 1, 3, or 4 in order to deduce that Marcus is dead since they do not seem directly relevant to that goal, but the computer has no way of knowing that. (On the other hand, if the initial set of assumptions included the additional fact that all mortals die before they reach the age of 120, then it would be possible to deduce that Marcus is dead using just facts 1, 3, 4, and 6, together with that important additional fact that when you have died, you are dead and you remain dead forever. There is often more than one way to deduce a conclusion from a given set of facts.)

The above example is extremely simple. And, to be honest, I have deliberately avoided going into a lot of details that are important even for that simple example—if you were to try to write an AI program based on the description given above, you would find yourself faced with a lot of issues I have not mentioned. But my aim is not to teach you how to write an AI program; rather, it is to give you a general sense of how such programs work—how a computer can be programmed so that its symbol manipulations correspond to logical deduction and problem solving. Devoid of any understanding of what is meant by the symbols they manipulate, it is only by virtue of their incredible speed that computers can (in some instances) make use of the crude and intrinsically inefficient approach of heuristic search-and-matching to arrive at an outcome for which humans require intelligence.

The above remark applies in particular to AI systems that process natural language. Natural language understanding and chess playing were the two problems that Turing regarded as key test cases for AI. The intervening years have seen significant advances in computer chess. In 1996, an IBM chess-playing computer called Deep Blue beat World Chess Champion Garry Kasparov in a game and drew two others, though Kasparov won the six-game series. In contrast, progress in natural language understanding has been far slower. Let's see what has been done and what the remaining problems are.

Machines that answer back

In the previous section, I argued that in the familiar sense of the word, computers do not 'understand' English or any other human language. They do not even understand in the sense of passing the Turing test, and it may well be that there will never be computers that do. Nevertheless, there are computer programs that do allow humans to carry on a conversation with a computer, using ordinary language to exchange information. How is this achieved?

In the case of ELIZA, the psychotherapist program described at the beginning of the chapter, the answer is that it is essentially a trick—the computer equivalent of an illusion performed by mirrors. In writing ELIZA, Joseph Weizenbaum was not trying to program a computer to pass the Turing test. Rather, he was showing that by using a few simple tricks, it was easy to produce the *illusion* of intelligent conversation, and by all accounts, he was horrified when others seemed to regard his program as the first step toward the development of an artificial psychotherapist.

By present-day AI standards, ELIZA is a very small and very simple program. All it does is scan the input looking for certain key words. For each key input word, the program has a number of preset replies. The responses are not always the same. In order to make the illusion a bit more realistic, Weizenbaum provided his program with a variety of responses to use in each case. Also, there are priority rules that the program follows when a sentence contains two or more key words. For instance, if the patient types in the sentence

My father hated me.

then ELIZA will spot the word *father* and respond with

TELL ME MORE ABOUT YOUR FAMILY.

If the patient then goes on to type

My father is a jerk.

then ELIZA will respond with

WHO ELSE IN YOUR FAMILY WAS A JERK?

The response "TELL ME MORE ABOUT . . . ," shown in the first reply, is a favorite response of ELIZA and is used on a wide variety of occasions.

Often the program will simply return the patient's input as a question, with *I* and *you* interchanged. For example

Patient: My boyfriend made me come here.
ELIZA: YOUR BOYFRIEND MADE YOU COME HERE?

If the patient's input includes the word *perhaps,* ELIZA may respond with the observation

YOU DON'T SEEM QUITE CERTAIN.

An input that includes *remember* can evoke the response

WHY DO YOU REMEMBER . . . JUST NOW?

or perhaps

WHAT ELSE DO YOU REMEMBER?

It says a lot about everyday polite conversation in general, and perhaps about certain kinds of psychotherapy in particular, that this canned-response approach can produce results that are uncannily realistic. ELIZA not only makes no attempt to understand the inputs it receives, it ignores most of that input and bases its response on a few key words. If it really runs into trouble and can find nothing in the input on which to base a response, it still manages to keep up the appearance of the caring psychotherapist by producing a reassuring response along the lines of

PLEASE GO ON.

However, if the patient strays away from matters of personal problems, then it is easy to lead ELIZA off course, and the illusion is shattered at once. Occasionally, even a 'legitimate' input will cause ELIZA to display its complete lack of understanding. For example, consider the input

I am happy. No, elated.

In some contexts, this produces the response

ARE YOU SAYING NO JUST TO BE NEGATIVE?

ELIZA sees the word *no* and responds to that, ignoring the rest of the input entirely.

Again, consider the input

I can't sleep at night.

This produces the reply

HOW DO YOU KNOW YOU CAN'T SLEEP AT NIGHT?

Clearly, ELIZA knows little about sleeping, nor about anything else for that matter. ELIZA does not understand language, and it is not an AI program. But it does remind us that with computers, as with many other things in life, it pays to look beneath the surface and not be fooled by a glossy exterior.

A far more sophisticated natural language system is Terry Winograd's SHRDLU, written in the early 1970s. (*SHRDLU* is the name spelled out by the first six keys on the top row of a Linotype typesetting keyboard, in the same way that the first six letters on the top row of a standard typewriter keyboard spell out *QWERTY.*) The SHRDLU program was designed with the deliberate intention that the computer should understand the input sentences. In order to stand even the remotest chance of achieving this goal, Winograd restricted his system to conversations about a very small, well-delineated, simple domain: a so-called *microworld.* SHRDLU's microworld—a hypothetical world displayed on a computer screen—consisted of nothing but blocks on a tabletop, together with a hand for moving them about. The blocks came in different shapes and different colors, and they could be stacked one on top of the other to form a tower, a pyramid, or whatever. An illustration of a blocks world is given in Figure 8. All conversation was about those blocks. The computer kept a continually updated database of which blocks were where, whether block *A* was on top of block *B,* which block was held in the hand, and so on, and used that store of information in communicating with the (human) user.

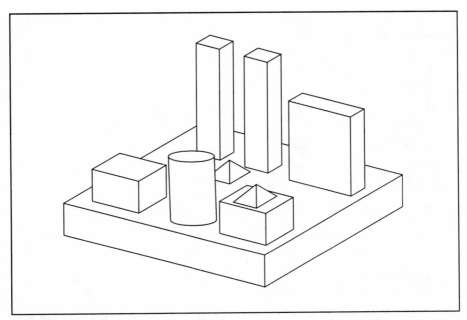

FIGURE 8 A Blocks World

SHRDLU could respond to English commands such as "Place the green pyramid on the red brick" and English queries like "What is sitting on the red block?" or "What shape is the blue block on the table?" It could cope with pronoun references such as

> *User:* Is there a red block?
> *SHRDLU:* YES.
>
> *User:* Pick it up.
> *SHRDLU:* OK. [SHRDLU picks up the red block.]

It can also handle ellipses such as

> *User:* What color is the block on the red brick?
> *SHRDLU:* GREEN.
>
> *User:* Shape?
> *SHRDLU:* PYRAMID.

The box on the following page provides part of an SHRDLU session, with Winograd's explanatory comments added.

Part of an SHRDLU Session

User: Pick up a big red block.
SHRDLU: OK.

(The system answers 'OK' when it carries out a command. In order to pick up the red block, it had to clear it off by finding a space for the green one and moving the green one away.)

User: Grasp the pyramid.
SHRDLU: I DON'T UNDERSTAND WHICH PYRAMID YOU MEAN.

(There are three pyramids in the scene, so the program does nothing.)

User: Find a block which is taller than the one you are holding and put it
              into the box.

(The system has to figure out what is meant by *one* and *it*, as well as use deduction to decide which block it is holding.)

SHRDLU: BY "IT" I ASSUME YOU MEAN THE BLOCK WHICH IS TALLER THAN THE
              ONE I AM HOLDING.

(Statement printed out to keep us informed.)

SHRDLU: OK.

(The hand has to set down the red block to pick up the taller blue one.)

User: What does the box contain?
SHRDLU: THE BLUE PYRAMID AND THE BLUE BLOCK.

User: What is the pyramid supported by?

(Earlier the system responded to "the pyramid" by saying "I DON'T UNDERSTAND WHICH PYRAMID YOU MEAN." Now it assumes that we mean the one just mentioned.)

SHRDLU: THE BOX.
. . .   . . .

SHRDLU was able to handle language in this fashion because it had complete knowledge of its blocks world and was able to keep track of the topic of conversation. Unlike ELIZA, SHRDLU made use of its stored knowledge of the blocks world to interpret the user's commands and questions and to respond to them—respond by language, by action, or by updating its knowledge of its world. In a limited sense, the program could be said to understand what the conversation was about. Of course, in the end, SHRDLU was simply manipulating symbols just like any other computer program. Thus, as with the person in Searle's Chinese room, there was no *real* understanding going on (in the sense of the understanding that occurs when a human being discusses a blocks world). What the program demonstrated was that given a small enough microworld and provided with sufficient knowledge of that microworld, a computer program could carry on a conversation in an intelligent fashion that could probably survive a microworld version of the Turing test.

Though each successful in its own way, SHRDLU and various other AI programs dealing with microworlds—whether concerned primarily with natural language understanding or having other goals—tended to sustain a belief in the possibility of genuinely intelligent computer programs for longer than would otherwise have been possible. With AI programs working well for microworlds, there was an expectation that by scaling up, the same kinds of program could be made to work for less restricted—and hence more useful—domains. But it never seemed to happen. The successful 'toy' examples never gave rise to useful working systems. The logician Yehoshua Bar-Hillel called the scaling-up belief 'the fallacy of the successful first step'. By the end of the 1960s, AI was in big trouble—though a further decade was to go by before there was widespread realization of the scale of the problem.

BURSTING BUBBLES

Toward the end of the 1970s, the AI and natural language understanding bubbles began to burst. The pattern was always the same. A promising new idea would lead to the development of a small-scale computer program that would work well, or at least tolerably well, for some artificially created microworld or some small, highly restricted fragment of natural language. But then all attempts to scale up to a more realistic scenario would run into trouble.

The problem had been pointed out ten years earlier, but few people bothered to listen. In his then controversial book *What Computers Can't Do,* published in 1972, the philosopher Hubert Dreyfus observed that not one of the successful microworld AI programs ever scaled up to anything close to a useful level. He went on to debunk claims that the success of those microworld programs signaled a first step toward genuine machine understanding, by likening them to a person climbing a tree and claiming to have thereby made the first step toward reaching the moon.

In 1993, Dreyfus published a new edition of his 1972 book, entitled *What Computers Still Can't Do*. In the introduction to the later book, he says the following:

> . . . now that the twentieth century is drawing to a close, it is becoming clear that one of the great dreams of the century is ending too. Almost half a century ago, computer pioneer Alan Turing suggested that a high speed digital computer, programmed with rules and facts, might exhibit artificial intelligence (AI). After fifty years of effort, however, it is now clear to all but a few diehards that this attempt to produce general intelligence has failed. This failure does not mean that this sort of AI is impossible; no one has been able to come up with such a negative proof. Rather, it has turned out that, for the time being at least, the research program based on the assumption that human beings produce intelligence using facts and rules has reached a dead end, and there is no reason to think it could ever succeed.

Dreyfus did not say that work in AI had failed to make interesting discoveries or to develop some useful software systems—though he did suggest that the successful systems were not AI systems in the sense normally understood by workers in the field. Rather, he said, AI failed to achieve the goal of machine intelligence as set out by Turing and the other early pioneers in the field. (Incidentally, Dreyfus's hedging remark about "for the time being" is the generosity of the academic critic. The evidence against AI he presents in his book and in another one written with his engineer brother Stuart in 1986, *Mind Over Machine: The Power of Human Expertise in the Era of the Computer,* is strong and convincing. We shall examine some of that evidence at the end of this chapter.)

Part of the reason why Dreyfus's words went unheeded for so long was that he was criticizing the enterprise from the outside—he was a philosopher, not a computer scientist. But within a few years of his 1972 broadside, some leading researchers within AI were also starting to express their doubts. SHRDLU designer Winograd was one of the first to publicly acknowledge the difficulties. Writing in *Artificial Intelligence and Language Comprehension,* published by the National Institute of Education in 1976, and fresh on the heels of his early success with SHRDLU, he says:

> The AI programs of the late sixties and early seventies are much too literal. They deal with meaning as if it were a structure to be built up of the bricks and mortar provided by the words. . . . This gives them a "brittle" character, able to deal well with tightly specified areas of meaning in an artificially formal conversation. They are correspondingly weak in dealing with natural utterances, full of bits and fragments, continual (unnoticed) metaphor, and reference to much less easily formalizable areas of knowledge.

A few years later, Winograd lost all faith in the AI enterprise and started to work along very different lines. We'll hear more of those new lines in due course.

In 1967, in his book *Computation: Finite and Infinite Machines,* MIT's Marvin Minsky predicted that "within a generation the problem of creating 'artificial intelligence' will be substantially solved." By September 1982, speaking to a reporter from *Science* magazine, he declared "The AI problem is one of the hardest science has ever undertaken."

And in 1985, Drew McDermott of Yale University, one of the stalwarts of the AI movement, made a dramatic defection with his paper "A Critique of Pure Reason" (reprinted in [4]).

The root of all the trouble, and the Achilles heel of AI that McDermott zeroed in on, was what had become known as the *common-sense knowledge problem.* When you or I or anyone else reason, we use all sorts of common sense knowledge of the world. We do so unreflectingly and in general unknowingly, and we do it all the time. The "if you die, then you are dead" and "if you are dead, then you stay dead" rules we noticed earlier are just two of what is literally an endless list of such common-sense knowledge facts. Without a base of such everyday knowledge, computers are quite unable to perform even quite elementary reasoning about real-world scenarios (as opposed to artificial microworlds) or to process natural language in an intelligent fashion. The question is, or rather, it was in the late 1970s: Is it feasible to program enough of these common-sense knowledge facts into a computer in order for the computer to function even tolerably well as an intelligent agent? Minsky had thought it was. In his introduction to the book *Semantic Information Processing,* a collection of his students' Ph.D. theses he edited and published in 1968, he wrote:

> If we . . . ask . . . about the common-everyday structures—that which a person needs to have ordinary common sense—we will find first a collection of indispensable categories, each rather complex; geometrical and mechanical properties of things and of space; uses and properties of a few thousand objects; hundreds of "facts" about hundreds of people, thousands of facts about tens of people, tens of facts about thousands of people; hundreds of facts about hundreds of organizations. . . . I therefore feel that a machine will quite critically need to acquire the order of a hundred thousand elements of knowledge in order to behave with reasonable sensibility in ordinary situations. A million, if properly organized, should be enough for a very great intelligence.

By the end of the 1970s, most workers in AI would have increased Minsky's figure of a million facts by quite a bit, but only a few questioned the underlying belief that machine intelligence could be achieved by constructing a sufficiently large database of stored facts about the world. Around 1979, British AI pioneer Patrick Hayes started work on his "Naive Physics Manifesto," an attempt to write down, in the language of formal predicate logic, all of our common-sense knowledge of the physical world: how solids and liquids behave, the effects of gravity on people and objects, properties of size and systems of measurement, the notions of force and energy, and so forth. It was pretty basic stuff. It had to be. Just think of all the basic facts about the physical world we take for granted: You need a container to store a liquid; if there is an opening in the container beneath the surface of the liquid then the liquid will run out; liquids cannot run upward; you can only put an object in a container bigger than itself; oil floats on water; most woods float in water; bricks and stones sink in water; and so forth. (Hayes's initial paper on the subject is reprinted in [4].)

However, even if you are able to list enough such basic facts to support—in principle—reasoning about the world, how on earth do you use all that stored information? More precisely, how will a computer use all those stored facts? For example, how do you respond when someone asks you if there is any water in the refrigerator? Almost certainly, you will simply assume they are asking if there is a bottle or jug of drinking water, and you will answer accordingly. But now imagine a computer is asked the same question. It will start to search through its database looking for references to water. Among the facts it finds are that all fruits consist largely of water and that apples are fruits. If it also finds a fact that says there are apples in the refrigerator, then the computer will say there is water in the refrigerator. Or maybe the computer first comes across the fact that when the temperature of water falls below 0°C, it turns to ice. It then finds the fact that there is ice in the refrigerator. So it tells you there is water in the refrigerator. Or maybe it finds the naive physics fact that the air always contains water vapor, and hence, as the refrigerator contains air, it contains water. All of the computer's responses are logically correct, but they do not answer the question asked. Unless there was a supply of drinking water in the refrigerator, an answer of "yes" to the question "Is there any water in the refrigerator?" would be quite wrong, even if logically correct. To give the appropriate answer it is necessary to know what a human being normally means by this question.

Though all of the computer responses we have just considered are logically correct, under normal circumstances, a human never considers them. It is not that we consider them and eliminate them; rather, they do not come into the reasoning process at all! Of course, you could always add to the database an additional fact that stipulates what a person means by water in the question "Is there any water in the refrigerator?" But that will not work, since there *are* circumstances when a human being might well have something different in mind. For example, suppose you and a friend are trapped in a building after an earthquake, and you need water to survive. Your friend asks if there is any water in the refrigerator. Under those circumstances, the ice in the freezer and the apples in the fruit tray are both acceptable sources of water, and you would respond accordingly. The point is, what is meant by the word *water* depends to a great extent on the circumstances of utterance. For the purposes of drinking, water in fruit may or may not count, depending on the circumstances; on the other hand, the water in battery acid never counts for that purpose.

Thus, if people do reason by accessing facts stored in memory, then those facts must be stored in the human brain in a manner that allows extremely rapid access that is highly dependent on circumstances. But no known means of organizing and storing data in a digital computer can support context-dependent data retrieval even remotely as efficient as the human brain.

Faced with the problem of how to access a large body of basic facts, a number of researchers attempted to provide appropriate data structures for organizing common-sense knowledge, most notably Minsky, who called his structures *frames,* and Roger Schank, who developed a similar notion called *scripts*. The idea in both cases was to provide the computer with structured knowledge about various stereotypical situations, such as dining in a restaurant, attending a birthday party, going to a football game, and so on. For example, here is Schank's own description of a restaurant script, vintage 1975:

Script: restaurant
Roles: customer, waitress, chef, cashier
Reason: to get food so as to go down in hunger and up in pleasure

Scene 1 entering
   go into restaurant
   find table
   go to table
   sit down

Scene 2 ordering
   receive menu
   look at it
   decide on order
   tell order to waitress

Scene 3 eating
  receive food
  eat food

Scene 4 exiting
  ask for check
  give tip to waitress
  go to cashier
  give money to cashier
  go out of restaurant

The idea is that, equipped with such a script, a computer will be able to reason about people going to restaurants: The various entries in the script and the order in which they appear are supposed to guide the computer as it searches for whatever facts it needs. But a few moments reflection should indicate that this approach is not likely to succeed. It is easy to imagine realistic restaurant scenarios in which any one of the above scripted steps is skipped or replaced by some other action, or any combination thereof. It might be an open-air restaurant, seating may be assigned, you might be refused entry for not wearing formal dress, the menu might be written on a wallboard, the 'waitress' may be a waiter, the food might arrive burned and inedible, you might pay by credit card, you might meet a friend who pays for you—the list of variations is, quite literally, endless.

Even if you regard such scripts as mere stereotypes that simply fit moderately well in most cases, there is still a problem. In real life, people move fluidly and effectively from one type of behavior to another. While waiting to be seated in a restaurant you might meet a friend and switch into your *greeting a friend* script; maybe you meet your boss and switch into your *meeting the boss* script; perhaps you see someone you are trying to avoid and go into *making a rapid, unseen exit* mode; maybe there is a fire in the kitchen, and you and all the other diners have to adopt the *emergency exit* script; or, perhaps you eat some badly prepared sushi and are propelled unwillingly into a *medical emergency* script. Again, the possibilities are endless, and it is hard to see how a computer equipped with scripts could be programmed to make all these script changes. Indeed, the original motivation for scripts makes it impossible to program such changes. The idea of a script is that, once invoked, it guides the reasoning processes. Thus, any potential deviations from the expected sequence of events would themselves have to be included in the script. But that would make even the simplest of scripts prohibitively long, thereby wiping out any gain in computational efficiency that the script was supposed to achieve in the first place.

No, scripts and frames did not solve the problem of how to store and utilize common sense knowledge, and AI was left with a blueprint for the creation of machine intelligence that MIT philosopher Jerry Fodor described in his 1983 book *Modularity of Mind* as providing "a picture of the mind that looked rather embarassingly like a Sears catalogue."

Oddly enough, the growing awareness that progress in AI was stalling did not lead to any lack of enthusiasm in the field. On the contrary, in 1981, AI was given a second chance when Japan announced a hugely ambitious ten-year program to develop the so-called Fifth Generation of computer technology.

By the end of the 1970s, computer scientists could divide the development of computer technology into four generations, based on the hardware used: First there was the vacuum tubes technology of the 1940s, then came transistors in the mid-1950s, followed by integrated circuits in the 1960s and early 1970s, and finally, in the late 1970s and the 1980s, very large-scale integrated circuits (VLSI). The Japanese adopted the name *fifth generation* to mark what they perceived to be the next step in the evolution of the computer, this time based primarily on advances in software rather than hardware. The development of powerful AI systems based on mathematical logic was to be central to the project. Writing in 1983, computer scientist and expert-systems pioneer Edward Feigenbaum of Stanford University summarized the new Japanese thrust as follows:

> In the kind of intelligent system envisioned by the designers of the Fifth Generation, speed and processing power will be increased dramatically; but more important, the machines will have reasoning power: they will automatically engineer vast amounts of knowledge to serve whatever purpose human beings propose, from medical diagnosis to product design, from management decisions to education. (*The Fifth Generation: Artificial Intelligence and Japan's Computer Challenge to the World*, co-authored with Pamela McCorduck.)

The major Western industrial nations were so in awe of the prowess the Japanese had already demonstrated in electronics that in order to protect their industrial independence, they each immediately launched their own lavishly funded research programs—Britain's Alvey program, Esprit in the European Community, and the Strategic Computing Initiative in the United States. So began another decade of almost feverish activity in the field of AI.

But all that was achieved by the sudden infusion of additional funding was a more widespread awareness of the problems that blocked further progress. Though AI met with limited success in constructing as that could play games, solve problems, and converse about worlds—tasks that for all their simplicity require intelligence when performed by a person—to this day, no one has been able to develop a computer system that could really be described as intelligent. Whether this is due to limitations in current technology and in our human expertise, or whether there is a more fundamental issue involved, remains a matter of considerable debate. The question is whether it is even *theoretically* possible to achieve intelligence by the manipulation of symbols.

The assumption that it is, in principle, possible to achieve intelligence by symbol manipulation was put forward by Newell and Simon in 1976 as the "Physical Symbol System Hypothesis." If this hypothesis is correct, then it is possible, in principle, to program digital computers to have intelligence.

On the other hand, if Newell and Simon's hypothesis is incorrect, and intelligence involves more than symbol manipulation, then the best that can be hoped for in AI is that further research will lead to computer systems more useful than those available today—computer systems that behave in a more intelligent way than today's—but the original goal of machine intelligence will be an impossibility.

However, the simulation of intelligence on a digital computer is just one goal of AI, albeit the original and most central goal. Another major area of AI research that developed in the late 1960s was *expert systems*. For a while, it appeared that in this particular branch of AI at least, real progress was possible.

Silicon experts

The idea behind an expert system is to capture in a computer program the expertise of a specialist in a particular domain, thereby creating an artificial expert that we may consult for advice. As with Winograd's concentration on a blocks world, by restricting attention to expertise in a relatively narrow area, it seemed more likely—at least on the face of it—that a usable and reliable system could be built. In restricted domains, the argument went, one would not get bogged down by the common-sense knowledge problem described in the previous section. Areas of expertise for which this approach was attempted included the diagnosis of infectious diseases, the exploration for oil and minerals, the analysis of organic compounds, income tax planning and calculation, the operation of an air defense system, the configuration of complex computer systems, and fault diagnosis in a modern automobile.

The kinds of questions one might want to put to an expert system are "What is wrong with this patient?"; "Would this be a good spot to drill an oil well?"; and "What is the molecular structure of this compound?" Such questions are not unlike our earlier "Is Marcus dead?" example, and this is no accident. That earlier example is a special case of an expert system—an expert system for history. Well, that is going a bit too far. A program would have to be quite a bit more complex than that simple example to warrant the title of expert system. But the fundamental idea is there. Here is how you would set about constructing an expert system.

First you build a *knowledge base*—a list of all the fundamental facts about the domain in question and the rules and rules of thumb that the human experts use in their daily work.

The basic facts in the knowledge base are generally easy to obtain—textbooks are a ready-made source of basic facts, such as "Substance X is deadly poisonous in doses above Y" and "Atom A joins to atom B to form molecule C."

The rules and rules of thumb might be in the form "If *this* and *that* then *some result*," or they may be more vague and involve probabilities, such as "If *this* (probability at least X) and *that* (probability at least Y) then *some result* (probability Z)." Getting those rules and rules of thumb is often no easy matter. Experts are frequently unaware of the heuristics they use when they reason about their domain of expertise, and even when they are aware they can find it hard to say when they use the rule or how to assign a numerical probability in the case of an imprecise rule. An entire new area of human science had to be developed in order to obtain this necessary information from the experts: *knowledge engineering*.

Once you have the knowledge base, two further things are required to produce an expert system: an *inference engine* that instructs the computer how to apply the rules in order to reason about the domain, and a *user interface* whereby the user can ask questions, provide information requested by the system, and obtain the sought-after answers. Expert systems technology was helped along by the fact that these two ingredients are essentially the same regardless of the domain of expertise, so there was no need to keep reinventing different versions of those particular wheels.

Given the uncertainties in the construction of knowledge bases, there was always a justifiable reluctance to rely completely and uncritically on the advice of expert systems in making life-or-death decisions. But when no irretrievable loss would follow from a poor decision, and a considerable gain would follow from a good decision, a successful expert system could be worth considerably more than its weight in gold. Or its weight in molybdenum, to take one particular example. According to reports at the time, a geological expert system called Prospector, developed by the Stanford Research Institute in the late 1970s, successfully predicted the existence of major deposits of the mineral at a specific location in the Mount Tolman area of Washington State. (But read the remainder of the section before you get too excited. The same caution applies to all the other expert systems mentioned here.)

Another expert system that operated in a low-risk area was Dendral, developed by Feigenbaum at Stanford University around 1980 to work out the molecular structure of complex organic compounds. The user provided the program with the chemical formula of the compound together with data from mass spectrometer analysis, and the program then suggested the most likely arrangement of atoms in each molecule.

Digital Equipment Corporation were particularly pleased with their expert system R1, developed in the early 1980s to configure VAX computer systems.

In the case of expert systems in medicine, the dangers of following unreliable advice prompted system designers to provide the user of the system with a means of querying any advice that they did not understand. The best-known system of this type was Mycin, developed at Stanford University in the mid-1970s. Mycin diagnosed infectious diseases such as meningitis. Information about the patient was fed into the system by a doctor or a medical assistant in answer to questions from the computer. Most of the answers the user entered were simply *Yes* or *No,* but instead of giving such an answer the user could type *Rule* and the system would display the rule it was currently using. This provided the user with the system's reasoning if it was not clear where the questions were leading. A further user response, *Why?,* could elicit more detailed information about the system's current line of reasoning. Part of a consultation session with Mycin is shown in the box on the following page. (The numbers shown in parentheses indicate the system's estimate of the probability that the statement concerned is correct. A figure of .1 represents a 1 in 10 chance of being right; .7 indicates a 7 in 10 chance of being correct.)

In addition to diagnosing diseases, Mycin could also recommend antibiotic treatment. In one trial, ten difficult cases were selected, and detailed clinical summaries of these were presented to a group of nine doctors of varying degrees of experience and to Mycin. The prescriptions each one came up with were then presented to a panel of meningitis experts to assess, with no clue as to the identities of the prescribers. The highest score was achieved by Mycin.

Part of a Mycin Consultation Session

Mycin: 22. WAS ANY CHEMOTHERAPY RECENTLY BEGUN SPECIFICALLY TO COMBAT ORGANISM-1?

User: No

Mycin: 23. IS PATIENT-1 A BURN PATIENT?

User: Rule

Mycin: RULE047

IF:

1. THE SITE OF THE CULTURE IS BLOOD, AND

2. THE IDENTITY OF THE ORGANISM IS NOT KNOWN WITH CERTAINTY, AND

3. THE STAIN OF THE ORGANISM IS GRAMNEG, AND

4. THE MORPHOLOGY OF THE ORGANISM IS ROD, AND

5. THE PATIENT HAS BEEN SERIOUSLY BURNED

THEN:

THERE IS WEAKLY SUGGESTIVE EVIDENCE (.4) THAT THE IDENTITY OF THE ORGANISM IS PSEUDOMONAS

User: No

Mycin: 24. IS THE PATIENT'S ILLNESS WITH ORGANISM-1 A HOSPITAL-ACQUIRED INFECTION?

User: Yes

Mycin: 25. DO YOU CONSIDER PATIENT-1 TO BE A COMPROMISED HOST? (ALCO-HOLIC, IMMUNOSUPPRESSED, ETC.)

User: No

Mycin: 26. HAS PATIENT-1 HAD ANY GENITO-URINARY SURGERY OR MANIPULATION OF THE URINARY TRACT? (E.G., INDWELLING CATHETER, CYSTOSCOPY, ETC.)

User: Why?

Mycin: I AM TRYING TO FIND OUT ABOUT THE IDENTITY OF THE ORGANISM.

I ALREADY KNOW THAT:

THE PORTAL OF ENTRY OF THE ORGANISM IS UPPER-GU

THE MORPHOLOGY OF THE ORGANISM IS ROD

THE STAIN OF THE ORGANISM IS GRAMNEG

THE SITE OF THE CULTURE IS BLOOD

THEREFORE, IF:

1. THE PATIENT HAS NOT HAD A GENITO-URINARY MANIPULATIVE PROCE-DURE, AND

2. URINARY-TRACT-INFECTION IS NOT A PROBLEM FOR WHICH THE PATIENT HAS BEEN TREATED

THEN:

THERE IS SUGGESTIVE EVIDENCE (.6) THAT THE IDENTITY OF THE ORGANISM IS E. COLI (RULE156)

The diagnosis system Puff, mentioned at the start of the chapter, was a derivative of Mycin, obtained by replacing the specific disease rules of Mycin by rules for the diagnosis of lung disease. As always with a medical expert system, a qualified physician examined the system diagnosis and signed off on it before any treatment began. According to reports from the Pacific Medical Center in San Francisco, where Puff underwent trials, in 85% of cases the physician made no amendment to Puff's diagnosis.

One thing to realize about expert systems is that they are not the same as database query systems, even in the case where the database is large. A database system, when queried for information, simply searches through its stored data until it finds what is required: An on-line railway timetable would be an example of such a database system. An expert system, on the other hand, actually *reasons* about the domain, as a glance at the Mycin dialogue in the box on the previous page will indicate. Thus, an expert system can produce new knowledge, knowledge that can surprise the user (or even the system designer). Expert systems may not be intelligent, but they are not simply passive storehouses of facts.

However, despite the initial high hopes and the early claims of success, expert systems soon ran into trouble, and it became clear that there was more to human expertise than could be captured in a list of facts and rules.

In preparation for writing their book *Mind Over Machine* in 1985, the Dreyfus brothers contacted several universities and industrial sites that carry out mass spectroscopy and were told that *none* of them used Dendral. Apparently it had never worked as well as had been hoped, and it had been replaced by a much more successful package called Congen. However, the new system does not use heuristics, nor can it be said to reason in any significant sense. It is thus not an expert system.

The geological expert system Prospector that had hit the *CBS Evening News* in September 1983 with its discovery of molybdenum in the Mount Tolman region also turned out to be less effective than was suggested by those breathless first news reports. There was no unexpected discovery of molybdenum. The system had made its predictions on the basis of information about prior drillings in the area where the mineral had already been found! What is more, though the system did correctly predict locations where further deposits of the ore might be found, all of the new deposits turned out to be too deep to mine economically, so it could not be claimed that Prospector had outperformed—or even equaled—the human experts.

A panel of experts evaluated the performance of the medical expert system Mycin, and reported their findings in the *Journal of the American*

Medical Association in September 1979. The human experts rated 7 out of 10 of Mycin's prescriptions as acceptable. That means that 3 out of 10 prescriptions were not acceptable. Just think about that. Would you be happy consulting a physician whose record was unacceptable 30% of the time? More to our present point, would you call such a person an expert?

And what about Mycin's offshoot, Puff? Remember that figure I quoted earlier, that the physician in charge was happy to leave unchanged some 85% of the program's diagnoses? That means that the human expert changed 3 out of every 20 diagnoses. Given the routine nature of much medical diagnosis, it is surely the diagnostic performance on the less straightforward cases that distinguishes the expert from the merely competent. Getting it right 17 out of every 20 cases might be no great feat at all. In fact, what the performance of Puff surely demonstrated was that human expertise was in fact very difficult, if not downright impossible, to achieve with a computer system.

This all seems very negative, so let me finish with a success. R1, the program that Digital Equipment developed in order to configure VAX computer systems, did perform well and was used for many years. But notice the highly specialized, nonhuman nature of the domain. The world of VAX computers was essentially a microworld, free of the complexities that come with human beings.

Another successful expert system is the one used by American Express to detect fraudulent use of credit cards by monitoring the patterns of use of each individual card and looking for suspicious, dramatic fluctuations in card spending. (The prudent cardholder should realize that "Don't leave home without it" should be supplemented with "Don't do anything particularly out of the ordinary with your card, or our expert system will get you." The expert system understands numerical and geographical patterns of spending, but not impulsive human behavior.)

And there are others. What characterizes the domains where successful expert systems have been developed and implemented is that they are essentially nonhuman, resembling well-delineated microworlds rather than the messy real world inhabited by people. Just as happened with AI in general, the original goal of expert systems research remains unattained. It's time to ask ourselves why.

REASONS OF THE HEART

Tennis coaches call it the *inner game:* the achievement of peak performance that comes when an expert player forgets everything he or she knows about the sport and plays the game of a lifetime by instinct alone.

Good skiers have a similar experience: those times when you forget you have skis on your feet and poles in your hands and you simply experience skiing in a smooth and effortless fashion, as if there was nothing else in the world. A similar, though less dramatic, experience familiar to most of us is when we arrive at our destination by car and realize that we have been completely unaware of our driving.

As with physical pursuits, so too can we conceive of an inner game for mental activity. Arguing in support of reliance on intuition and emotion in making a decision, the great French mathematician Blaise Pascal said, "The heart has its reasons that reason does not know."

In a similar vein, Albert Einstein, referring to his great insights into the laws of physics, wrote, "To these elementary laws there leads no logical path, but only intuition, supported by being sympathetically in touch with experience." (Quoted in Gerald Holton, *Thematic Origins of Scientific Thought: Kepler to Einstein,* Harvard University Press, 1973, p. 357.)

As anyone who has achieved a level of true expertise in some activity will know, peak performance is quite effortless and instinctive. It does not involve consciously following rules. According to Dreyfus and Dreyfus, expert performance does not involve rule-based behavior *in any way,* conscious or otherwise. In their book *Mind Over Machine,* they present a five-stage model of human performance, which they based on a study of the skill-acquisition process of airplane pilots, chess players, car drivers, and adult learners of a second language. Against this model, they then evaluate the performance of the best expert systems.

Stage 1 of skill acquisition is what the Dreyfuses call *Novice,* and is where the beginner simply follows the rules in an unquestioning, context-free fashion. In the case of learning to drive a car with a manual transmission, this would involve following rules such as changing gears at such-and-such a speed, following the car in front at such-and-such a distance, and so on. Novice performance is generally easily recognized as such. In the case of the novice car driver, the driver's movements are sudden and jerky, the changing-gear rule is applied rigidly with no account taken of contextual factors such as the sound of the engine or the degree of slope and other road conditions, and the driver tries to maintain the recommended separation distance regardless of the traffic density.

Stage 2 is that of the *Advanced Beginner.* The feature that distinguishes the advanced beginner from the novice is that while both act in a rule-following fashion, the advanced beginner modifies some of the rules according to context. For example, the advanced beginner driver will consider engine sound in deciding when to change gears and will adjust the separation distance from the car in front according to traffic density.

Stage 3 is called *Competence.* The competent performer still follows rules, but does so in a fairly fluid fashion—at least when things proceed normally. Instead of stepping from one rule to another, making a conscious decision of the next step at each stage (behavior characteristic of the novice and advanced beginner stages), the competent performer has a much more holistic understanding of all the rules. In the case of driving a car, the competent performer drives with a particular goal in mind and pays attention to engine sound and traffic density in making choices of gear and vehicle position. However, since the act of driving still occupies the full attention of the competent driver, he gives little thought to passenger comfort, road courtesy, or even safety and the law. Moreover, he is unlikely to be able to respond well to a sudden emergency. Because the competent performer has an overall sense of the activity and chooses freely among the rules for the appropriate one, he tends to feel a sense of involvement in the activity and to feel responsible for its outcome. The novice or advanced beginner, on the other hand, is likely to absolve himself of any responsibility when things go wrong, claiming that he was, after all, simply doing what he was supposed to do (according to the rules).

Stage 4 is termed *Proficiency.* For much of the time the proficient performer does not select and follow rules. Rather she has had sufficient experience to be able to recognize situations as very similar to ones already encountered many times before, and to react accordingly by what has become, in effect, a trained reflex. For instance, the proficient driver may realize, quite subconsciously, that she is approaching a sharp corner too fast, given the rainy conditions, and so may decide to ease off the accelerator or to apply the brakes. Though the action of slowing down or braking involves making a conscious decision and following a rule, the driver comes to make that decision as a result of a quite unconscious 'instinct', based on past experience of similar circumstances.

Stage 5 is that of the *Expert.* Terms such as *rule following, decision, mechanical,* and *knowing facts* do not really apply to the expert performer; rather one speaks in terms of *skill, know-how, intuition, instinct,* and *expertise.* The expert performer does not follow rules and indeed is generally not consciously aware of any rules governing the activity. Instead, she performs smoothly, effortlessly, and subconsciously. The expert driver is not aware of the car she is driving, rather she becomes one with her car and simply experiences driving. She may not even be consciously aware of her driving. When things proceed normally, the expert performer does not make decisions, follow rules, or solve problems; she simply *does what normally works.* In the case of an unexpected change in circumstances, the expert may react instinctively and without thought.

On the other hand, the change might cause her to revert to an earlier, lower level of expertise, resulting in a corresponding lowering of performance standard. Indeed, at any stage of expertise, unexpected and novel circumstances can lead to a regression to earlier stages of skill development.

Notice that the Dreyfuses are making a very strong claim with regard to expert performance. They do not claim that the expert is someone who has learned to follow the rules in a highly efficient and rapid fashion. Rather, they assert that *the expert is not following rules at all,* not even subconsciously. Rules, they say, are there to help us *learn* how to perform a task. When we become expert at performing that task, we no longer need the rules. According to this view, rules are like the training wheels we sometimes use in order to help young children learn to ride a bicycle. At first, the training wheels are set to be in contact with the ground, where they provide constant support. A little later, when the child has had some practice, the training wheels are set a little higher. This way, the child can learn to feel what it is like to ride without the constant support of the wheels but is still protected from the danger of falling over. Then, finally, when the child has learned how to ride the bicycle, we remove the training wheels altogether. At that stage, the child's skill has eliminated any need for the training wheels.

The suggestion that much human activity is not based on rules has enormous implications for the logicians' rule-based view of human thought that has influenced two thousand years of study. Saying that driving a car or riding a bicycle are not (for the expert) rule-based activities might not seem so shocking. But what if the human mind does not follow rules? What if our logical thinking and our use of language are not rule-based actions? Where does that leave logic as a science of reasoning, and what do Chomsky's syntactic theory and his Universal Grammar tell us about the human mind?

Having grown up in a culture whose intellectual traditions are heavily influenced by the ancient Greeks, in particular, Plato and Aristotle, most people find the very notion of rule-free expert performance hard to accept. On a number of occasions I have explained the Dreyfuses' theory of expertise to classes of college students, and I have always met with considerable opposition. Fresh on the heels of many years of fact- and rule-based high school education, most college students seem to find the idea of rule-free expertise completely counterintuitive. "Experts simply know the rules better and are much better at following those rules," they assert. They seem shocked that a mathematician such as myself could even entertain the suggestion that human beings are equipped to acquire skills that eliminate the beginner's need to follow rules. Even students that have themselves achieved expert performance—at skiing, tennis, basketball, playing chess, driving, or whatever—seem convinced that they are simply following rules they have learned, albeit subconsciously for the most part.

"But what about chess?" I ask, mentioning that the very greatest players say they play chess not by a process of rational analysis but by instinct; that although they must stop and ponder the next move from time to time, for the most part they simply look at the board and sense what is the best move to make. "No," my students reply, "all this shows is that the expert chess player simply analyzes the situation subconsciously and very rapidly—the grand master does it much better than the average chess player, but the process is the same." Generally speaking, even the good chess players in my class hold this view.

"How about walking?" I ask my students next. "Computer scientists have put enormous efforts into trying to design and build robots that can walk and have not yet managed to achieve a performance level that resembles a toddler a week after he or she first learns to stand upright. Robotic walking requires the solution of difficult mathematical equations and involves many complicated rules. Surely, a toddler cannot master all that mathematics?"

This generally gives my students pause, and for some, this example can be quite decisive. But for many of them, the compulsion to have a rule-based theory is so strong that, in the end, they prefer to settle for an explanation along the lines that the young human toddler must have some sort of hard-wired ability to subconsciously solve all of those equations. Those same students likewise prefer to think of bicycle riding as involving many rapid, subconscious, mathematical computations, rather than as a basic skill that humans are able to acquire through practice.

I generally make one desperate last-ditch attempt to convince them. "Look, there is a difference between following various rules and acting in a manner that is consistent with those rules," I say. "The person walking certainly acts in a manner that is consistent with all of the rules of physics, as does the bicycle rider. They are not breaking the rules. What's more, those rules can be reliably used by scientists who wish to *study* the physics of walking and bicycle riding. But the person walking or cycling neither needs to *know* nor *uses* those rules."

My attempts are generally quite in vain; most of my students remain unconvinced. The ones who most steadfastly stick to the rule-based view are invariably the ones who have had a solid science education.

What on earth is going on? Why are most of my students so reluctant to admit the possibility that humans are able to acquire *skills,* skills that may be learned through a process of following rules, but which, once fully acquired, neither require nor involve the following of rules?

The clue is probably to be found in the fact that the science students are generally the ones most wedded to the rule-based theory.

Western culture is dominated by an approach to knowledge that goes back to Plato, and to his teacher, Socrates. Their love of mathematics and of precise definitions led them to discount any human talent, ability, activity, or skill that could not be defined and explained and subjected to rational argument.

Though Aristotle mounted something of a defense against this view—pointing out that some fundamental human skill must surely be required in order to select and apply the facts and rules sought by Socrates and Plato—it was the Platonic view that came to dominate.

In the seventeenth century, Galileo provided support for the rational approach by showing it could be applied very successfully to the physical world. At about the same time, Descartes argued that the rational approach provided the 'right' way to look at the activity of the human mind. According to Descartes, understanding consists of the formation and use of appropriate representations.

Descartes's view was taken further by Leibniz, then later by Kant and Boole, and on into the present century, where the scientific method dominates much of contemporary Western thought and where the coolly logical 'rational man' is generally regarded as far more reliable than the much maligned woolly-minded, intuitive thinker.

To anyone steeped in this rationalist tradition—and that includes most people brought up in a Western culture and a Western educational system—there is always a desire to explain *knowing how* in terms of *knowing that,* to reduce skills to facts and rules, to explain the *composite* in terms of its *constituents.* It was this Cartesian approach to understanding that Pascal railed against with the cry I mentioned earlier: "The heart has its reasons that reason does not know."

The same objection was raised again a half century later by the British philosopher David Hume, who argued against Leibniz that knowledge is *not* grounded in principles and theories but rather is based on habits formed from experience. In other words, knowing how is not reducible to knowing that.

Into this two-thousand-year-old tradition, and fresh on the heels of the logical positivists and the mathematical linguists and logicians of the early twentieth century, came Alan Turing, Allen Newell, Herbert Simon, John McCarthy, Marvin Minsky, and the other pioneers of AI, all with a firm grounding in mathematics, and all brought up in a culture of rationalist science. To such people, the development of machine intelligence was a perfectly reasonable scientific goal. And make no mistake about it, the project was regarded as a *scientific* one. Indeed, the successful application of the methods of science to our understanding of the physical world provided a model to guide the research, as indicated by Terry Winograd in reference to the problem of representing knowledge in a computer:

> We are concerned with developing a formalism, or "representation," with which to describe . . . knowledge. We seek the "atoms" and "particles" of which it is built, and the "forces" that act on it. (*Artificial Intelligence and Language Comprehension,* National Institute of Education, 1976)

And yet the effort failed: Machine intelligence was not achieved. Of course, it could be that people have simply not tried long or hard enough. There is no watertight argument against that possibility. But there is another explanation: The original goal of machine intelligence is not possible, at least in terms of a program running on a digital computer, because human intelligent behavior involves *knowing how,* and *knowing how* cannot be reduced to *knowing that.* One circumstantial argument in favor of this conclusion that I personally find appealing is that right from the word *go,* the field of AI attracted some of the smartest thinkers around. When so many very bright minds, provided with enormous resources, failed to achieve their goal, it makes sense to look for a reason. And the most obvious explanation in this case is that the goal is an impossible one.

Pascal put the point quite clearly—and bluntly—in his collection *Pensées,* written in 1670:

> These principles [involved in reasoning] are so fine and so numerous that a very delicate and very clear sense is needed to perceive them, and to judge rightly and justly when they are perceived, without for the most part being able to demonstrate them in order as in mathematics. . . . Mathematicians wish to treat matters of perception mathematically, and make themselves ridiculous . . . the mind . . . does it tacitly, naturally, and without technical rules.

Pascal's words might seem unnecessarily cruel when quoted in reference to twentieth-century work in AI, but remember that Pascal was himself a mathematician. He was not decrying mathematics or mathematicians. He was simply pointing out that, although mathematical thinking has many uses, it cannot be applied to everything, and the functioning of the human mind is one of the things to which it cannot be applied.

This anti-Cartesian theme will come up again frequently in the remainder of this book, as we explore some of the abilities of the human mind and the ways in which it operates. Just as we have seen the limitations to a rule-based approach to various kinds of expertise, so too we will discover evidence that Chomsky's rule-based approach to language also fails to account for many important features. And if that is the case, if Descartes was wrong and Pascal was right, what are the possibilities of a science of mind and language, and what kind of a theory should we be looking for?

8

COMMUNICATION
IS THE KEY

Fie, fie upon her!
There's language in her eye, her cheek, her lip.
Nay, her foot speaks; her wanton spirits look out
At every joint and motive of her body.

—William Shakespeare[1]

BEYOND CHOMSKY

Chomsky called his approach to linguistic investigation *Cartesian linguistics* in order to emphasize its scientific nature as the study of language in a rational manner, free of any messy context, like culture. The characteristic features of Cartesian investigation, as advocated by Descartes in his treatise *Discourse on Method,* are that it is objective, dispassionate, rational, and context free. Two of the leading proponents of this approach were Galileo, in the case of the natural sciences, and Descartes himself—after whom the approach became named—in the case of philosophy and the theory of knowledge. Following Plato, these great thinkers emphasized that the object of a scientific study should be examined free of context, with the study carried out in a rational fashion. Today, the terms (*natural*) *science* and *Cartesian science* are virtually synonymous.

For awhile, Chomsky's Cartesian approach—inspired by the dramatic advances in logic of the early twentieth century—dominated linguistics,

---

1. *Troilus and Cressida,* Act IV, Scene V, l.54.

particularly in North America. However, in the early 1970s, the study of language changed once again, under the influence of sociology (to form the subject known as *sociolinguistics*) and psychology (to give *psycholinguistics*). Chomsky's hard-science, context-free approach to language was complemented by the soft-science investigations characteristic of the social sciences. Turning their backs on Chomsky's approach, sociolinguists and psycholinguists demonstrated that context plays a highly significant role in even the simplest of linguistic utterances. Whereas Chomsky had concentrated on what might be called the *internal mechanics* of language, the new linguists viewed language as just one of many ways in which two people can communicate. Using language to communicate requires much more than having a mastery of the syntactical rules of a given language, these new researchers argued. Accordingly, the focus should be widened from language itself to the much more general notion of language as a component of a communication process.

For the student of communication, there are a number of features involved when two people engage in conversation, for example, eye movements and physical gestures. Researchers who approach language as a component of the process of communication would agree with Shakespeare in the quote that opened this chapter, that there can be language in the gaze, the eyes, the lips, and in the "motive" of the body.

Indeed, communication can take place using just those other means, without any use of language at all. Animals communicate with each other through shrieks, cries, whistles, barks, thumping the ground, body motion, and displays of plumage. People can communicate with a glance of an eye, with a raise of one eyebrow, with a smile or a frown, by markings in the sand or on a tree, by music, visual art, and mime.

So from now on, as we examine our language ability, the emphasis will be very much on *communication* using language, as opposed to a de Saussure- or Chomsky-style study of the structure of language taken out of context. The developments we will follow are part of an emerging new science of communication. This new science is presenting many new challenges, as well as revelations, into what our minds are doing as we reason and use language.

As is usually the case with an emerging science, there are many different ways to proceed, each one the product of a particular school or research group. And each group can usually provide a persuasive argument to demonstrate why their approach is better than all the others. In the account I present here—which is about to move from the past to the present day and to what lies beyond—I make no attempt to remain faithful to any one particular group. I just give a general outline of the new science, taking ideas from many different schools of thought and occasionally blending different approaches that their adherents would claim could not possibly be combined. And why not? No single approach has yet been shown to be the correct one. There is, after all, one very obvious explanation for why there are so many different schools trying to analyze communication: We do not yet have a proper understanding of the phenomenon.

Our exploration of the new science of communication begins with a look at some fascinating research that helped point the way toward understanding what the key questions are that must be investigated. Some of that research involved studying the difference between human and machine abilities to communicate, in particular, the problems that can arise when humans attempt to communicate with computers. We understand how machines communicate—they follow the rules we give them. The problems people have in using computers can give us a good indication of the extent to which we follow rules—or not.

Photocopy Machines and Air-Traffic Control

In the early 1980s, researchers at the famed Xerox Palo Alto Research Center (Xerox PARC) developed a computer self-help facility designed to assist users in operating a large and relatively complex new photocopier. The idea was that the system would prompt the user for an action or inform the user of any problem. If necessary, the user could type in a request for instructions, and the system would give the appropriate response. The system ought to have worked well. Just think of everything that was in its favor:

- With Xerox, you have the company that pioneered photocopying technology, a world leader in the design and manufacture of photocopiers, whose very company name is synonymous with photocopying.
- The company's major research center, Xerox PARC, was, at the time, the acknowledged leader among computer research centers around the world. To mention just two of the many innovations that came out of Xerox PARC, it was PARC (as the center is affectionately known to many computer scientists) that created the personal computer desktop interface that Apple Computer subsequently made famous with its Macintosh computer, and it was at PARC that the *Ethernet,* the method by which most computer workstations are nowadays connected together in a network, was developed.
- PARC sits right in the middle of Silicon Valley, which, in the early 1980s, was the center of the world as far as computer innovation was

concerned. Within a five-mile radius could be found many of the world's leading computer scientists. The very air was thick with ideas and innovation.

■ Though the task involved human–machine communication, all communication was about the single task of photocopying using that one machine—a more simple, constrained, and well-defined task would be hard to imagine. Surely, there would be no problems in designing the system so anyone could use it.

Well, there were problems and plenty of them. In her now-classic book *Plans and Situated Action: The Problem of Human–Machine Communication,* published in 1987, Xerox PARC anthropologist Lucy Suchman described in detail just what went wrong with this seemingly simple information system. By videotaping and audiotaping groups of people trying to use the new copier, Suchman and her colleagues showed just how hard it is to design a computer system that people can communicate with, even when the communication is restricted to simple and predictable tasks of a very constrained kind. Put simply, most people found the copier help facility impossible to use. In particular, the system's responses to requests for information often seemed inappropriate or unhelpful, and there were constant communication breakdowns between user and machine.

Here is just one short section of the dialogue that Suchman recorded between two users (*E* and *F*) trying to understand what the current instructional display wants them to do. The display in question was designed to instruct them how to raise the document cover in order to copy a bound document. Quotation marks indicate that the person is reading text from the display.

E: "Pull the latch labeled—" We did that. "Raise—" We did that. (Studies display.) Okay. Okay.

F: "Lift up on the latch." We did that.

E: Now let's change . . .

F: "Change the task description?"

E: Yes.

F: (Selects "Change" on the display menu.) "Describe the document to be copied." Oh, we already did—no, we don't want to do that.

E: Maybe we have to do it to copy that [i.e., the next page].

F: (Looks around machine and laughs) I don't know.

The document, needless to say, does not get copied.

In her book, Suchman tries to point the way toward designing better systems. The key to such advances, Suchman suggests, is to achieve a better understanding of the way humans communicate with each other. Even if they do not speak each other's language very well, people are able to *negotiate* their way to an understanding in a way that was not possible with the Xerox photocopier help facility.

Besides photocopiers, office information networks are another area where there is a pressing need for computer systems that people find easier to use. A year before Suchman's book appeared, Terry Winograd and Fernando Flores published their landmark book *Understanding Computers and Cognition: A New Foundation for Design,* in which they also argued that real progress in information-systems design could only come about through a proper understanding of human communication. In Chapter 6 of their book, they write (p. 75):

> If we begin with the implicit or explicit goal of producing an objective, background-free language for interacting with a computer system, then we must limit our domain to those areas in which the articulation can be complete (for the given purposes). This is possible, but not for the wide range of purposes to which computers are applied. Many of the problems that are popularly attributed to 'computerization' are the result of forcing our interactions into the narrow mold provided by a limited formalized domain.

Echoing (a year in advance, as it happens) the point raised by Suchman in her book, Winograd and Flores continue:

> At the other extreme lies the attempt to build systems that allow us to interact as though we were conversing with another person who shares our background. The result can easily be confusion and frustration, when breakdowns reveal the complex ways in which the computer fails to meet our unspoken assumptions about how we will be understood.

Incidentally, the Winograd just mentioned is the same Winograd we met earlier as one of the early advocates of AI and natural language processing, who became one of the first proponents of AI to argue that it could never achieve its stated aims.

Winograd and Flores's aim, then, was not to develop computer systems that are able to carry on a conversation with a person in the usual sense. Rather, their goal was more subtle—to make use of an increased understanding of how people produce and understand language in a conversation, in order to design a computer system that is tailored to the way humans communicate. In other words, don't try to *mimic* the way people communicate, just try to design the system so it *complements* human communicative skills.

Following the work of Suchman, Winograd and Flores, and others, the late 1980s saw an increasing effort being put in to the development of a scientific understanding of communication. Much of the momentum was provided by a new research discipline that was emerging at the time from some of the world's leading information-systems research laboratories (including Xerox PARC). The name of the new field was *Computer-Supported Cooperative Work* (CSCW). As the title suggests, the new field sought to understand the way human organizations function in performing various tasks that involve the use of computer information systems, and then to use such understanding in order to design and build better computer support systems.

CSCW was—and still is—one of the most eclectic research fields you will ever encounter. The large, annual, international CSCW conference, held at various locations around the world every summer, attracts researchers in sociology, linguistics, cognitive science, psychology, computer science, systems design, systems engineering, philosophy, management science, and probably other disciplines as well.

Air-traffic control was one of the first tasks that attracted the attention of the CSCW crowd, including Suchman and her colleagues at Xerox PARC. With thousands of lives at stake every day, as jet aircraft thread their way along the world's airways at heights up to thirty-nine thousand feet, the crucial importance of reliable information systems is obvious. Computer system designers are always seeking to develop better systems to track and help control aircraft in flight. But if you can run into trouble with something as simple as a photocopier information system, imagine the challenge raised by the complexity of an air-traffic control room, where there is constant and sometimes highly technical communication between pilots and controllers, between controllers and other controllers—either in the same room or at different control sites—between aircraft and flight-control computers, and between controllers and flight-control computers. In order to try to understand the information flow involved in air-traffic control, the PARC team and others videotaped and audiotaped many hours of work in air-traffic control rooms around the world. The aim was to analyze the communications that were recorded on the tapes, so that it would be possible to develop a scientific understanding of communication that could lead to improvements in systems design. This analysis is still going on.

So there you have the two classic motivations for the development of a science. On the one hand, there is a simple, human desire to understand; on the other hand, there is a technological need that can only be met by the development of an appropriate science. The new science of communication is still in its early stages, and there are those who think it might never fully materialize—though that probably hinges upon what you mean by the word *science*. But there has been definite progress. In this chapter and the next, I'll tell you something about the advances that have been made—advances that have already led to better photocopiers, more reliable air-traffic control procedures, and personal computers that are easier to use than their predecessors.

Those advances depend on new understanding about four key features of communication that were explicitly ignored in Chomsky's logic-inspired analysis of language:

- Meaning
- Context
- Cultural knowledge
- The structure of conversation

By taking into account these features of communication and the role they play, we are going beyond the framework of logic. This does not mean we have to completely abandon logic, or more generally, other rule-based frameworks. It may be possible to extend some of the ideas of logic to include these additional features. For example, techniques of logic have been developed (by Tarski and others) to study meaning. And as we shall see, it is possible to extend some of those ideas to analyze the role played by context in communication, and there have been attempts to formulate *axioms for conversation*. However, whereas logic set out to provide the *theory of* reasoning, the role played by logic and its extensions in studies of communication is very much that of a tool that is used in the analysis—just one tool among several.

I'll consider the first two of the above four key features in the remainder of this chapter, and then look at the other two in Chapter 9.

THE MEANING OF IT ALL

During the 1970s, linguists were at long last able to give a precise answer to a question that had been troubling humankind for thousands of years: What is the meaning of life?

In order not to keep you on the edge of your seat for a moment longer than necessary, let me give you their answer right away. Here it is: The meaning of life is

$$\wedge life'.$$

Chances are, the significance of the above piece of mathematical notation—for that is what it is—has eluded you, so let me translate it into plain English. What it says is that the meaning of life is a function from possible worlds to life in those worlds.

Still no wiser? Well, it's time to stop teasing the linguists and come clean. The above 'explanation' of the meaning of life assumes a very technical notion of *meaning,* indeed, one that is mathematical. The mathematical theory in this case is known as *intensional logic,* a framework to study meaning developed by the logician Richard Montague in the early 1970s. How meaning is created and conveyed by language is one of the key aspects of language that Chomsky's analysis did not address. It is one of the most elusive of the features that researchers have turned attention to, and as we shall see, though progress has been made, many questions remain unanswered.

Montague's intensional logic was the first really successful attempt to develop a mathematical framework that incorporates the notion of meaning. Successful, that is, in a mathematical sense. No one familiar with Montague's work would claim that his theory says very much about *meaning* as we normally understand the word—Montague's notion of *meaning* only captures part of what we normally understand by the word.

Roughly speaking, when an ordinary person says that a word *means* such and such, he or she is referring to what it is that the word *signifies*— what its significance is for a human being who speaks and understands the language concerned. However, though it may seem natural, this idea of meaning (or significance) is notoriously difficult to pin down and explain.

Contrary to popular belief, dictionaries don't tell you what a word means in the sense of "what does this word mean to speakers of the language who know the word." Rather, they provide some kind of *description of* the meaning—usually a description that involves words whose meaning can be far less familiar than the word you started with.

For instance, try to say exactly what the word *dog* means. (And I pick *dog* as an example that ought to be easy—judgmental words such as *good* or *justice* or *fair* seem far harder to grasp.) "Look in a dictionary," you might suggest. Okay, here is what you find under the heading *dog* in the *Concise Oxford Dictionary:*

> **dog** *n.* **1.** carnivorous quadruped of genus *Canis,* of many breeds wild and domesticated; one used for hunting; male of dog, wolf, or fox. **2.** despicable person; (colloq.) fellow.

Ignoring the second, alternative meaning given, does the above paragraph really provide you with the *meaning* of the word *dog?* Surely not in any but a fairly convoluted sense of the word *meaning.* For one thing, most two-year-olds know full well what the word *dog* 'means', but few, if any, of those youngsters would know what a "carnivorous quadruped of genus *Canis*" is. For another thing, what about the proverbial dog that has lost an eye and a leg in an accident and answers to the name Lucky? Surely, a three-legged dog is still a dog, whether it was born with four legs and lost one or, by some accident of nature, was born with only two or three legs.

Whatever meanings are then, they must lie in our heads, not in a book.

Though Chomsky initially avoided the issue of meaning, declaring it to be unamenable to a mathematical approach, many linguists who came later attacked the problem by creating limited notions of meaning, which capture some of the more important aspects of meaning. *Semantics* is the name given to such studies.

One approach to semantics takes as its starting point the dictionary definitions just mentioned. In this approach, the meaning of the word *dog* is taken to be the aggregate of the notions *carnivorous, four-legged, of genus* Canis, and so forth.

Another way to go is to postulate a collection of abstract concepts that are the meanings of words. For example, the concept of a dog would be the meaning of the French word *chien,* the German *Hund,* and the English *dog.* According to this approach, the concepts provide some kind of *lingua franca* that transcends all the individual languages. (A variation on this approach takes the abstract concepts to be defined within mathematics, and it is a version of this approach that leads to the meaning-of-life joke given above.)

In semantics, one studies not just meanings of words, but meanings of phrases and of whole sentences. In fact, present-day semantics is concerned almost exclusively with phrase and sentence meaning, and, in particular, the way the meaning of a phrase or sentence is somehow built-up from the meanings of its constituent words, which are often assumed as given or understood—an approach known as *compositional semantics.*

Compositional semantics can be made very mathematical, tying linguistics back into logic. For example, take the classic linguistic example *The cat sat on the mat.* The compositional approach to the meaning of this sentence works like this. The phrase *the cat* refers to a particular object c in the world, a certain cat. The verb *sat* refers to a certain activity, S, the activity whereby one object sat on top of another. And the phrase *the mat* refers to a particular object m, a mat. From these three references, c, S, and m, you arrive at the meaning of the entire sentence. The sentence meaning is that c stands in the relation S to m. This could be written in the form *cSm,* which reflects the linguistic order in the original sentence, or in predicate logic fashion as *S(c, m),* which displays the logical structure of the sentence. Whatever notation is chosen, the point is that the meaning of the whole sentence is constructed from the individual references of its constituent words and phrases, in much the same way that a wall may be constructed by cementing together its constituent bricks.

So, using predicate logic, it is possible to write down a formula that represents the meaning or the semantics of a simple sentence such as *The cat sat on the mat.* What about a more complicated sentence? Consider

John loves Mary but Mary loves someone else.

To obtain a typical rendering of the meaning of this sentence in predicate logic, let *L* represent the relationship of loving, let *J* represent the person John, and let *M* represent the person Mary. The meaning can then be given as:

$$L(J,M) \; \wedge \; \exists x[x \; \neq \; J \; \wedge \; L(M,x)]$$

Read literally, this predicate logic expression says the following:

"*J* loves *M* and there is an individual *x* who is not *J* such that *M* loves *x*."

This is quite a mouthful and a far cry from the original sentence.

Linguists generally refer to the logical expression you get from a sentence of a natural language in the above manner as the *logical form* of the sentence. Logical form provides the basis of many of the attempts in AI to develop computer systems that can process natural language. The computer program begins by translating an input sentence to its logical form. Further processing is then done with the logical form, which is in an ideal format for computer manipulation.

Logical form is a useful device not only for the computer processing of natural language but also for the linguist who is trying to understand language. The logical form provides a sort of stripped-down version of the sentence, a logical skeleton of what the sentence says. Some cognitive scientists have gone even further and suggested that logical form is not just a useful analytic tool, but that it, or something very much like it, must be involved in the way people really do think and understand language. The American cognitive scientists Jerry Fodor and Ray Jackendoff are particularly well-known proponents of this view, which they have each put forward in a series of books. Roughly speaking, the argument Fodor, Jackendoff, and others advance goes something like this.

As we have seen already, Chomsky believes that we human beings must be equipped with a Universal Grammar that enables us to learn and use whatever specific language we are exposed to in our childhood. Universal Grammar is concerned with the syntactic structure of language, but, the argument goes, we must likewise have some sort of internal meaning structure in our heads, a facility which enables us to think and reason and to learn and utilize the meanings of words and sentences. Fodor refers to that fundamental mental framework as a *language of thought;* Jackendoff uses the term *conceptual structure.* The natural languages we all speak are simply external manifestations of our common internal mental language or conceptual structure. Since the internal language of thought, or conceptual structure, has to be more or less the same for all people, whatever language or languages they speak, Fodor and Jackendoff argue it will surely be something like logical form. Even if it isn't—and at present no one has any way of finding out for certain one way or the other—then logical form is a reasonable working model to work with.

The language-of-thought approach is certainly appealing, not the least reason being that it does provide us with some way to think about the otherwise mysterious process that goes on in our heads when we think or use language. However, there is considerable evidence to suggest that logical form (or any variation of logical form) provides, at best, a very poor picture of mental activity, and at worst is both misleading and a completely inappropriate way to think about mental and linguistic activity.

One problem is that, more often than not, the logical form distorts the linguistic structure of the sentence so much that it is more like a caricature drawing of the exterior than an X-ray of the skeleton. For instance, to get to the logical form of a sentence such as

> *Max knows everyone in the room and so does Naomi.*

you have to first rewrite the sentence as

> *Max knows everyone in the room and Naomi knows everyone in the room.*

and then you get to the logical form

$$\forall x[I(x,r) \rightarrow K(M,x)] \land \forall x[I(x,r) \rightarrow K(N,x)].$$

The result is that you get a complicated logical form that is difficult to understand, coming from a fairly simple-looking sentence that is easy to understand.

Logical forms of sentences where the verb is in the past or future tense are particularly messy. A simple English sentence such as

> *John will run.*

has a logical form that reads roughly as

There exists some time t *later than now such that John runs at that time* t.

The sentence

John had run.

has an even worse form that reads like this:

There is a time t_1 *earlier than now such that there is a*
time t_2 *earlier than* t_1 *such that John runs at time* t_2.

This seems so far removed from the way we generate and understand the simple sentence *John had run* that it is not clear that the logical form reflects the way we think, or that it really helps us to understand the meaning of sentences in a scientific fashion.

Complexity is not the only problem with logical form. A far more serious difficulty is that the use of logical form assumes that words have fixed, definite, and unique meanings. But this is just not true. Meaning is a much more complicated phenomenon than that. In fact, meaning generally depends on context—the second of the four key features of communication that Chomsky ignored but which many present-day linguists take very seriously.

How big is big?

Most everyday words have different meanings, depending on the context. For example, the word *big* does not have a fixed meaning in terms of size—big does not invariably mean over six feet tall or having a volume greater than 10 cubic meters. Just think of the phrases *big elephant, big mouse, big house, big mountain,* and *big country.* The meaning of each of these does not arise by combining the property big with the property of being an elephant, being a mouse, et cetera. A big elephant is not an object that is both big and is an elephant. A big elephant is an elephant that is big, as elephants go. However, the logical form approach to meaning simply requires that there be a single property B (big) that works in all cases. Thus, the logical form of the sentence *That is a big mouse* would be

$$B(a) \land M(a)$$

where a is the object referred to by the word *that* and M is the property of being a mouse. The logical form of the sentence *That is a big elephant* would be

$$B(a) \land E(a)$$

where *a* is the object referred to by the word *that* and *E* is the property of being an elephant. But as we just observed, the property *B* cannot possibly be the same in both cases.

If this kind of example were rare and exceptional, there would be no problem. However, far from being exceptional, it is the way most everyday language works. It is only in mathematics and the sciences that you find words having fixed, unique, and unchanging meanings—and then because mathematicians and scientists *define* the technical words they use precisely in order to avoid ambiguity. With everyday language, in contrast, the meaning of a word can depend on a whole range of factors.

Take the word *red*. According to the standard definition provided by physics—which is the definition you will find in the dictionary—red refers to the color seen at the least-refracted or long-wave end of the visible color spectrum. But this definition does not apply to any of the following uses of the word: red hair, red wine, red wood, red potatoes, red sunset, red skin (as in natural pigmentation), red skin (as in blushing), and red skin (as in sunburnt). In none of these uses does the *word* red refer precisely to the *color* red as described in the dictionary.

The above observations do not imply that word meanings are at all arbitrary or chaotic. People exhibit a high degree of agreement as to the meanings of words in various contexts. What varies are the meanings a particular word has in different contexts. For example, how many are *several*? How many are *few*?

The dictionary definitions are not much help. For instance, *Webster's Dictionary* gives the meaning of several as "an indefinite number more than two and fewer than many." If you try to unravel this definition by looking up the definitions of fewer and many, you find that the former is defined to mean "a smaller number of persons or things" and the latter is listed as "a large number of persons or things." In other words, according to *Webster's*, *several* means "an indefinite number more than two and a smaller number than a large number." We are clearly starting to go round in circles here. The only thing for sure that the dictionary tells us is that several implies more than two. It does not give us any idea of the typical numerical values Americans will attach to the word *several* in different contexts, the mental image conjured up in the average American mind by a phrase such as *in front of us were several mountains* or *there were several women in the room*.

A German study carried out in the early 1980s showed that the numbers people attached to words such as *several* and *few* depends on a number of factors, including what the objects are, where they are situated, and how they are observed. In the study, people were given sentences containing *several* and *few* and asked to provide in each case a numerical estimate of the number of objects involved. Though the numbers the respondents gave varied from context to context, within each context the responses were remarkably consistent from person to person.

In the case of the word several, the number given became smaller as the objects became larger. For *several crumbs* the median estimate was 9.69; for *several paperclips* it was 8.15; for *several pills*, 7.27; for *several children*, 5.75; for *several cars*, 5.50; and for *several mountains*, 5.27.

Just as it makes a difference what the objects are, so too, the answer varies depending on where the objects are located. Here are translations of some of the German *few* sentences used in the study, with the median figure reporting how many few indicates in each case:

- In front of the hut are standing a few people. (4.55 people)
- In front of the house are standing a few people. (5.33 people)
- In front of the city hall are standing a few people. (6.34)
- In front of the building are standing a few people. (6.69)

The German study also indicated that it makes a difference what that 'few' people are doing:

- In front of the city hall there are a few people standing. (6.34)
- In front of the city hall there are a few people working. (5.14)

Another relevant factor identified is the viewpoint of the observer:

- Out of the window one can see a few people. (5.86)
- Through the peephole one can see a few people. (4.76)
- Out of the window one can see a few cars. (5.45)
- Through the peephole one can see a few cars. (3.95)

We have to be careful in how we interpret this data. As we saw in Chapter 5, when we translate from one language to another, meanings of words often change in subtle ways. (See the *hot–warm* discussion on page 109.) A study of the use of the terms several and a few carried out in the United States might produce a different range of numbers. A similar study carried out in England might produce different numbers again. But the key point is that, whatever the actual numbers are, they will vary depending on the context.

Observations such as those above would appear to strike a death blow to the compositional theory of meaning. However, there is a standard counterargument to this conclusion. It goes like this.

Admittedly, words have different meanings in different contexts. However, the range of possible meanings is finite in each case, and in order to 'get it right', all you need to do is make sure that the dictionary definition for each word lists all the possibilities. For example, in the case of the word *red,* the dictionary should list all of the different meanings of the word mentioned earlier, as in red wine, red skin, red sunset, et cetera. (In fact, most comprehensive dictionaries do list the more common alternative meanings, usually by giving examples of use, such as "red as in red hair" to mean a gingery–orange color.) The linguist then has the task of investigating the manner in which, in any given instance, a person chooses the correct or appropriate meaning from among the finitely many listed possibilities. This is exactly the approach adopted by the more sophisticated computer systems to process natural language.

Such computer systems can perform well when presented with pairs of sentences such as

> *We went to the bank to get the money.*
> *We sat by the bank and watched the boats sail by.*

The computer dictionary lists (at least) two possible meanings for the word *bank:* a financial institution and the edge of a river. The mention of money in the first of the above sentences suggests that the appropriate meaning for *bank* in this case is a financial institution; similarly, mention of boats in the second sentence suggests that *bank* means river bank in this case. However, neither of these readings is written in stone. Consider the following two scenarios:

- *We went to the bank to get the money. Bob had buried it by the river some months earlier.*
- *After we had cashed the check at the bank down by the bay, we sat by the bank and watched the boats sail by.*

These examples would confuse most computer systems.

Still, you might think, the situation is not completely hopeless. Admittedly words such as *big, red, few,* and *bank* have different meanings depending on context. Indeed, when you look closely, you discover that most words have more than one meaning. But if each word has a small, fixed range of possible meanings—as a quick glance at a dictionary might suggest—then it could still be possible to develop a clean, crisp theory of meaning fashioned after Tarski's analysis of meaning for the formulas of mathematics. Each word would require several analyses, one for each possible meaning, and there would have to be some way to indicate the circumstances under which each meaning applies. But, on the face of it, such an approach seems feasible.

In fact, linguists have analyzed meaning this way. But for the researcher investigating communication (and not just the structure of language), this approach will not work. The problem is, for many words, the list of their possible meanings is, for all intents and purposes, endless. There can be no list of all possible meanings given in advance. In their daily conversations, people often create one-time meanings on the fly.

Linguists in a playful mood sometimes use the term *nonce sense* to refer to such one-time meanings created *for the nonce—nonce* being a Middle English word and the phrase meaning "for the moment" or "for the one occasion."

An illustration of nonce sense is provided by psychologist and linguist Herb Clark, in his 1992 book *Arenas of Language Use*. The example is taken from an article in the *San Francisco Examiner* by columnist Erma Bombeck. Bombeck is talking about her daughter's difficulties in finding a roommate:

> We thought we were onto a steam iron yesterday, but we were too late. Steam irons never have any trouble finding roommates. She could pick her own pad and not even have to share a bathroom. Stereos are a dime a dozen. Everyone's got their own systems. We've just had a streak of bad luck. First our Mr. Coffee flunked out of school and went back home. When we replaced her, our electric typewriter got married and split, and we got stuck with a girl who said she was getting a leather coat, but she just said that to get the room.

As Clark points out, there is nothing remarkable about this passage. It is easy to read and to understand. And yet six of the eight sentences in this passage contain words or phrases used in a nonce sense: *a steam iron, steam irons, stereos, our Mr. Coffee,* and *our electric typewriter.* In each case, the phrase refers not to the object (the usual meaning) but to a person—the person who owns such an object. In all likelihood, this is the first time you have seen these particular phrases used in this manner, but that did not prevent you from understanding the meanings. You *created* the appropriate meanings, just as Bombeck intended.

Again, it would be possible for the linguist to ignore such examples if they were fairly rare. But as Clark and others have observed, they are not at all rare—everyday language is full of such novel uses of words and phrases: In a restaurant we ask for 'one water' or 'one orange juice' to mean one glass of water or one glass of orange juice; we say we are going to 'do the lawn' to indicate that we are about to mow the lawn; we refer to certain kinds of people as 'very San Francisco' or 'very Boston'; and so on. Such uses of language are ubiquitous. Just pick up any newspaper or magazine or listen to people talking to each other. Sometimes, novel uses of words become so common they find their way into the regular lexicon. Obvious examples are the verbs *to fax* and *to telephone.*

With the ubiquity of nonce sense, there seems little hope that the re-searcher investigating communication can develop a relatively simple compositional theory of meaning along the lines of Tarski's theory of mathematical meaning. So, if we want to develop a science of communi-cation, we need to adopt a different approach.

A good place to start is with the observation that, in human terms, the role played by context in communication is, for the most part, fairly unproblematic. People don't have to be taught how to make use of con-text to understand each other's words. We do it automatically. We only become aware of the huge role that context plays in our day-to-day con-versations when something goes wrong—when we fail to communicate. So, if we want to understand how context affects communication, why not start with an examination of the causes of communication break-down?

A number of recent studies have done just that. The aim of these stud-ies is not to help people communicate better, though that would be a wor-thy goal. Rather, the motivation once again comes from the information systems industry. Breakdowns in human–machine communication are all too frequent: The ATM steadfastly refuses to give you the money you know is in your account; the photocopier machine seems incapable of do-ing what you want; and the airline reservation system can defy the efforts of even the best-trained airline agent. By closely examining cases of com-munication breakdown, perhaps we can learn how to design better sys-tems. And, indeed, this has happened on a number of occasions, including the ATM and the photocopier.

A FAILURE TO COMMUNICATE

"What we have here, is a failure to communicate." So says the sadistic prison guard in the final scene of the movie *Cool Hand Luke,* moments before blowing away the wrongly imprisoned hero—played by Paul New-man—with a shotgun. What the prison guard meant by his remark was that Newman refused to do things the guard's way—to do what the guard wanted.

Differences in backgrounds, goals, or outlooks on life can hinder or even prevent effective communication between two people every bit as much as their not speaking the same language.

Here is an example of a simple case of miscommunication. Suppose that Peter, in San Francisco, promises to phone Emily, in New York, at 6 o'clock. At 6 o'clock, Emily waits by the phone, but there is no call. At 7 o'clock, in desperation, Emily phones Peter. "Why didn't you call at six as you promised?" she asks him. "Because it's only 4 o'clock," Peter replies. The problem, of course, is that for Peter, in California, it *is* 4 o'clock, whereas for Emily, in New York, it is 7 o'clock. When people are in different time zones—in different physical *contexts*—miscommunication of this kind can result.

Notice that the communication breakdown between Peter and Emily does not result from either one of them saying something that is false. The sentence each one says is true in the relevant context. The problem is that the two contexts are different. The only way to completely avoid such communication breakdowns is to be explicit about which context is meant. For example, Peter should have said something like "I'll call you at 6 o'clock California time" or "I'll call you at 6 o'clock Pacific Standard Time."

Notice also, that in order to resolve the confusion, you don't have to know exactly where the 'lines' are that separate Pacific time from Mountain time from Central time from Eastern time—the exact borders of the time zones are not important. Nor do you need to know how many people there are in each time zone, or what the weather is in each region. The only crucial facts are (1) that time is always set within a time zone, and (2) Eastern Standard Time is three hours ahead of Pacific Standard Time.

Another instance where we become aware of context is when we travel for the first time to another global hemisphere. For instance, an American grows up knowing that June is a summer month. When Americans travel to Australia for the first time, they discover that the Australians know that June is a winter month. So who is right, and who is wrong? The answer, of course, is that they are both right. When in the United States, the American has no need to mention the environment when talking about the seasons, and likewise for the Australian in Australia. It is only when there is some kind of crossover from one country to another, either a physical crossover or an informational one by communication, that it is important to specify the environmental context.

Here is one final example of context, connected not with language but with behavior. Most of us behave very differently at work and in our homes. We dress differently, we speak differently, we do many things differently. Does this mean that each of us has a dual personality—that we are all Dr. Jekylls and Mr. Hydes? Of course not. What changes is our context—our environment. Our work environment and home environment each supports a whole range of behavior patterns. When at work, we behave one way, when at home, we behave another way. If I went into my office one day wearing slippers, my colleagues would find my behavior extremely odd. Not because there is some unwritten rule that says "It is not appropriate to wear slippers." After all, I do often wear slippers. Rather the crucial issue is that *in my office context*, it is not appropriate to wear slippers, whereas *in my home context,* it is.

COMING TO TERMS WITH THE SITUATION

One of the more intriguing developments in recent years has been an attempt to develop a mathematics of contexts. Actually, there have been a number of such attempts. The one I shall describe in the remainder of this chapter has been one of the most successful, and that is a good reason to include it here. Furthermore, it is the only approach that begins with the clear intention of working out of the classic tradition of logic (though it rapidly takes some turns that make it very different from classical logic). Finally, it is the approach I myself have been involved in—though my involvement came about *because* I thought it was the most promising approach in the first place. However, from now on in this book, we are dealing largely with science in the making, and only time will tell which is the "right" method, or even if there is a single "right" method.

Whatever flavor of theory one chooses to try to understand contexts, the first step is to decide on a name to refer to them. Of course, we could simply call them contexts. As the saying goes, a spade is, after all, just a spade. Unfortunately, as we have observed already in this chapter, a spade is, in fact, *not* just a spade. What a word means can depend very much on the context in which it is used. That is true of the word *spade*. It is also true of the word *context*.

One problem with using the word context in a new scientific study of communication is that the word is used in a semitechnical way in a lot of work in linguistics and artificial intelligence, in many cases with different meanings. A term that suffers less in that way (though there are still some conflicts with other schools of research) is *situation*. This is the term I shall use in this account.

Having chosen our name, our next step is to try to understand just what kinds of objects these situations are. We have to come to terms with their inherent, amorphous nature. For example, among the situations that could arise as contexts—or topics—for a conversation are such amorphous entities as "the current political situation in the Middle East" or "the Vietnam War." These both have some geographical focus, but many of their constituents are spread across the globe. It is clearly impossible to specify everyone who is a constituent of either of these situations and to specify everyone who is not a constituent—though it is possible to be precise about some individuals.

The term *situation* was first used to refer to a background context or to a topic for an utterance or a conversation by the American logician Jon Barwise in the late 1970s and early 1980s. Barwise was trying to adapt the mathematical methods of predicate logic (described in Chapter 4), in particular, Tarski's theory of mathematical truth, to apply not just to the formal languages of mathematics but to natural language as well. The name he gave to his new theory of meaning was *situation semantics*. His idea was as follows.

As Tarski observed, a mathematical statement is about a mathematical structure or object and makes a claim about that structure or object that is either true or false for that structure or object. As described in Chapter 4, Tarski used this observation in order to give precise definitions of meaning and truth for mathematics. Taking his lead from Tarski, Barwise observed that many statements of ordinary English are about a part of the world and make a claim about that part of the world that is either true or false for that part of the world. That part of the world could be very small, say, a desk top with pens, papers, computer, and telephone, or it could be larger, such as a meeting taking place in a room, or larger still, such as an entire country or even the whole world. Barwise then tried to mimic Tarski's definitions of meaning and truth to give definitions of meaning and truth for natural-language sentences that are about a part of the world and make a claim about that part of the world that is true or false. His effort was partially successful. He used the word *situation* to refer to a part of the world about which a statement could be made.

Barwise even adopted Tarski's algebraic notation, which we met in Chapter 4. Using the Greek letter σ (sigma) to denote a statement of the kind he was considering (i.e., a statement about a part of the world that makes a claim about that part of the world that is true or false), he wrote

$$s \models \sigma$$

to mean that the statement σ makes a claim about the situation *s* which is true about that situation. He suggested that we should read this formula as "*s* supports sigma." For example, if the situation *s* is a meeting taking place in some conference room, and John starts to address the meeting at 4 o'clock, then Barwise would write:

$$s \models \textit{John starts to speak at 4 o'clock.}$$

(In words, "The meeting situation, *s*, supports the fact that John starts speaking at 4 o'clock.")

As I have just presented it, the above example is ambiguous. What exactly goes on the right of the 'supports' symbol? What is written is a sentence, that is, a piece of language. But do we mean the sentence itself or do we mean the information expressed by the sentence? This is the familiar logician's problem of syntax versus semantics. What Barwise really meant in such an example is that the situation *s* supports *the fact of the matter* or *the item of information* that John starts to speak at 4 o'clock. This is another place where the use of mathematical notation can be an advantage. A less ambiguous way to express the same example is to write it in a purely algebraic form, without any words, like this:

$$s \vDash \sigma$$

where the symbol σ denotes *the fact* or *the item of information* that John starts to speak at 4 o'clock. Then it is clear that what is meant is the information expressed by the sentence (the semantics), not the sentence itself (the syntax).

However, Barwise and his followers quickly tired of having to write the phrase "the fact that . . ." or "the item of information that . . ." all the time, so they introduced a further algebraic notation to mean the same thing. Using that new notation, the item of information that John starts to speak at 4 o'clock is written like this:

⟨⟨*John starts to speak at 4 o'clock*⟩⟩.

In general, if we enclose any English sentence in the double angle-brackets, ⟨⟨ and ⟩⟩, the resulting expression denotes the fact or the item of information expressed by that sentence. Thus the double angle-bracket notation provides a simple way to distinguish between a sentence and the information it expresses.

Using the bracket notation, the original, ambiguous formula involving the situation *s*, where it was not clear whether the item on the right should be understood as a sentence or the item of information expressed by the sentence, can now be written in the unambiguous form:

$$s \vDash \langle\langle \textit{John starts to speak at 4 o'clock} \rangle\rangle.$$

In 1987, I coined the word *infon* to refer to a single item of information, such as the one in the above example, and that name has stuck.

One advantage of Barwise's framework, and in particular, his algebraic notation, is that it separates the soft entity *s* (the situation) from the hard entity σ (the infon). The formula that says an item of information σ (an infon) is true in a situation *s* (i.e., *s* supports σ) looks like this:

$$s \vDash \sigma.$$

The situation (the soft entity) is on the left of the 'supports' symbol (⊨); the infon (the hard entity) is on the right. And never the twain shall meet.

(At least, not in the elementary part of Barwise's theory described here.) You can do things to the left-hand side of such a formula that you cannot do to the right, and you can do things to the right that you cannot do to the left.

This is very different from high school algebra. When you have to solve an equation such as

$$x^2 - 5x + 3 = 2x - 7$$

the way to proceed is to follow the rule "whatever you do to the expression on the left of the equals sign, you must do to the expression on the right." (In this particular case, your first move should be to subtract $2x - 7$ from both sides of the equation.) This rule works because the expressions on both sides of the equation denote objects of the same kind, namely, polynomial expressions involving an unknown number x. With Barwise's notation

$$s \models \sigma$$

the symbols on the left and the right denote different kinds of objects, and in this case the notation tells you to "Treat the things to the left of the supports sign ($\models$) very differently from the way you treat the things to the right."

Barwise and his followers (I was an early disciple) worked out the algebraic rules for manipulating formulas involving situations and infons, giving rise to a new branch of mathematics known as *situation theory*.

One of the things Barwise was able to do with his new situation theory was provide a scientific description of the information conveyed by a statement such as "John sees Mary run," where the object of the verb is not a noun but a clause. Classical approaches ran into trouble with examples such as this, because there is no single object that John sees. Predicate logic can handle a sentence such as "John sees the car." If J denotes John, and C denotes the car, the information conveyed by an utterance is

$$\text{See}(J, C).$$

This formula is what we have called the *logical form* of the sentence. However, for the sentence "John sees Mary run," there is no object to go into the empty slot in the formula

$$\text{See}(\text{John}, \underline{\quad}).$$

However, in Barwise's theory, there is such an object, namely, the situation John sees. So, the analysis of an utterance of this sentence takes place in two steps:

- See(John, *s*)
- *s* ⊨ Run(Mary).

These two formulas describe—in Barwise's new framework—the information conveyed by the utterance.

In fact, Barwise was able to apply his approach to a variety of examples that could not be handled using classical techniques such as logical form. The key in each case was being able to use situations as subjects of verbs, direct or indirect objects of verbs, and so on.

In many respects, situation theory is an extension of classical logic that takes account of context. The truths of situation theory are the *propositions:*

$$s \models \sigma.$$

In terms of this notation, classical logic concentrates entirely on the right-hand side of the supports relation; the situation on the left is held fixed—indeed, in classical logic it is rarely mentioned.

As mentioned earlier, situation theory is just one of a number of attempts being made to take account of context in the analysis of communication via language. Situation theory models itself on classical logic, in particular, Tarski's theory of meaning, but it does not assume that communication is rule based. Other mathematically based treatments currently being developed (such as the theory of context being developed by AI pioneer John McCarthy) take a more rule-based approach, trying to formulate rules that explain how people make use of context in order to communicate. Just how far we can get with any such approach is not yet clear. What does seem clear is that the result of these efforts is unlikely to be a clean, precise theory such as propositional logic. Real communication in a context appears far too complex for that.

So much then (for now) for meaning and context. It is time to turn to the other two key features of communication that Chomsky ignored: cultural knowledge and the structure of conversations.

9

VERBAL
TANGOS

*I feel that if a person can't communicate, the very
least he can do is to shut up!*

—Tom Lehrer[1]

ER, UMM, MAYBE, ALL RIGHT THEN

As we have observed already, Chomsky restricted himself to the syntactic
structure of grammatical sentences, isolated from their context. The perfectly grammatical sentences he studied exist in much—though not all—
written language but are less common in spoken language. Consequently,
Chomsky's analysis tells us relatively little about everyday communication, such as a conversation between two people. Everyday speech not
only involves context, it can include ungrammatical utterances. In fact,
when they first read transcriptions of spoken conversations, most people

---

1. From the introduction to the song "Who's Next" which appears on the deliciously
funny satirical album *That Was the Year That Was*, recorded at The Hungry I in San Francisco in July 1965 and released on the Reprise record label. Though a lot of the humor is
lost in transcribing the spoken word to the written text, the full quotation goes as follows:

". . . Speaking of love, one problem that recurs more and more frequently these days, in
books and plays and movies, in the inability of people to communicate with the people
they love, husbands and wives who can't communicate, children who can't communicate
with their parents, and so on. And the characters in these books and plays and so on, and
in real life I might add, spend hours bemoaning the fact that they can't communicate. I feel
that if a person can't communicate, the very least he can do is to shut up!"

are surprised by just how ungrammatical a lot of everyday speech is. Here is part of an interview between a college counselor (C) and a student (S):

C: Well, let's start from scratch. What did you get in your English 100 last semester?

S: A 'C'.

C: Biology 101?

S: 'A'.

C: Reading 100?

S: 'B'.

C: Med tech . . . 'B'?

S: 'B'.

C: Gym?

S: 'A'.

C: Was that a full credit hour? What was it?

S: It was wrestling . . . two periods.

. . . . . .

For another example, here is part of a conversation two people are having about a wedding.

B: How . . . how was the wedding?

A: Oh it was really good, it was, uh, it was a lovely day.

B: Yes.

A: And . . . it was a super place . . . to have it . . . of course.

B: Yes.

A: And we went and sat on, sat in an orchard, at Granchester, and had a huge tea afterwards (laughs).

B: (laughs)

A: Uh.

B: It does sound . . . very nice indeed.

The above conversations make perfect sense, but they hardly constitute grammatical English.

To try to handle issues of context and ungrammatical utterances, many linguists separate the study of meaning into two categories: semantics and pragmatics. *Semantics* concentrates on the canonical meanings of words and phrases; *pragmatics* deals with issues of particular uses of language, the effect of various contextual features, nonce sense, and the like.

For example, pragmatics investigates the factors that distinguish the two possible readings of the sentence

He informed the woman that he knew.

Does the phrase *that he knew* refer to the woman or is it a complement of the verb *informed*?

The semantics–pragmatics approach is analogous to the way scientists work. For example, physicists first study frictionless motion of perfectly shaped objects and then try to make use of their results by taking into account the effects of friction and shape. Likewise, the linguist might try to study the semantics of grammatical sentences, free of context, and then add in the various pragmatic effects. But does such an approach work? In physics, experience has justified making an initial study of idealized, friction-free cases, followed by an investigation of the changes that result when shape, friction, and the like, are taken into account. For one thing, the idealized, friction-free case is often a very good approximation to what actually occurs in the world. Moreover, it is often possible to quantify the changes that result when the effects of shape and friction are taken into account. But can the same be said of linguistics? Is there anything to be gained by an initial study of the context-free, 'perfect' cases? The answer is that there probably *is* something to be gained, though some linguists dispute this point. What is certainly the case is that many issues of pragmatics are not minor additions that must be made to a pure semantic theory. Looking first at the semantics of grammatical sentences, and then looking at the modifications resulting from pragmatics, will not work. A proper study of communication has to begin with a fresh look at real, everyday conversations. This was done in the early 1970s by a group of sociologists who referred to their study of everyday conversation (and other everyday activities) as *ethnomethodology*—from the Greek word stem *ethno*, which means pertaining to people or culture, and *methodology*, meaning a collection of rules or practices.

One of their first observations was that even the simplest acts of communication will, in general, involve not only context but a huge amount of cultural knowledge of the society we live in. Cultural knowledge is the third in our list of the four key features of communication that Chomsky ignored. The fourth feature—the structure of conversations—was also examined by the ethnomethodologists, and we'll come to that in due course.

THE FINE POWER OF A CULTURE

You get some idea of the degree to which linguistics—which in the United States, at least, grew largely out of sociology and anthropology—was taken over by Chomsky's mathematical approach when you consider the fact that studies of language from a sociological point of view are referred to nowadays by a separate name: *sociolinguistics*. Whereas linguists study language—its syntactic structure and, more recently, its semantics—socio-linguists focus on communication. The sociolinguist examines the way people use language to communicate and what information is communicated when they do. In contrast, the linguist only incidentally gets involved with issues of communication.

One of the first people to study communication from the sociolinguistic perspective was the sociologist Harvey Sacks, one of the founders of ethnomethodology. In a short paper entitled "On the Analyzability of Stories by Children," published in 1972, Sacks showed how even the simplest uses of language depend on large amounts of cultural knowledge of the society we live in.

In fact, the data Sacks looked at is about as simple as you can find: It consisted of the first two sentences produced by a young girl, nearly three years old, who was asked to tell a story. The child began

The baby cried. The mommy picked it up.

"Is that it?" I hear you cry. "Did this fellow Sacks write an entire paper about that? Surely, it's too trivial to bother about. After all, anyone can understand what the child said. It doesn't take any effort. You don't have to think about it. It's obvious."

Indeed, the *data* is trivial. It does require no effort to understand what the child said. It *is* obvious. And that's the point. One of the most significant contributions Sacks made to our understanding of language and communication was to realize that the very obviousness of data such as this is what makes it worth studying. The fact is, we do find almost all everyday language trivial and obvious. We use our native language in an immediate and unreflective manner. Apart from special occasions, such as listening to a speech or a lecture, we do not have to concentrate or think in order to understand what someone is saying to us. We simply understand. Sacks's question was, *how* do we do it?

His answer was that we rely upon cultural knowledge—and large amounts of it. To support this claim, Sacks made a number of observations about the way you—or any native English speaker—understand those two sentences. Imagine, says Sacks, that those two sentences were spoken to you by a small child. What do you understand them to mean? Do not consider the understanding you might achieve after you have thought about the two sentences; rather, concentrate on your *immediate, unreflective* understanding.

For one thing, you hear the word *mommy* as referring not to just any mother but to the mother of the baby. Why do you do this? There is no genitive in the second sentence, and it is certainly possible for the mommy to be some other child's mother. For example, suppose that the child had begun

> *Emily's mommy was looking after Jonah and his baby sister.*
> *The baby cried. The mommy picked it up.*

This time, you hear *mommy* as referring to Emily's mother, not the baby's.

You also hear the two sentences to say that it is the baby that the mother picks up. Why do you hear it that way? After all, the *it* in the second sentence could refer to some object other than the baby. For example, the child could have started the story this way:

> *The baby dropped its pacifier. The baby cried. The mommy picked it up.*

This time you understand *it* to refer to the pacifier.

To go back to Sacks's original example, you hear the second sentence as describing an action (the mommy picking up the baby) that follows, and is caused by, the action described by the first sentence (the baby crying). Once again, why do you understand it that way? There is no general rule that says sentence order corresponds to temporal order or to causality of events (though it often does so). For example, the passage

> *John fell. Bill pushed him.*

is normally heard as describing a pair of events where the second one mentioned precedes and causes the first.

Finally, you hear the two sentences as describing a scene. Indeed, they conjure up a visual picture in your mind. But there are plenty of examples of pairs of simple sentences that are related—that is, are about the same thing—but do not evoke mental images of scenes. For instance, the following pair of sentences are about the same thing, namely, capitals of countries, but they do not describe a scene:

> *Madrid is the capital of Spain. Paris is the capital of France.*

As Sacks observed, though we all understand the child's utterance in exactly the same way, none of the observations he enumerated are explicitly stated in the sentences themselves. Indeed, in different contexts, each and every one of his observations can be false. Rather, our understanding depends on our cultural knowledge: our knowledge of how people behave, what kinds of things babies do, how mothers relate to their babies, and so forth. The child's words describe something familiar to us. For instance, we know that a common response to hearing her baby cry is for the mother to pick it up and comfort it, and in the absence of any information to the contrary, we hear the child's utterance as describing that familiar behavior.

Speaking and understanding a language, Sacks says, requires not only an implicit knowledge of the grammar of that language—how to string words together to form meaningful expressions—but also an implicit knowledge of the relevant culture. After enumerating (most of) the observations listed above, he wrote:

> My reason for having gone through the observations I have so far made was to give you some sense, right off, of the fine power of a culture. It does not, so to speak, merely fill brains in roughly the same way, it fills them *so that they are alike in fine detail*. The sentences we are considering are after all rather minor, and yet all of you, or many of you, hear just what I said you heard, and many of us are quite unacquainted with each other. I am, then, dealing with something *real* and something *finely powerful*. (Italics added.)

But you know what I mean!

Nowhere is the influence of culture on communication more obvious than in the problems men and women often have in understanding each other, and the past few years have seen a plethora of self-help books by psychotherapists, describing the common misunderstandings in man–woman relationships. Typical of the examples presented in such books are exchanges such as:

> *She:* You never listen.
>
> *He:* What do you mean? I'm listening now, aren't I?
>
> *She:* You weren't listening to me.
>
> *He:* Yes I was. I can repeat every word you said.
>
> *She:* My job is stressing me out too much.
>
> *He:* Well why don't you quit? You don't have to work.

Examples such as these are intended to indicate the different approaches to various life issues taken by men and women, resulting in differences in what each means by the seemingly simplest of remarks.

The studies that led to such books originated in part with research carried out by the American sociologist Harold Garfinkel in the 1960s. Garfinkel, who introduced the term *ethnomethodology*, was an academic at the University of California at Los Angeles. In one celebrated experiment, he used the students in one of his classes as a source of information. He asked the students to write a report on an everyday conversation. The next time they found themselves in a conversation, he instructed them, they were to note down everything that was said. When the conversation was over, they were to add explanations to their notes, describing the thought processes behind their statements. The resulting report would then provide an account of what was actually said, what was assumed, and what was meant.

When the class next met, one of the students reported on the following conversation between himself and his wife. What was actually said is written in Roman type; the speaker's subsequent interpretation follows in italics.

Husband: Dana succeeded in putting a penny in a parking meter today without being picked up.

This afternoon as I was bringing Dana, our four-year-old son, home from the nursery school, he succeeded in reaching high enough to put a penny in a parking meter when we parked in a meter zone, whereas before he has always had to be picked up to reach that high.

Wife: Did you take him to the record store?

Since he put a penny in a meter that means that you stopped while he was with you. I know that you stopped at the record store either on the way to get him or on the way back. Was it on the way back, so that he was with you or did you stop there on the way to get him and somewhere else on the way back?

Husband: No, to the shoe repair shop.

No, I stopped at the record store on the way to get him and stopped at the shoe repair shop on the way home when he was with me.

Wife: What for?

I know of one reason why you might have stopped at the shoe repair shop. Why did you in fact?

Husband: I got some new shoe laces for my shoes.

As you will remember I broke a shoe lace on one of my brown oxfords the other day so I stopped to get some new laces.

Wife: Your loafers need new heels badly.

Something else you could have gotten that I was thinking of. You could have taken in your black loafers which need heels badly. You'd better get them taken care of pretty soon.

A number of things are obvious about this particular exercise. First, the original conversation is remarkably everyday and mundane and concerns an extremely restricted domain of family activity. Second, the degree of detail given in the subsequent explanations or elaborations of what each person said seems quite arbitrary. It is easy to imagine repeating the exercise over again, this time providing still further explanation. And then it could be repeated a third time. Then a fourth. And so on, and so on, and so on. Apart from boredom or frustration, there does not seem to be any obvious stopping point.

Indeed, this issue of *how much* detail to provide was raised by the students themselves. As Garfinkel himself reported:

> Many students asked how much I wanted them to write. As I progressively imposed accuracy, clarity, and distinctness, the task became increasingly laborious. Finally, when I required that they assume I would know what they had actually talked about only from reading literally what they wrote literally, they gave up with the complaint that the task was impossible.

The dilemma faced by Garfinkel's students was not simply that they were being asked to write everything that was said, where that 'everything' consisted of some bounded, albeit vast, content. It was, rather, that the task of enumerating what was talked about itself *extended* what was talked about—the horizon of understanding continued to recede with every cycle of increased explanation. Quite simply, the task was endless.

So, what exactly is going on when two people get together and talk?

The traditional view of linguistic communication goes like this. The speaker uses words to convey information to the listener (or listeners). By putting words together according to the rules of grammar, the speaker constructs meaningful expressions. These meaningful expressions can be thought of as railroad boxcars into which the speaker loads the information to be transmitted. By uttering the appropriate meaningful expression, the speaker sends the intended information to the listener, who unloads the information from what she hears. All that is required for the listener to recover the information from the expression she hears is the ability to understand the language. For obvious reasons, this way of viewing linguistic communication is sometimes called the *boxcar model*. It is essentially the approach used in attempts to program computers to understand natural language. With this approach to communication, we can use the logical form of a sentence to denote the information conveyed by that sentence.

The boxcar model seems reasonable when restricted to simple one-sentence examples, such as "Fred painted the house." But it fails miserably when applied to most real-life examples. As indicated by Sacks's analysis of the baby–mommy story and by the conversation reports of Garfinkel's students, the information conveyed by a meaningful expression can be far more extensive than, and even quite distinct from, the logical form. Furthermore, the listener may require a considerable amount of cultural knowledge in order to acquire the information the speaker intended to convey from the expression she hears.

For instance, the students in Garfinkel's class had little trouble communicating with their spouses, partners, or other family members. And yet, when they repeatedly tried to fill in all the details Garfinkel asked for, it became clear that their conversations depended on an endless chain of unspoken information. Indeed, both the information that the conversation depended on, and the information that was communicated, seemed to be infinite. Since people do manage to communicate all the time and without effort, we seem to have stumbled onto a modern linguistic analogue of Zeno's paradoxes of the infinite. How can communication take place if it depends on an endless list of prior knowledge, and how can a finite sequence of words transmit an effectively infinite amount of information? After all, our minds are finite, and communication takes place in a finite amount of time.

As with Zeno's paradoxes, the way out of the dilemma is to recognize the hidden false assumption. The source of the confusion is to think of conversation simply as two people exchanging information. The solution is to take into account the last of our list of crucial features of communication: the structure of conversations.

The Elephant's Trunk

Recall Steven Pinker's description of our facility with language as an instinct, discussed in Chapter 6. According to Pinker, in his book *The Language Instinct,* we should think of our language facility as an organ with which we manipulate various features in our environment (mostly people, sometimes animals, and occasionally machines), just as we use our hands and arms to manipulate objects in our environment. Pursuing this example a little further, think of two people engaged in conversation as analogous to them shaking hands. Their two 'language organs' come together for a limited period of time. During that period of contact, they coordinate sufficiently to produce a single, joint action: a conversation. A linguistic handshake, if you will.

The coordinated linguistic action that we call a conversation does not suddenly materialize out of nowhere. It takes a considerable amount of linguistic skill to engage in a meaningful conversation—far more skill than we can produce in any computer. If you were to try to list all of the prior experiences that contributed to that level of skill, you would almost certainly find that the list was endless, just as you would discover if you tried to list all the actions performed with your hands that contributed to your last handshake. As we have already observed, everything that we do is done in, and influenced by, a context. Moreover, the context of any action—including a conversation—potentially includes everything that has happened to us in our lives up to that moment. But context (including the cultural background that Sacks investigated) is only part of the story.

When two people successfully engage in a conversation, they use their language organs in order to achieve a shared understanding—what I have just called a linguistic handshake. That such a shared understanding is possible is a result not of shared knowledge (at least, not directly so) but of their having compatible communicative organs, of which they have developed skillful use in the same environment (i.e., culture). This is why Garfinkel's students had so much difficulty trying to list the information content of their conversations.

For most people, thinking of conversation in terms of interacting language organs is a radical departure from how they are used to thinking about it. As a result of over two thousand years of intellectual development, starting with the ideas of Plato and Aristotle and strongly influenced by Renaissance thinkers such as Leibniz and Descartes, twentieth-century man finds it very difficult to break free of trying to understand human conversation as an exchange of information. Certainly, people do use language to convey information, and it can be argued that this is its main purpose. But even if these two claims are true (and the second is almost certainly not true), it does not follow that the information-conveying aspect of language will provide the single key to understanding how it works. Looking at conversations as exchanges of information will give just part of the picture. We must also look at the manner in which the two conversationalists are able to establish the linguistic handshake that enables that information to be exchanged.

In *The Language Instinct,* Pinker compares the human language capacity with an elephant's trunk. As he observes, the six-feet-long and one-foot-thick trunk of the adult elephant contains three thousand muscles and can be used to uproot trees, stack timber, or carefully place huge logs in position when recruited to build bridges. An elephant can curl its trunk around a pencil and draw characters on letter-sized paper, remove a thorn, pick up a pin or a coin, and uncork a bottle. The tip of the trunk is sensitive enough for a blindfolded elephant to ascertain the shape and texture of objects. Elephants can use their trunks as snorkels to breathe while walking underwater on the beds of deep rivers. They communicate through their trunks by trumpeting, humming, roaring, piping, purring, rumbling, and pounding their trunks against the ground. In short, the elephant's trunk might have begun as a simple nose with which to breathe, but, over time, it has evolved into an extremely versatile organ used for many purposes besides breathing in air.

As with the elephant's trunk, whatever the original function of our (invisible) language organ, evolution has developed it to the point where it is an extremely versatile device. We can use it to argue, to persuade, to plead, to explain, to command, to greet, to ask questions, to amuse, to create social and legal contracts, and so forth. Each one of these uses *may be described* in terms of the information conveyed. However, to do so is to take one particular view of each of these different uses to which language is put—albeit an important use in some circumstances—and there is no reason to expect that such a view will lead to an understanding of how language works. For example, describing the information contained in a legal contract is to completely miss what it is about legal contracts that makes them special—namely, the status they are given in society and the role they play in our lives.

Among the many uses to which we put our language organ is one for which we have become extremely skilled—to engage in the joint activity known as conversation. This, according to many of today's language avant garde, is how we should view language and its use. In fact, some of them make an even bolder claim. What we need, they suggest, is a *logic of conversations,* which describes the abstract patterns of conversation—the unconscious rules that we follow when we engage in conversation.

But wait a minute. Haven't we all but abandoned the rule-based approach to thought and language? Surely, the main lesson we learned from the failures of artificial intelligence and natural language processing is that reasoning and linguistic communication are not rule-based endeavors.

Well, yes, if by 'rule-based' you mean that thinking and using language involve nothing more than the mechanistic application of rules. But that does *not* imply that there are no rules of rational thought, or when two people engage in a conversation, that they do not follow some rules. Even the world-class tennis player, whose level of expertise has reached that of an instinct—the highest level in the Dreyfuses's classification of expertise—still plays according to the rules of the game. Human logical thought and our use of language almost certainly involve more than the mechanistic application of rules. But that does not mean that there are no rules. What it does mean is that the rules are not sufficiently comprehensive so that we can program a computer to reproduce those human activities.

Thus, in trying to formulate the rules of conversation or to develop an algebra of conversation, our goal is not a comprehensive axiomatization of conversation. Rather, it is the more modest—but far more realistic—goal of trying to increase our understanding of the activity. Such an approach means that we will not end up with a hard science of conversation. But as we shall see, there is still a role for logic and the techniques of mathematics to play.

CONVERSATION—FROM LOST ART TO NEW SCIENCE

Critics of contemporary society often complain that conversation is a lost art. Whether or not they are right, it is certainly at the heart of the emerging science of communication. The reason is this. Conversation (talking to one another), particularly face-to-face conversation, is the form of human communication most familiar to us. It is the first method that most of us learn to exchange all but the most rudimentary items of information; we master the basics at a very early age, around two or three years old. Talking to each other face to face is surely the prototypical method by which people exchange information. It is certainly the one with the longest history. Written communication and the more recent forms of remote communication—radio, telephone, voice mail, television, and electronic mail—all developed toward the end of many thousands of years of face-to-face verbal communication. Indeed, all those other kinds of linguistic communication are surely just derivations of face-to-face verbal conversation. If we can understand how we manage to convey information by means of conversation, then we will be well on the way to understanding other kinds of communication.

Most analyses of conversation concentrate almost entirely on two-person conversations. Though conversations involving three or more participants cannot be regarded as a collection of two-person conversations—they have special features not shared by two-person conversations—most of the crucial issues already arise in the two-person case. In other words, there is some loss of generality in ignoring conversations with three or more participants, but not a huge loss. Accordingly, in this account I shall also focus on two-person conversations.

A common, naive view of conversation is that two people take turns speaking to each other—person *A* speaks, person *B* responds, then *A* says something else, and so on. But this is not a realistic picture. Real conversations are generally full of false starts, overlaps, and simultaneous utterances by both participants. What is more, many of those features may be relevant to the development, and any eventual success, of the conversation.

However, while acknowledging such features of real-life conversation, many theorists decide to ignore them, at least 'for the time being', and concentrate on other aspects of conversation. This is akin to the physicist who ignores friction when studying the motion of various objects. As I mentioned earlier, whether such simplifying assumptions are justifiable depends on the results that thereby follow. In the case of conversations, it does appear to be fruitful to ignore the false starts and the overlaps and to assume that a conversation consists of discrete utterances, one after the other. Indeed, it seems useful, and harmless, to concentrate on conversations that are largely made up of complete, grammatical sentences, or at the very least of meaningful expressions.

What cannot be ignored, however, is the essentially *collaborative* nature of conversation—the verbal handshake aspect of conversation mentioned earlier. A study of conversation that ignores this feature will not be a study of real conversation.

A collaborative or joint act is more than two individual acts performed at the same time. Handshakes are not the only familiar examples of joint acts. Playing a duet is also a joint act. The two players in a duet are indeed performing individual actions—each is playing an instrument. But in order for the result to be recognizable as a *duet,* they have to be playing as one. If we were to make a study of duets, that single joint act would be the object of study, not its constituents.

Joint acts are intriguing. They are examples of phenomena where the whole is greater than the sum of the parts. Though shaking hands and playing a duet are obvious examples, perhaps a better example to compare with conversation is two people dancing a tango. As the old saying goes, "It takes two to tango." A well-coordinated tango requires that the two partners move in perfect coordination, each one receptive and responsive to the other's every move.

One of the main tasks involved in analyzing conversation is to see how it is that the contributions of the two participants fit together to produce a single, joint communicative act. What are the basic steps and body movements in the verbal tango we call conversation, and what are the rules of the dance that govern the way those verbal steps and body movements are put together? What is the logic of the verbal tango?

THE LOGIC OF CONVERSATION

In a lecture given at Harvard University in 1967—and subsequently published under the title *Logic and Conversation*—the British philosopher and logician H. P. (Paul) Grice formulated a set of *maxims* that participants in a conversation implicitly follow. It was a bold and brilliant attempt to apply a mathematical approach to the structure of conversation, very much in the spirit of Euclid's formulation of axioms for plane geometry. (Though, as we have observed before, the aim of anyone who tries to apply the methods of mathematics to the analysis of human activities such as thinking and communicating is simply to increase our *understanding* of those activities. Euclid's goal of a set of assumptions from which all the facts of geometry *follow* is almost certainly not possible for the human domains of thought and language.)

Grice was, then, looking for the logic of everyday conversations, the structure that any conversation must have, regardless of its topic and purpose. He began his analysis by observing that a conversation is a cooperative act, which the two participants enter into with a purpose. He tried to encapsulate the cooperative nature of conversation by what he called the *Cooperative Principle:*

> Make your conversational contribution such as is required, at the stage at which it occurs, by the accepted purpose or direction of the talk exchange in which you are engaged.

In other words, "Be cooperative."

The next step Grice made was to derive more specific principles—his maxims—from the Cooperative Principle, by examining consequences of the Cooperative Principle under four different headings: quantity, quality, relation, and manner. Grice illustrated these four headings by means of nonlinguistic analogies, similar to those given below.

Quantity. If you are assisting a friend to repair her car, your contribution should be neither more nor less than is required; for example, if your friend needs four screws at a particular moment, she expects you to hand her four, not two or six.

Quality. If you and a friend are making a cake, your contributions to this joint activity should be genuine and not spurious. If your friend says he needs the sugar, he does not expect you to hand him the salt.

Relation. Staying with the cake-making scenario, your contribution at each stage should be appropriate to the immediate needs of the activity; for example, if your friend is mixing the ingredients, he does not expect to be handed a novel to read, even if it is a novel he would, at some other time, desire to read.

Manner. Whatever joint activity you are engaged in with a friend, your partner will expect you to make clear what contribution you are making and to execute your contribution with reasonable dispatch.

In terms of conversation, the category of *quantity* relates to the amount of information the speaker should provide. In this category, Grice formulated two maxims:

1. Make your contribution as informative as is required.
2. Do not make your contribution more informative than is required.

Under the category of *quality*, Grice listed three maxims, the second two being refinements of the first:

1. Try to make your contribution one that is true.
2. Do not say what you believe to be false.
3. Do not say that for which you lack adequate evidence.

Under the category *relation*, Grice gave just one maxim:

1. Be relevant.

However, Grice observed that it would take a great deal more study to come up with more specific maxims that stipulate what is required to be relevant at any particular stage in a conversation.

Finally, under the category of *manner*, Grice listed five maxims, a general one followed by four refinements, though he remarked that the list of refinements might be incomplete:

1. Be perspicuous.
2. Avoid obscurity of expression.
3. Avoid ambiguity.
4. Be brief.
5. Be orderly.

As Grice observed, his maxims are not laws that have to be followed. They are not like mathematical axioms. If you want to perform an arithmetical calculation in a proper manner, you have to obey the rules of arithmetic. But it is possible to engage in a genuine and meaningful conversation and yet fail to observe one or more of the maxims Grice listed. The maxims seem more a matter of an obligation of some kind. In Grice's own words: "I would like to be able to think of the standard type of conversational practice not merely as something which all or most do *in fact* follow, but as something which it is *reasonable* for us to follow, which we *should not* abandon" (emphasis as in the original).

One of the more interesting parts of Grice's analysis is his discussion of the uses to which people may put his maxims in the course of an ordinary conversation. Indeed, it was this part of his work that makes it a contribution to a science of communication. In science, the real tests of a new theory come when the scientist (1) checks the theory against further evidence, (2) attempts to base explanations on the theory, and (3) tries to use the theory to make predictions that can then be tested.

Grice made successful use of his maxims in analyzing a widespread conversational phenomenon he called *conversational implicature,* and it was this application of his maxims that established their status as scientific principles.

Conversational implicature occurs when a person says one thing and means something other than the literal meaning. For example, suppose Naomi says to Melissa, "I am cold," after Melissa has just entered the room and left the door wide open. Literally, Naomi has simply informed Melissa of her body temperature. But what she means—or what she probably means—is "Please close the door." Naomi's words do not actually say this; rather this is implicated by her words. Grice used the word *implicate* rather than *imply* for such cases since Naomi's words certainly do not imply the "close the door" meaning in any logical sense. Assuming Melissa understands Naomi's remark as a request to close the door, she does so because of cultural knowledge, not logic.

Conversational implicatures are ubiquitous in our everyday use of language. They can be intended by the speaker or can be made by the listener. Traditional methods of analyzing language say virtually nothing about the way conversational implicature works. Grice used his maxims to analyze the phenomenon. Let's take a look at his analysis.

The Hidden Meanings in What We Say

Suppose Mark meets Naomi and says, "How is the car your brother lent you?" Naomi replies, "Well, it hasn't broken down so far."

Mark's question seems straightforward enough. What about Naomi's reply? Assuming both Mark and Naomi are obeying Grice's Cooperative Principle, that is, they are engaged in a genuine attempt to have a conversation and not trying to mislead each other, what are we to make of Naomi's words? Presumably Naomi is implying—in a roundabout way—that she does not expect her brother's car to be in good order. She is *implicating* this unspoken meaning. Most people in Mark's position would probably take Naomi's reply that way. But what is the logic behind this particular use of language? After all, Naomi certainly does not come out and say "My brother's car is likely to be unreliable."

In terms of the maxims, here is Grice's analysis of the Mark-and-Naomi example. On hearing Naomi's reply, Mark could reason as follows:

1. Naomi's remark appears to violate the maxim "Be perspicuous."
2. On the other hand, I have no reason to suppose she is opting out of the Cooperative Principle.
3. Given the circumstances, I can regard the irrelevance of Naomi's remark as appropriate if, and only if, I suppose she thinks her brother's car would be likely to break down.
4. Naomi knows I am capable of working out step 3.
5. Thus, Naomi is *implicating* that her brother's car would be likely to break down.

Of course, few if any of us would actually go through such a reasoning process. But that is not the point. In a similar vein, people rarely consult the axioms of logic when putting forward a logical argument, but that does not prevent a logician from analyzing their argument and checking to see if it is valid by seeing if it accords with the rules of logic. Though scientists like to understand how something 'really' is, they often settle for a plausible explanation of the phenomenon that fits the known facts. In explanations of human activities such as reasoning and conversing, one way to see if a particular explanation fits the facts is to see if it would provide a reasonable response to a challenge of "How did you reach that conclusion?" In the case of Mark and Naomi's conversation, imagine that a bystander asks Mark what he understood by Naomi's concluding remark and to explain how he reached that conclusion. Most people in Mark's position would probably respond with an explanation something like the one just given, though perhaps much shorter and, unless they knew about Grice's maxims, not using his technical terminology.

Though Grice makes no claim that people have any conscious awareness of his maxims, his discussion of conversational implicature establishes a strong case that the maxims capture part of the abstract structure of conversation. They do, after all, enable the linguist to provide satisfactory, after-the-event explanations of a variety of conversational gambits.

According to Grice, a participant in a conversation, for example, Bill, in conversation with Doris, may fail to fulfill a maxim in various ways, including the following:

1. Bill may quietly and unostentatiously *violate* a maxim. In some cases, Bill will thereby mislead Doris.

2. Bill may *opt out* from the operation both of the maxim and the Coopera-tive Principle, making it plain that he is unwilling to cooperate in the way the maxim requires. For example, he might say, "I cannot say more. My lips are sealed."

3. Bill may be faced with a *clash*. For example, he may find it impossible to satisfy both the quantity maxim "Be as informative as required" and the quality maxim "Have adequate evidence for what you say."

4. Bill may *flout* or blatantly fail to fulfill a maxim. Assuming that Bill *could* satisfy the maxim without violating another maxim, that he is not opting out, and that his failure to satisfy the maxim is so blatant that it is clear he is not trying to mislead, then Doris has to find a way to reconcile what Bill actually says with the assumption that he is observing the Coopera-tive Principle.

Case 4 is the one that Grice suggests most typically gives rise to a con-versational implicature. Let's take a look at some more examples of everyday conversational implicatures.

For some implicatures, no maxim is violated. For example, suppose Roger drives up to a policewoman and says, "I'm almost out of gas," and the policewoman replies, "There's a gas station around the corner." By the maxim "Be relevant," Roger can infer that the gas station is open.

In contrast to the gas station scenario, the next example involves ap-parent violation of the "Be relevant" maxim in a very clear way in order to produce the intended implicature.

Arthur says, "Bill doesn't seem to have a girlfriend these days." Susan replies, "He has been spending a lot of time in Denver lately." Susan's re-sponse will violate the "Be relevant" maxim unless she intends her reply to implicate the fact that Bill has (or at least she suspects that he has) a girlfriend in Denver, and she wants her remark to suggest that that is the reason for his frequent visits there.

For another kind of example, suppose Greg has been telling Melissa of his intention to visit Europe and has mentioned that he would like to visit her friend Yannis. He asks, "Where does Yannis live?" and Melissa replies, "Somewhere in Greece." Clearly, Greg was asking for the name of the location where Yannis lives, in order to see if it would be possible to visit him. Hence Melissa's reply violates the quantity maxim "Make your contribution as informative as is required." Assuming that Melissa is not violating the Cooperative Principle, the conclusion Greg can draw is that Melissa violates the quantity maxim because to say more would require that she violates the quality maxim "Do not say that for which you lack adequate evidence." In other words, Greg concludes that Melissa does not know the city or town where Yannis lives. Indeed, assuming Melissa is being as informative as she can, Greg may conclude that Melissa cannot be more specific than she has been.

People sometimes flout maxims in order to achieve by implicature an information exchange they would, for some reason, prefer not to state explicitly. For example, suppose Professor Alice Smith is writing a testimonial for her linguistics student Mark Jones, who is seeking an academic appointment at MIT. She writes a letter in which she praises Jones's well-groomed appearance, his punctuality, his handwriting, and his prowess at tennis, but does not say anything about his ability as a student of linguistics. Clearly, Professor Smith is flouting the quantity maxim "Make your contribution as informative as is required." The implicature is that Professor Smith has nothing good to say about Jones's ability in linguistics but is reluctant to put her opinion in writing.

Irony is often achieved by a violation of the quality maxim "Do not say what you believe to be false." For example, suppose Jane has been telling Richard how badly her friend Sally had let her down, and Richard comments, "Well, Sally certainly is a great friend." The implicature is that Sally is a very poor friend.

Metaphor is another linguistic affect that may be achieved by flouting the same quality maxim. For example, if Tom says to his wife, "You are the cream in my coffee," the implicature is that Tom thinks his wife is the completion to his life.

Violation of the quality maxim "Do not say what you believe to be false" may also be used to achieve the effect of understatement. An example of this is where Barbara and George have an enormous fight, in which Barbara ends up flinging crockery all over the kitchen. The next morning, Barbara approaches George and says, "I was a bit annoyed last night." The implicature is that Barbara was, as George knows full well, thundering mad. In this case, George probably takes her words as an acknowledgement of, or even an apology for, her behavior.

So far, none of the examples have involved the maxims of manner. Here are three that do.

Parents of young children sometimes flout the manner maxim "Avoid obscurity of expression" in order to communicate with each other in a manner that their children cannot comprehend, saying things like "Did you pick up the you-know-what on your way home?"

Politicians sometimes try to violate the "Avoid ambiguity" manner maxim in order to mislead their audience. In a notorious case in Britain some years ago, a Prime Minister promised not to take a certain action without "the full-hearted consent of the British people." Most people took this to be a promise of a referendum, but, in the end, the issue was decided by a single vote in Parliament. In the furor that followed, the Prime Minister pointed out that in a parliamentary democracy, this did amount to full-hearted consent.

Neither of the above two examples results in an implicature. However, suppose John says to Sally, "Mary produced a series of sounds on the piano that sounded like 'Home on the Range'. " This violates the manner maxim "Be brief," and the implicature is clearly that Mary's piano playing was not very good.

Though I skipped the details, the above examples should illustrate ways a person can make (implicit) use of Grice's maxims to convey a meaning other than the literal meaning of the words actually spoken. The maxims provide some of the logic of conversation, just as Aristotle's syllogisms provided some of the logic of reasoning.

Here is one final example of implicature. In this one, the "Be relevant" maxim is violated. The scene is a cocktail party at a company headquarters. Not knowing that the company president is within earshot, Theresa says, "The president really is a pompous ass." Max replies, in a purposeful tone, "Where did you say you are going for your vacation this year?" Provided Theresa has her wits about her, she will realize that Max must be violating the relevance maxim for some reason, in this case, to cover the fact that she has just made a terrible social gaffe. With a bit of luck, and Max's help, she might just manage to escape with her job intact. Thanks to conversational implicature and one of Grice's maxims.

BUILDING ON COMMON GROUND

We can regard Grice's maxims as some of the unconscious rules that we all conform to when we engage in conversation. They constitute a first step toward a logic of conversation. But remember, our goal now—the goal of most contemporary work of this nature—is to increase our overall understanding. We do not assume that conversation consists solely of the mechanistic application of rules. Indeed, we do not assume that people follow rules at all when they talk to each other; the word I used above is conform. What we are doing is making use of well-developed and highly successful techniques of mathematics and logic in order to cast some light on that mysterious process we call communication.

Even in the terms just outlined, Grice's theory is only a first step. Though the maxims are all based on Grice's Cooperative Principle, and thus take account of the collaborative nature of conversation, they are ultimately directed at the individual speaker in a conversation. More recent work has concentrated more on the whole conversation, considered as a single joint act, and takes account of the observations of the ethnomethodologists.

Much of this recent work has concentrated on conversations that are entered into with the deliberate intent to exchange information. Moreover, in many cases the goal of the research has been to identify the information that is actually transmitted during the conversation. This is not to say that these studies regard the conversation as simply an exchange of information. For reasons I have already explained, they do not. A conversation can be entered into in order to convey information, but the conversation itself can involve all of the complexities considered by the ethnomethodologists. And when a conversation is completed, we can reasonably ask what information has been exchanged.

The reason for the interest in conversations motivated by information exchange and in the information they convey is simple. As I mentioned at the start of the chapter, much of the more mathematical work on conversations has been motivated by the needs of the information-systems industry, and the ultimate goal of that industry is to facilitate the flow of information in a modern society. Nevertheless, such research has led to general insights into conversation, insights that apply to all of our everyday conversations.

For instance, the results of an information-motivated investigation into what is called the background of a conversation apply to any conversation, whatever its purpose. *Background* is the term used to refer to that collection of experience, skills, and information that the two participants bring to the conversation. In general, much of the background is shared by the two participants.

For example, the rules of the English language (or at least enough of those rules) constitute part of the shared background for a conversation between two participants carried out in English. (The shared mastery of the language would not normally be regarded as *part of* the conversation; it is, as the term indicates, part of the background to the conversation.)

Another aspect of the background that supports any everyday conversation comes from our common sense knowledge of the everyday world. This aspect of the background illustrates, in a dramatic way, just how extensive—and how impossible to pin down—is the common background that supports even the most mundane of conversations. Just consider those conversation reports of Harold Garfinkel's students. As Garfinkel's students discovered, it is not possible to list all the facts in the background that are pertinent to a particular utterance. The more you examine the background, the more extensive you discover it is.

The background for a particular conversation *is* certainly extensive and in many ways impossible to pin down. On the other hand, it does not consist of everything. If you and I have a conversation about football, the background certainly includes a knowledge of the English language and some familiarity with football, as well as our general common sense knowledge of the world. But it does not include a knowledge of Russian or Chinese, or experience in chemical engineering, or an ability to wind-surf.

One way to think of the background to a conversation is by comparing a conversation to two people building a wall. The building skills and experience the two individuals bring to the task are part of the background. So too is the supply company that delivers the bricks, sand, and cement. All of these contribute to the building of the wall, and some of them are essential to the task. But none are part of the actual building work. The one part of the background that can be regarded as part of the actual building process is the preparation of the foundations for the wall, since the foundations are, in a sense, a part of the wall. The construction of the wall then proceeds in a step-by-step fashion, as the two persons add one brick after another in a coordinated and cooperative fashion. The bricks in the first row rest on the foundations. Thereafter, each new brick builds upon those that have been laid previously. The attention of the two people building the wall is focused entirely on the wall and its foundations, not on anything in the background.

In an analogous fashion, a conversation between two individuals may be regarded as a process whereby they cooperate to add information to a common pool. At the outset of the conversation, the information each person supplies rests upon some common foundation—the initial pool. Thereafter, each new contribution builds upon the aggregate of information that has been contributed up to that point.

The name linguists give to the common information pool for a conversation—the wall to which the two participants contribute—is the *common ground* for the conversation. Not only does each contribution to the conversation add new information to the common ground, but the common ground also provides a context and a resource for each contribution.

For example, going back to our hypothetical conversation about football, knowledge of English and a layperson's familiarity with gravity and Newtonian mechanics are clearly part of the background, and the conversation could not take place without them, but they are hardly *relevant* to the conversation. On the other hand, an adequate knowledge of football surely is relevant to what is said. The conversation depends on that knowledge in an immediate way, and may well contribute to our shared knowledge about football. Our shared knowledge of football is part of the common ground for our conversation.

One of the constraints a speaker must satisfy in order to successfully initiate a conversation is to ensure that the listener is able to identify (that is to say, to be aware of) the relevant common ground. An investigation of how two people determine the common ground that supports a conversation is one of the main tasks facing present-day conversation analysts.

For example, if John and Alice are both on the faculty at Saint Mary's College, and if they meet in the college cafeteria, John may open a conversation with Alice with an utterance such as:

The chapel looks much nicer now the repainting has been done.

In this case, John's use of the phrase *the chapel* is perfectly adequate to identify—for Alice—the college chapel, since a basic knowledge of the college architecture and the names of the main buildings is part of their relevant common ground as Saint Mary's faculty.

Now, it could also be the case that John and Alice travel regularly to Stanford University, some fifty miles away, to participate in a linguistics seminar. Relative to a different common ground, one dependent on their familiarity with, and possibly their presence on, the Stanford campus, John could use the phrase *the chapel* to refer to the Stanford chapel. Indeed, if the two were standing in the Stanford Main Quad, directly in front of the chapel, John could open a conversation with the same utterance as before, only this time in reference to the Stanford chapel. John's sentence is the same, but it refers to a different chapel. What has changed is the common ground.

One of the important features of common ground is that it involves *common* (or *mutual*) knowledge. That is to say, the two participants have *joint knowledge* of the common ground. As in the case of joint action, joint knowledge involves more than the two individuals having the same knowledge. Not only do the two participants in a conversation have the knowledge in the common ground; in addition, they both know that they both have this knowledge.

Though the concept of common knowledge is an ubiquitous one, in the past, analysts found it very difficult to analyze. Early attempts to make sense of the phenomenon led to an infinite regress. Here is the fine print that accompanies common knowledge. (As always with fine print, you might want to skip over it. The issue will come up again in the next chapter.)

The Fine Print. According to the traditional explanation, if you and I have common knowledge of a fact *F*, then we must each know (in some implicit sense) an infinite chain of facts, namely:

I know *F*.
You know *F*.
I know you know *F*.
You know I know *F*.
I know you know I know *F*.
You know I know you know *F*.
I know you know I know you know *F*.
You know I know you know I know *F*.
And so on, *ad infinitum*.

Since neither of us can really know an infinite number of facts, this explanation is clearly unsatisfactory. The source of the problem is that the explanation tries to explain our common knowledge in terms of what each of us knows individually. More recent approaches have taken common knowledge as a phenomenon in its own right. In this case, our mutual knowledge of *F* is an item of information *K* such that:

$$K = F \wedge [\text{I know } K] \wedge [\text{You know } K].$$

This approach regards common knowledge as an intrinsically self-referential notion. The equation describes *K* by stipulating what *K* is equal to, but since *K* also occurs on the right-hand side of the equation, that description is in terms of *K* itself.

According to the common-ground view of a conversation, the speakers have to design their utterances so that the listener can readily identify the relevant common ground and what is to be added to it as a result of the utterance. Indeed, it is part of the collaborative nature of a conversation that the participants work together to establish the common ground on which the particular conversation depends, and they are aware that the conversation creates common knowledge.

The common ground for a conversation can depend on a number of features, including being members of the same community, being in the same physical location, and being referred to in the same utterance. Examples of community membership include both being mathematicians, both working for the same company, both reading the same newspaper, both having seen the same movie. And if Alice and John are in the same physical location, they can refer to any number of items: "this chair," "the clock on the wall," "the temperature," and so forth.

It should be stressed that common ground is *local* to a particular conversation. John and Alice may have a great deal in common: They are both Americans, they were both brought up and educated in California, they both support the San Francisco 49ers football team, they both own a house in San Francisco, they both have children at the same elementary school, they both read the *San Francisco Chronicle,* and so forth. Each one of these may provide part of the common ground for a conversation; more likely, a number of these commonalities in their lives may contribute to that common ground.

Linguists use the term *audience design* to refer to the way in which speakers construct their utterances to be appropriate for their intended audience (or audiences). In the case of two-person conversations, what this amounts to is the manner in which the speaker ensures that his or her utterance can be readily understood by the recipient.

In large part, what audience design means in a two-person conversation is that the participants have an obligation to ensure that the relevant common ground is readily established *as a common ground* for that conversation. Conversation openings generally fulfill the task of establishing an initial common ground on which the subsequent utterances depend. In simple terms, what this means is that a speaker should make utterances that the listener can readily understand, choosing the words he or she uses in order to achieve this goal. Grice's maxims are relevant in this connection, but there is a lot more than can, and should, be said. Audience design is still a wide-open research topic.

For an example of audience design, an utterance of the sentence

> *He did a Richard Nixon to the tape of the meeting.*

would likely be perfectly appropriate for an American listener who was an adult in the 1970s. Such a person would know that this meant erasing part of the recording in a deliberate attempt to hide the truth. However, an utterance of the linguistically similar sentence

> *Johnny did an Aunt Lucy to the cream cake.*

would not be appropriate for such a general listener. Such utterances are not at all uncommon, but they are generally restricted to conversations within a family, where the listener knows just what it was that Aunt Lucy did—say, sitting on a dessert on some occasion in the past.

STEPS IN THE VERBAL TANGO

The common-ground view of a conversation is that the two participants in a conversation begin by assuming, or somehow establishing, a common ground, and this common ground then grows and changes as a result of the accumulation of additional shared information contributed by the utterances of the two participants. But how on earth do they do it? How are they able to identify the common ground on which the conversation depends in so many crucial ways? Answers to these questions will also form part of our desired logic of conversations.

Instead of regarding a conversation as made up of utterances, we need to think of it in terms of a series of joint acts. The term linguists sometimes use to refer to such a joint act is a *contribution*. (Thus, the word contribution becomes a technical term.) An *utterance* is an act performed by one person (the other person being the recipient), and, in principle, the same utterance could be made in the absence of any recipient. On the other hand, a contribution, in the new technical sense, is a joint act that cannot be performed by one person alone.

In the simplest case, a *contribution* to a conversation is a joint act that consists of the current speaker (the *contributor*) uttering a sentence or sequence of sentences, and the listener providing confirmation that the utterance has been adequately understood. This view of conversation means that in order to proceed, the speaker must obtain *positive* confirmation from the listener that his or her utterance has been adequately understood. In the absence of such confirmation, the speaker will generally assume a communication breakdown has occurred and will try to correct it—a common occurrence in everyday conversation. In other words, even no action on the part of the listener amounts to a response, which the speaker will take note of. In a joint act, there is no possibility for either partner to opt out.

Speakers in a conversation continually monitor the course of the discourse, looking for confirmation that they may continue, and this is in part what makes conversations collaborative joint acts. In making a contribution, the contributor and his or her partner will work to ensure that they mutually believe that the partner has understood what the contributor meant, to a degree adequate for their current purpose. This mutual belief is then added to the common ground, in addition to the information the contributor intended his or her utterance to supply.

The term *confirmation devices* is sometimes used to refer to the methods the listener uses to indicate that he has correctly, or adequately, understood the utterance and to ensure that the mutually assumed common ground remains just that—a *common* ground. In the most straightforward cases, a contribution to a conversation will involve an utterance plus a confirmation device.

There are a number of confirmation devices that people regularly use in the course of a conversation. The ones listed below are among the most common. Since we all use these devices all the time, none of them will come as any surprise. The reason for spelling them out and introducing technical language (*common ground, confirmation device,* etc.) is that we are trying to come to grips with the key features that make conversation possible.

Assume Alice is the speaker, and Brian, the listener. Brian, then, uses the confirmation device to indicate to Alice that she may continue.

- *Continued attention.* Brian shows he is continuing to attend and thereby signals that he is satisfied with Alice's utterance thus far.
- *Acknowledgement.* Brian nods or says "uh huh," "yeah," "right," or the like.
- *Facial expression.* Brian raises an eyebrow to indicate surprise, or shows puzzlement or confusion. In the case of a raised eyebrow, Alice may infer that her utterance has been understood. If Brian shows puzzlement or confusion, Alice will realize she has not made herself fully understood and will act accordingly, perhaps paraphrasing what she has said or else offering an explanation.
- *Initiation of a relevant next contribution.* Brian utters a sentence, or chain of sentences, that makes a relevant and appropriate contribution to the discourse. This includes obvious signals of failure, such as Brian asking for clarification. In such a case, the appropriate response for Alice is not to continue as before, but to provide a repair or clarification of the utterance that Brian has not adequately understood. A not infrequent response is for Brian to inform Alice of his failure to understand by uttering a phrase such as "Pardon?" or "What was that?" Alice is then obligated to repeat her original utterance, possibly with some rephrasing. Alternatively, if Alice's utterance consisted of her asking a question, then the utterance by Brian of an appropriate answer constitutes confirmation that he has understood Alice's original utterance.
- *Demonstration.* Brian demonstrates all or part of what he has understood Alice to mean, perhaps by presenting a paraphrase. Alternatively, an appropriate action by Brian indicates that he has understood. For example, if Alice says "Pass the salt," then Brian's performance of the physical action of passing the salt indicates understanding.

■ *Completion.* Brian completes Alice's utterance, or rather what he takes that utterance to be. This requires confirmation or rejection by Alice. Alice's confirmation would normally take the form of an utterance such as "Right," followed by Alice initiating another contribution. Alice's rejection of Brian's completion would normally be followed by Alice attempting to repeat her first utterance, possibly with some rephrasing.

■ *Display.* Brian displays verbatim all or part of what Alice has said. For instance, a common way to acknowledge that one has understood the presentation of a telephone number is by reading it back aloud.

Having carried our analysis of conversation to the point where we have, at least in a loose sense, started to write down rules (axioms would be too strong a word) that we unconsciously follow when we engage in conversation, it is tempting to see if we can capture some of the structure of a conversation by algebra, in much the same way that Boole captured certain patterns of reasoning by means of an algebra.

After all, modern logic—the mathematical science of reasoning—began with Boole's development of an algebra of thought, and modern linguistics—the mathematical science of language—began with Chomsky's introduction of an algebra of syntactic structure. Faced with two clear successes, who would argue against our trying to make it three in a row and develop a science of communication based on an algebra of conversation? (Actually, it would be four in a row, since computer science—the mathematical science of computation—began with an algebra of computation developed by the mathematicians Alan Turing, Kurt Gödel, Stephen Kleene, and Alonzo Church in the 1930s. That algebra of computation is generally known as *recursion theory,* a topic we have not considered in this account.)

CAN THERE BE AN ALGEBRA OF CONVERSATION?

Anyone trying to develop an algebra of real, live, face-to-face conversation is faced with a significant problem. Mathematics rests upon precision. But all the evidence, from Garfinkel, from Sacks, from Suchman, from Clark, and from countless other researchers who have examined real, everyday conversations, shows that even the most mundane everyday conversation involves a whole range of skills, experience, and knowledge that cannot be specified. And as Garfinkel's students painfully discovered in the assignment described earlier, it is quite literally an impossible task to list everything that lies behind a particular conversational utterance or to enumerate exactly what information the utterance conveys to the other person. On the other hand, the other lesson Garfinkel's students learned from their assignment is that even with the endless nature of the background for a conversation, the two participants usually have a very clear sense of what is, and what is not, in that background. So maybe the endless nature of the background is not a total barrier to a mathematical analysis after all.

Another problem facing the would-be conversational logician is that there seems to be no limit to the course a particular conversation can take. But again, this is an illusion. Conversations are generally far more constrained than they might first appear. Any attempt by either party in a conversation to step outside certain boundaries—say to elicit greater precision—will almost certainly be regarded as out of place. Garfinkel's students learned this lesson the hard way as well. In another assignment he describes in his book *Studies in Ethnomethodology* (pp. 42–44), Garfinkel asked each student to go home that evening and to engage in an ordinary, everyday conversation with a family member, friend, or acquaintance. Without indicating that anything unusual was going on, they were to respond to every utterance directed toward them with a request for elaboration, for more specific detail, for definitions of terms used, and so forth. As Garfinkel expected, the results were highly consistent: The family members, friends, et cetera allowed at most one round of such requests, often none at all, and they clearly regarded such questions as unwarranted. Here are some of the exchanges Garfinkel reported:

First case

Subject: I had a flat tire.

Student: What do you mean, you had a flat tire?

Subject (Stunned silence followed by hostile answer): What do you mean, 'What do you mean'? A flat tire is a flat tire. That is what I meant. Nothing special. What a crazy question!

Second case

Subject: How are you?

Student: How am I in regard to what? My health, my finances, my school work, my peace of mind, my . . . ?

Subject (Out of control): Look! I was just trying to be polite. Frankly, I don't give a damn how you are.

Third case

The student is watching television with the subject, her husband.

Subject: [I'm tired.]

Student: How are you tired? Physically, mentally, or just bored?

Subject: I don't know, I guess physically, mainly.

Student: You mean that your muscles ache or your bones?

Subject: I guess so. Don't be so technical.

(Later, after watching some more television.)

Subject: All these old movies have the same kind of old iron bedstead in them.

Student: What do you mean? Do you mean all old movies, or some of them, or just the ones you have seen?

Subject: What's the matter with you? You know what I mean.

Student: I wish you would be more specific.

Subject: You know what I mean! Drop dead!

Obviously, the participants in a conversation not only have no need for an elaboration of the background, they also have a very clear sense of what is a permissible contribution, and they will object strongly to any attempt to go beyond what they consider reasonable. Perhaps there are enough constraints on the course a conversation can follow to allow some kind of mathematical analysis. It might seem a long shot, but why not give it a try?

Why not, indeed? It would, after all, be similar to the approach toward reasoning adopted by the Greeks and still later by Boole. Propositional logic is mathematically precise in terms of the way it treats the logical connectives *and, or,* and *not,* but it is completely imprecise as to the structure or meaning of the propositions that are combined using those connectives. All that is known about the constituent propositions is that they are either true or false. The theory simply gives them names, p, q, r, et cetera, and thereafter treats those names as algebraic unknowns, unknowns to be manipulated but not 'solved for'. By the simple process of giving the constituent propositions algebraic names, all of their complexity is swept under the algebraic rug, leaving the logician to examine the logical patterns that connect those algebraically named propositions.

So, maybe we should take inspiration from the successes of the logicians of the past and adopt a similar approach to everyday conversation, using algebraic symbols to denote various features of a conversation and sweeping the complexity of those features under the rug of algebra. What features of a conversation would our algebraic symbols have to denote?

According to the model of conversation discussed in the previous chapter, a conversation involves two contextual elements: the background (call it B) and the common ground (call it G). Supported by B, the conversation consists of a sequence of contributions, c_1, c_2, c_3, on up to some final contribution c_n. Each contribution, c_i, consists of an utterance, u_i, by one participant followed by a response, r_i, from the other participant. The common ground, G, grows as the conversation proceeds. In particular, after each c_i, the information conveyed by c_i (call it σ_i) is added to G.

Already we have algebraic symbols denoting contributions, utterances, responses to utterances, items of information, and the contextual features denoted by B, G, G_0, G_1, . . . , G_n. This is quite a bit more complicated than having algebraic symbols denote just numbers (as in high school algebra) or just propositions (as in propositional logic). But it is not unusually complicated as mathematical theories go. In predicate logic we use algebraic symbols to denote predicates, functions, constants, and variables, and in physics algebraic symbols are used to denote all kinds of different entities—mass, energy, velocity, force, momentum, gravity, electric charge, radiation, temperature, entropy, and so on.

Having decided what the algebraic symbols should denote, the next step would be to write down the appropriate algebraic rules—the rules of conversation. Grice has already done some of that work for us, and so too have the ethnomethodologists, with their analyses of conversations. This is encouraging, but Grice's maxims and the observations of the sociolinguists don't seem to give us anything as clean and precise as Boole's algebra of thought. In terms of mathematical depth, a reasonable analogy would be Leibniz's algebra of concepts, which we met in Chapter 3. On the other hand, Leibniz's work led eventually to Boole. In the case of speculative early work, there is really no way of knowing where it will lead. That is the very nature of science in the making. It may well be that attempts to develop an algebra of conversation never lead to a clean, precise mathematical theory. Mathematics may simply be the wrong tool. But these attempts might lead to valuable insights resulting in a quite different kind of theory of conversation and communication.

One thing that has already emerged from the various investigations into communication is a realization of just how little we know about information. Coming to grips with the nature of communication forced us to examine one of mankind's earliest skills: talking to one another. When we started to do that, we found ourselves talking about information—background information, the information in the common ground, the information added to the common ground by a contribution, and so forth. Now, talk about "the information in the background" or "the information added to the common ground by a contribution" is all very well at an intuitive level. But when such remarks are supposed to be part of a scientific analysis, a rigorous definition of information is needed. Unfortunately, for all the talk of the present era being an Age of Information, there is as yet no such definition.

And so our investigation—the age-long quest for a science of reasoning and communication—has led to still another question: What is information? Having widened our focus once, from language to the more general domain of communication, we now have to make a second adjustment. In order to develop a science of communication that builds on the tradition of logic, it seems we will have to come to grips with the nature of information. What is it? How is it acquired? How do we pass it on? What does it mean to say that information is processed?

In broadening our investigation to include information, we will also discover a new and fruitful way to think about human reasoning—a focus of mankind's logical odyssey that has tended to take a back seat in our account of late, as we followed the trail of the late-twentieth-century linguists.

So what exactly is this stuff called information?

10

THE CHESHIRE
CAT'S GRIN

"All right," said the Cat; and this time it vanished quite slowly, beginning with the end of the tail, and ending with the grin, which remained some time after the rest of it had gone.

"Well! I've often seen a cat without a grin," thought Alice; "but a grin without a cat! It's the most curious thing I ever saw in all my life!"

—Lewis Carroll[1]

THE INFORMATIONAL STANCE

New developments in human understanding often come from seeing things in a different way, from looking at things in a manner that highlights a common thread across what previously seemed like different phenomena. In the case of our attempts to understand reasoning and communication, some of the most significant present-day advances have arisen from what I will call the *informational stance*. This starts from the view of the human brain as an information processor, a device that can acquire, store, and process information.

To view the brain as an information processor is not the same as saying that the brain *is* (just) a fancy digital computer or (just) a neural network. Certainly, the brain can be regarded as a digital computer and as a neural network. But it is not *just* either of these things; it is much more.

---

1. From the oft-quoted story of the Cheshire Cat in *Alice's Adventures In Wonderland*, Chapter 7, "Pig and Pepper."

(Exactly how much more, and in what ways, has yet to be discovered.) To say that the brain is a device that can acquire, store, and process information is not to say anything about the way the brain performs these feats. It is simply one way to think about the brain and what it does, and while by no means the only way, it has proved to be a useful one, particularly when the goal is to understand reasoning and communication.

One useful consequence of adopting the informational stance is that it provides a uniform way to look at cognition, reasoning, and communication, as simply different ways that the brain processes information.

Cognition can be regarded as a process of acquiring information, and reasoning can be regarded as a means of enlarging our stock of information by deriving new information from existing information. For example, from the observation that the sky is filled with dark clouds (cognition—information acquired by means of our eyes), we can deduce that there is a strong likelihood of rain (reasoning—new information derived from existing information). Thinking of reasoning in this way, as a form of acquiring additional information, is quite different from the way Aristotle approached reasoning, which was as a process to establish truth—true consequences of true assumptions.

Likewise, communication can be regarded as a means for conveying information from one person to another. This could consist of making a straightforward informational statement, such as giving your name to someone you have just met. But other forms of linguistic communication can also be regarded as transmissions of information. For example, questions—quests for information—can be regarded as conveying information. If I ask you "What is the time?" I convey to you the information that I want to be told the time. (Incidentally, analyzing communication in terms of the transmission of information does not prevent us from regarding human language capacity as an organ, as described in the previous chapter or from adopting techniques of the psycholinguists or sociolinguists in order to study the mechanics of conversation. The informational stance gives us a way to analyze *what* is done with language; the psychologists and sociologists can help explain *how* it is done.)

Since I have mentioned the view of the brain as a computer, I should perhaps mention in passing that there is a closely related informational stance toward computing, which can be thought of as a systematic way of *processing* information. Indeed, what a computer does is often referred to as information processing or data processing, so an information approach to computing seems very natural. However, when computing first began, a mere fifty years ago, it was conceived of as a way to automate arithmetic calculation, and the very word computing reflects that approach.

Over the past forty years or so, the view of computers as automatic calculators gave way to thinking of them as devices for manipulating formal languages, and this is how computing is generally described in present-day textbooks.

But, to repeat the question we raised at the end of the last chapter, what exactly is this stuff, information, that has brought logicians, linguists, and computer scientists—and a host of other '-ians' and '-ists'—together? Surrounded as we are by information, the question at first seems superfluous—until you try to put it under the microscope. Then, like the Cheshire Cat's grin, it tends to disappear before your eyes.

THE CHESHIRE CAT'S GRIN

It is more than journalistic hype to say we are living in the Age of Information. We clearly are. In an era of global communications—including radio, telephone, fax, computer networking, and satellite broadcast television—information is the thread that ties us all together. The ability to transmit vast amounts of information rapidly from continent to continent has transformed a diverse world into a Global Village. The messenger on foot or on horseback has given way to the Information Superhighway.

Information can be a precious commodity, to be collected, guarded, duplicated, sold, stolen, and sometimes killed for. Millions of people spend their entire working day gathering, examining, and processing information. Some of the world's largest companies do nothing other than manufacture equipment to store and process information. Still other companies are devoted to the development of information-processing software. The music we play on our CD players and the movies we watch on videodisk reach us after going through a phase of being abstract information, where the sounds or pictures are first converted to a sequence of 0s and 1s (binary encoding of information), and then converted back into audible or visual form.

It is impossible to open a newspaper without reading the word information. Libraries are full of books that have the word in the title, and likewise, many people have the word in their job titles. We are, so we are told, in danger of drowning in information. There certainly does seem to be a lot more of it than there used to be.

With information all around us, it should be a simple task to say just what it is. But, like the Cheshire Cat, when you start to look closely at this stuff called information, it seems to disappear before your eyes, leaving only a tantalizing grin. In fact, the analogy with Lewis Carroll's cat is particularly appropriate. As Alice says,

> "I didn't know that Cheshire Cats always grinned; in fact, I didn't know that cats *could* grin."
>
> "They all can," said the Duchess; "and most of 'em do."

Information *is* all around us. All people have some information. And, as will be explained in this chapter, absolutely any physical object can— and does—carry or store information. But information itself is not physical; it is abstract. Information is like the Cheshire Cat's grin; it is stored or represented by physical objects but appears to have an abstract existence beyond those physical objects. All physical objects store information in the same way that all Cheshire Cats have grins. When the Cheshire Cat vanished, all Alice was left with was the grin; similarly, take away the physical representation of some piece of information and all you are left with is the information.

Our Age of Information is an age of information *technology.* There is, as yet, no science of information. Our ancestors have been in this position before.

Imagine yourself suddenly transported back in time to the Iron Age. You meet a local ironsmith and you ask him "What is iron?" How will he answer? Most likely, he will show you various implements he has made and tell you that each of those was iron. But this isn't the answer you want. What you want to know, you say, is just what it is that makes iron *iron,* and not some other substance. What does your Iron-Age man say in response to this question? For all his talent as a first-class ironsmith, he cannot provide you with the kind of answer you are seeking. The reason is that he has no frame of reference within which he can even understand your question, let alone give an answer. To provide the kind of answer that would satisfy you, he would need to know about the atomic structure of matter—for surely the only way to give a precise definition of iron is to specify its atomic structure.

Information-Age folk—us—trying to understand information are in the same position as the Iron-Age man trying to understand iron. There is this stuff called information, and we have become extremely skilled at acquiring and processing it. But we are unable to say exactly what it is because we don't have an underlying theory upon which to base an acceptable definition.

Before going any further, I should clear up a couple of potentially confusing terminological issues. First of all, there is already a discipline called information science. It used to be called library science; however, to many people, this title conjured up an unflattering image of elderly ladies staffing the checkout desk of the local library on a voluntary basis, rather than the sophisticated field of information organization, searching, and retrieval that is part of the tasks of today's librarian. So the name was changed to the sexier title of information science. Name change or not, this discipline does not deal with the fundamental question of the nature of information, and it therefore has relatively little to do with the kind of investigation I am talking about on these pages.

In addition to information science, there is another field called information theory. This is a branch of engineering mathematics developed over the past fifty years that investigates the amount of information that may be transmitted via a particular communication channel. The focus of attention is not on information as such but on signals: How complex a signal can be transmitted through a particular channel? However, as we shall see momentarily, there is no fixed connection between a particular signal or configuration of objects and the information it represents. It all depends on the way the information is encoded. A complex signal might not represent any information. On the other hand, the transmission of a single pulse along a wire—one 'bit'—could represent an enormous amount of information. As a result, information theory is extremely useful for the folks who design telephone and computer networks, but it is of almost no relevance to the linguist or the sociologist who wants to study the way people communicate with each other.

Having cleared up—I hope—the terminological confusion that surrounds the term *science of information,* let's try to see what kinds of issues the information scientist of tomorrow will have to grapple with.

One of the most common misconceptions about information is to confuse information with its representation, whether that representation be words on paper, bits on disks, or whatever. "Libraries," we say, "are full of information." But this is not the case. What libraries are full of are books. "But books contain information," you protest. No, that's not true either. Books contain pages, and on those pages there are various markings—little lines, curves, squiggles, dots, and the like. But no information. Where the information gets in is by being *encoded* or *represented* by those markings on those pages. Being encoded or represented in is not the same as being contained in. Your encyclopedia may contain the following sequence of markings on one of its pages

The capital of the United States is Washington, D.C.

This particular sequence of markings encodes a certain item of information, information about the relationship between a particular city and a particular country. That city is not 'in' the encyclopedia, though a sequence of markings that denotes that city (namely, the sequence *Washington, D.C.*) is in the encyclopedia. Likewise, the country is not 'in' the encyclopedia, though a sequence of markings that denotes that country (namely, the sequence *the United States*) is there. And, in a similar fashion, the *information* that the city Washington, D.C., is the capital of the country the United States is not 'in' the encyclopedia, though a sequence of markings that denotes that information is there. Words are not the same as the things they refer to—cities, countries, people, or whatever—and likewise, sentences are not the same as the information they refer to, if indeed they do refer to information.

How is it that we can store and process information with ever-increasing efficiency, and yet still have difficulty understanding what information is? Part of the reason is that we do not process and store information; rather, we store and process *representations* of information, representations such as words on paper, bits on magnetic disks, and so forth. So a first step in trying to understand information is to take a close look at the way information can be represented.

Though we generally think of information as being stored in books and computer databases, any physical object may store information, and both we and our fellow creatures regularly acquire information from a variety of physical objects and from the environment. If we see dark clouds in the sky, we may take an umbrella as we leave for work, the state of the sky having provided us with the information that it might rain. On Halloween night in North America, a light in the porch provides the information that it is acceptable for children to approach the house and ask for candy; a dark porch indicates that the household does not want to be disturbed. Also in North America, in rural areas setting the flag on the mailbox in the upright position indicates that the mail carrier should pick up outgoing mail. Furthermore, animals too can acquire and act upon information. For instance, many animals are aware that smoke indicates fire and that fire represents danger. It is arguable that plants and certain physical devices also acquire information and react accordingly. For example, a flower opens when it detects the sun's rays in the morning, and a thermostat will switch on the heating when it detects a drop in temperature.

Already these few examples indicate one significant factor concerning information: Different agents—people, animals, perhaps plants and certain physical devices—are capable of extracting different information from the same source. A person can pick up a great deal of information about the surrounding air—how clean it is, the presence of any smells, whether it is warm or cool, how humid it is, and so on. A simple thermostat, on the other hand, can only pick up one piece of information from the surrounding air—whether the temperature is above or below the value set.

Going in the other direction, different objects or configurations of objects can represent the same information. For example, dark clouds in the sky, the reading on a barometer, and the weather report in the newspaper can all represent the information that it is likely to rain.

So what is it that enables an object or a collection of objects to encode or represent information? How can a part of the environment encode or represent information? And would all of this encoded and represented information exist if no people or other information-sensitive creatures were around to perceive it?

In the case of smoke providing information that there is fire, or dark clouds providing information that it is likely to rain, part of the explanation is that this is the way the world is: There is a systematic regularity between the existence of smoke and the existence of fire and a systematic regularity between dark clouds in the sky and rain. Human beings and other creatures able to recognize those systematic regularities can use them in order to extract information. And information is definitely what they get, not what the information is about. For example, people or animals who detect smoke do not necessarily see fire, but they nevertheless acquire the *information* that there is a fire. And the sight of dark clouds can provide the information that rain is likely, even if there is no rain at the time.

Thus, one way information can arise is by virtue of systematic regularities in the world. People (and certain animals) are able to recognize those regularities, either consciously or subconsciously, possibly as a result of repeated exposure to them. They may also utilize those regularities in order to obtain information from aspects of their environment. For example, people learn to associate dark clouds with a likelihood of rain, and plan their day accordingly. And animals in the wild learn to associate smoke on the horizon with fire—or at least with danger—and react by taking flight.

The case of acquiring information from books, newspapers, magazines, and radio, and from being spoken to by fellow humans, is similar in that it too depends on systematic regularities. In this case, however, these regularities are not natural in origin like dark clouds and rain or smoke and fire—they do not arise 'because the world is that way'. Rather, they depend on manmade regularities, regularities of human languages. In order to acquire information from words and sentences of English, you have to understand English. More specifically, you need to know the meanings of the English words and you need an implicit, working knowledge of the rules of English grammar. In addition, in the case of written

English, you need to know how to read, that is to say, you need to know the conventions whereby certain sequences of symbols denote certain words. Those conventions of word meaning, grammar, and symbol representation are just that: conventions. Different countries have different conventions: different rules of grammar, different words for the same thing, different alphabets, even different directions of reading—left to right, right to left, or top to bottom. The linguistic conventions for any one country or population have evolved over thousands of years. In many ways, those conventions are quite arbitrary and liable to further change. What makes the entire system work is that the conventions of language are, at any one period, regular and systematic. The symbol sequence *cat* means the same thing to people all over the English-speaking world, and it means the same thing today as it did yesterday, and it will mean the same thing tomorrow.

The systematic regularities in language are not natural regularities, as are smoke and fire or dark clouds and rain. Rather, they are social regularities, determined by a linguistic community. As such, they may be used by anyone in that linguistic community. At an even more local level, there are the conventional information-encoding devices that communities establish on an ad hoc basis. For example, a school may designate a bell ring as providing the information that a class should end, or a factory may use a whistle to signal that a shift is over.

And there are even the one-person information storage devices, such as the knot in one corner of your handkerchief that today is supposed to remind you to pick up the laundry on the way home from work, but which yesterday encoded the information that your wedding anniversary was coming up and you should remember to book a table at the *Chez Louis* restaurant.

The plain fact is, anything can be used to store information. All it takes to store information by means of some object—or more generally, a configuration of objects—is a convention that such a configuration represents that information. The conventions that may be used to store information range from conventions adopted by an entire nation to a convention adopted by a single person. In order to cope with the many different ways that information may be represented, the people who carry out fundamental research into the nature of information have introduced a special term for them: They call them *constraints*. This is strictly a technical use of the word, unrelated to its everyday meaning as some kind of limit to our behavior.

A knowledge or an awareness of the relevant constraint, or an adaptation to it, is what enables a person to acquire the information represented by way of that constraint. For example, familiarity with the constraint that smoke comes from fire enables a person or an animal to infer the presence of fire from the appearance of smoke. In the case of mechanical devices, they are constructed to act in accordance with the relevant constraint. For example, the simple, mechanical thermostat is constructed to act according to a constraint linking the position of its bimetallic contact strip to the temperature of the surrounding air, a constraint that depends upon a physical relationship between temperature and the expansion rates of various metals.

In most cases it is not necessary to know anything about the origin of the constraint in order to use it to obtain information. In fact, you don't need any real awareness of the constraint. After all, the thermostat is not in any sense aware of how and why it operates the way it does. It is just a simple, mechanical device, so it is not aware of anything. Nevertheless, it can process information well enough to maintain the room at a constant temperature. And though considerably more aware than the average thermostat, the logger who can tell the age of a tree by counting the rings on its trunk does not need a deep knowledge of botany to do this. All he needs to know is the constraint that links the number of rings to the age of the tree.

Constraints are among the notions that a science on information will have to come to grips with—what they look like and how they work.

At the moment, there is no fully worked-out analysis of constraints. What we have are various observations about constraints. Using those observations, let's see where the informational stance leads us in terms of understanding how the human mind works. To do this, we need one further concept: that of a situation *type*.

ACTING ACCORDING TO TYPE

I'll introduce the notion of a situation type by way of our earlier example about wearing slippers. As I observed, when I am in an office situation *s*, it is not appropriate to wear slippers, but it is when I am in a home situation *h*. What makes this a particularly good example is that I can be fairly confident that the same is true for you: In your office or work situation it is inappropriate for you to wear slippers, whereas in your home, wearing slippers is entirely appropriate.

Now there is something interesting going on here. Here are all of these quite distinct office or work situations—one for each reader of this book, one for myself, and one for every person in the world who goes out to work—and in practically every one of them, it is inappropriate to wear slippers. Likewise, there are all these quite distinct home situations, and in practically every one of them, it is appropriate to wear slippers. It must be the case that all these individual office situations have something in common, and, likewise, all these individual home situations have something in common. Indeed, the common features are reflected in the very language that we use: "office or work situations" and "home situations." Given the enormous variety of possible office or work environments and the equally large variety of homes, there is probably little else office or work situations have in common other than that they are office or work situations, and there is probably not a great deal in common between the different home situations apart from the fact that they are home situations. These are certainly the common features that determine whether slippers are inappropriate footwear. It is by virtue of our being able to recognize these common features that we generally avoid violating the associated patterns of footwear behavior.

The situation-theory research community refers to such common features of situations as situation types. The type of all home situations is what all home situations have in common—whatever that is. This sounds a bit mysterious, and it is. But it is no more mysterious than are the counting numbers that we learn to use when we are two or three years old: 1, 2, 3, et cetera. When you ask what the number 5 really 'is', the only answer is that it is what all collections of five objects have in common—five apples, five oranges, five elephants, five languages, and so on.

Whatever types 'are', it is by recognizing (often subconsciously) situation types that we generally act in a manner appropriate for our given environment at any moment. For example, you are driving a car in an unfamiliar city and you come to an intersection controlled by a traffic light. You have never before been at that particular intersection and have never before seen that particular traffic light. Nevertheless, you know how to behave: If the light is red, you stop; if it is green, you proceed. Your behavior cannot be based purely on the circumstances of the particular situation you find yourself in, for this is a situation you have never encountered before. Rather, the situation is of a type you are very familiar with. You know how to behave in *any* intersection-controlled-by-traffic-lights situation. Your behavior is determined by the situation *type*.

The ability to recognize types of things lies at the basis of much of human cognition and communication. Humans are type recognizers. So too, it appears, are various animals—bees seem able to recognize the types of certain flowers, and cats and dogs seem able to recognize the type of feeding bowls and the type of doorways.

Many of the words in our language refer to types: types of object, types of action, and so forth. For example, nouns that denote things do so by making reference to types: *house* refers to any house, not one particular house; *car* refers to any car, not one particular car; *mountain* refers to any mountain, regardless of its exact shape or size or location; and so on. Similarly, for verbs, *walk* refers to walking action by any person or legged animal; *run* refers to any running action; *climb* refers to any climbing action; et cetera. Such nouns and verbs can be used on any particular occasion to refer to a particular thing or action, but such reference is only possible because their meaning refers to types of things or actions.

The recognition of types lies behind much of our ability to obtain information from our environment and from things in our environment. To take a previous example, you look up and see dark clouds in the sky, and you say to yourself, "It looks like it might rain today." On the basis of one situation, the cloudy sky right now, you infer information about another, future situation—the weather in that region later in the day. The basis for this inference is that you are aware of a systematic relation between skies of a certain type and subsequent weather of a certain type. When the sky is of the type 'dark clouds', it is often the case that the weather will subsequently be of the type 'raining'. The actual dark-cloud formation that you see on that particular occasion does not, in itself, tell you anything. It is a one-off event. It is by virtue of the sky being of a recognizable type that you can obtain the information you do. If we were not able to recognize types, the world would always be presented to us anew, and we would be unable to make any reliable inferences based on prior knowledge or past experiences.

The same is true for conventional signals such as the ring of the bell indicating that a class or work shift is over. Each particular ring of the bell is a brand new event. What makes it useful as an informational device is that each ring is a particular type of event, a type of event that we learn to associate with another type of event, the ending of the class or shift. In fact, many places have a more extensive code for bell rings, perhaps with a single short ring indicating the end of class, a double ring indicating the end of morning break, and a long ring signifying the end of the school day. In such cases the relevant type is not just that of a bell ringing but the particular kind of bell ring.

Likewise for spoken and written language. For example, how many words are there on the following line?

APPLE APPLE APPLE APPLE Apple apple *apple* **apple**

There are two possible answers: one and eight. The linguist would say that there is just one word, the word *apple,* because to a linguist, a word is a type. What you see on that line, the linguist would say, are eight *in-*

stances (or *tokens*) of the single type apple. Likewise for phrases and sentences: To the linguist, these are types. Any particular utterance or written expression of a phrase or sentence is a token of that phrase or sentence type.

We can use the word *apple* to refer to an actual apple since there is a relation that connects the word-type apple (i.e., the linguistic type that linguists say is the word *apple*) to the object-type apple (i.e., the type that all apples have in common). More generally, language serves to refer to things and events in the world and to convey information about the world by virtue of relations between types, specifically, between linguistic types and types of things and events in the world.

The constraints that were mentioned in the previous section are precisely these links between types that enable objects and situations to encode and provide information. The constraint that links the type of situation in which there is smoke to the type of situation in which there is fire is the constraint that enables us to obtain from the fact that we see smoke the information that there may be a fire. To take another example, there is a legally imposed constraint that connects the type of traffic situation where there is a red traffic light to the type of action where we stop the car. A law-abiding driver who comes to a particular traffic light that is red (a situation of the appropriate type) stops the car at that moment (an event of the appropriate type). And so forth.

The notion of a situation type enables us to start to analyze expertise, that key to smooth, effortless behavior discussed in Chapter 7. In terms of situation types, expertise simply amounts to becoming accustomed to react to certain situation types in certain ways. In other words, expert behavior is behavior governed not by any particular situation but by situation types. The expert is able to recognize (often subconsciously) certain situation types and to react accordingly.

Of course, this does not provide a detailed explanation of what expertise amounts to, or how people acquire it. It simply provides, at most, a *framework* within which to further analyze and study expert behavior. In order to provide a complete explanation (if such a thing exists), the use of the theoretical apparatus of situation theory has to be combined with other kinds of analysis, for instance, cognitive or behavioral psychology.

IT'S COMMON KNOWLEDGE

Very often, a scientific theory developed for one purpose turns out to have applications in a quite different area. For instance, situation theory was designed to investigate issues of natural-language semantics, but it was subsequently found useful in the study of communication in general, including human–human conversations and human–computer interaction. Perhaps more surprising, the theory was successfully applied to a problem of great concern in the political arena—the so-called problem of common knowledge—and to solve a classic logical paradox from ancient Greece, the Liar Paradox. To end this chapter, I'll describe, briefly, these two results. Readers who find the going getting tough (and it does get tough) can simply skip ahead to the final chapter.

Common knowledge means knowledge shared by two or more people, whereby shared means that not only do they both *have* that knowledge, but they both *know* that they both have it.

We have already encountered the concept of common knowledge in the discussion of conversations in the previous chapter.

The fact that the common ground of a conversation consists of common knowledge is an important feature of the conversation. The participants in a conversation make essential and frequent use of the fact that the common ground consists of common knowledge. When John makes a comment to Alice about 'the chapel', not only do they both have to know which chapel John is referring to, they have to know it *jointly*. Their knowledge of which chapel John is referring to has to be common knowledge. Without such mutual knowledge, the conversation cannot properly proceed. For without that common knowledge, neither participant can be sure that they are talking about the same building. They can find themselves faced with uncertainties, such as John thinking, "I know Alice is thinking about the same chapel I was referring to, but I am not sure if she knows I know, so maybe she will not follow what I say next." In fact, such uncertainties rarely arise, because, as we observed in the previous chapter, participants in a conversation constantly monitor the progress of the conversation and seek clarification or repair as soon as there is a communication breakdown. In other words, they make sure that the common ground remains common knowledge.

Besides the role it plays in conversations, common knowledge is a crucial feature in a number of other important activities.

For instance, common knowledge plays a significant strategic role in modern political, military, and commercial life. It was common knowledge that maintained the global balance of power between the United States and the Soviet Union for fifty years, after the end of World War II. As the two superpowers built their stockpiles of nuclear weapons, each knew that they both had the capability to destroy the other, and they each knew that the other knew—it was common knowledge between them that they each had that capability. The result was a standoff. As with nuclear (and non-nuclear) weapons and national defense, in the political and commercial arenas common knowledge can also result in a standoff. Such an equilibrium might make us nervous, but it is actually remarkably stable. In fact, what makes us feel uneasy about such a standoff is not the common knowledge that sustains it but the possibility of one side gaining an advantage by acquiring knowledge that is not common.

Clearly then, it makes sense to try to understand this phenomenon of common knowledge.

The first thing to realize is that common knowledge is not the same as the two individuals knowing the same thing, as the following story indicates.

Picture the following scenario. Three logic graduate students, Tom, Dick, and Harry, are working in their professor's garden one summer afternoon. It is a hot day, and from time to time each student wipes the sweat from his brow with the back of his hand. By the end of the afternoon, each student has a grimy mark on his forehead, though none of the students know this. Of course, each student can see that the other two have muddy foreheads, but being exceedingly polite students, none of them makes any remarks about another's appearance. Finally, their day's work done, the students go into the house and join their professor for a glass of lemonade. Seeing the marks on the three students' foreheads, the professor remarks, "Aha, at least one of you has mud on your forehead." Now this is a pretty odd thing to say, unless you are a professor of logic trying to test your students' reasoning powers. So each student thinks about the situation for a moment. Then, suddenly, all three students get up and head for the bathroom to wash their faces, each having independently realized that all three of them have muddy foreheads.

So much for the scenario. The question is, how was each student able to figure out that he had a muddy forehead? (By the way, in this scenario, there are no mirrors or glass surfaces in which the students can see themselves. And we'll suppose that they are so hot and sweaty, with dirty hands, that they cannot simply reach up and feel their foreheads to find out if there is mud there. They reach their conclusions by pure reasoning.)

The situation seems odd. Just think about it. Each of the three students can see that both of the other students have muddy foreheads. So the professor's remark that at least one of them has a muddy forehead does not seem to tell them anything new. In fact, the professor is surely telling them *less* than they already know! And yet, it is only by virtue of the professor's remark that each student is able to deduce that his forehead is also muddy.

The key is that, after the professor's remark, it is *common knowledge* among the three students that at least one of them has a dirty forehead. It is not the information itself that makes the difference, it is the fact that, after the professor makes his remark, that information becomes common knowledge—knowledge that is mutually known by all three students. It is also important that each student knows that his two companions are as capable as he at logical reasoning—it is no accident that this scenario is presented using logic students. Here is how each student reasons. Take Tom, for example.

Tom thinks to himself: Suppose I have a clean forehead. Then, when the professor spoke, Dick would have looked at my clean forehead and Harry's dirty forehead and said to himself, "The professor could have been referring to Harry's forehead." Likewise, Harry would have looked at my clean forehead and Dick's dirty one and thought, "The professor could have been referring to Dick's forehead." But then, surely the following thought would occur to Dick. "Harry can see, as I can, that Tom's forehead is clean. So if my forehead is clean, he should conclude that his own head must be the dirty one. And yet he has not gotten up and headed for the bathroom. Hence my forehead must be dirty." Likewise, Harry will have gone through a similar thought process to deduce that *his* forehead is dirty.

Remember, the above paragraph is the reasoning process Tom goes through, starting with the assumption that he has a clean forehead. That reasoning process leads Tom to the conclusion that Dick will reason that his forehead is dirty and Harry will reason that his forehead is dirty. And yet, as Tom can plainly see, neither Dick nor Harry has moved. So Tom's original assumption that he has a clean forehead must be wrong. Faced with this realization, he stands up and heads for the bathroom.

Meanwhile, Dick and Harry have each been going through the same reasoning process. So they too jump up to wash their faces. Presumably they grin to each other as they all try to squeeze through the bathroom door at the same time, each inwardly pleased that his reasoning was no slower and no less accurate than the other two. (If one of the three students reasons too slowly, then the above argument breaks down, since there are points where the inactivity of the others plays an important role.) The professor's smile is probably the widest, as he reflects on his good fortune at having three students who are not only very good logicians but are also prepared to spend an afternoon working in his garden.

Common knowledge, then, is something different from individual knowledge held by two or more people, and, as a result, it has long been a puzzle. Attempts to explain it in terms of individual knowledge lead at once to an infinite regress:

> A knows X,
> B knows X,
> A knows that B knows X,
> B knows that A knows X,
> A knows that B knows that A knows X,
> B knows that A knows that B knows X,
> A knows that B knows that A knows that B knows X,
> B knows that A knows that B knows that A knows X,
> And so on, *ad infinitum.*

One thing is clear: When people make use of common knowledge, they do not pursue an infinite regress of this kind. Thus, this kind of analysis is not really getting at the heart of the matter. And the heart of the matter is that common knowledge is, as the name says, common.

To see how situation theory can be used to understand common knowledge without leading us into an infinite regress, consider the case where two people, John and Mary say, have common knowledge about some fact, event, or circumstance, X. Then the act of John and Mary having common knowledge of X constitutes a situation; call it s. What exactly does it mean to say that "s is a common knowledge situation for John and Mary to have common knowledge of X"?

Well, first of all, John and Mary must individually know X. Expressed in the algebraic notation of situation theory:

$$s \models \langle\!\langle \text{John knows } X \rangle\!\rangle \wedge \langle\!\langle \text{Mary knows } X \rangle\!\rangle.$$

Second, and this is the key observation, both John and Mary know that s, the situation they are in, is one of common knowledge. In symbols, this is written as:

$$s \models \langle\!\langle \text{John knows } X \rangle\!\rangle \wedge \langle\!\langle \text{Mary knows } X \rangle\!\rangle$$
$$\wedge \langle\!\langle \text{John knows } p \rangle\!\rangle \wedge \langle\!\langle \text{Mary knows } p \rangle\!\rangle,$$

where p is the very proposition that this formula expresses.

This is not easy to fathom. The underlying idea is one of knowing about a situation—John and Mary know that the knowing situation they are in is one of common knowledge. What makes it particularly hard to follow is that the proposition that they each know, p, is the very proposition about their knowing p. Thus, we have eliminated the infinite regress of older theories, only to be faced with a circular, self-referential analysis using situations. However, when you stop to reflect on common knowledge as we experience it in our daily lives, it seems clear that it is very much a circular, self-referential notion. One of the strong points of the analysis just outlined is that it works by honing in on the way of knowing, and that is surely what distinguishes common knowledge from individual knowledge. Hence, the situation-theoretical analysis is much closer to reality than the old infinite-regress approach.

The application of situation theory to the phenomenon of common knowledge is just one of a number of ways that an information-based approach can lead to fruitful new ways of looking at old problems. A particularly dramatic illustration of the potential power of the informational approach was its use to resolve one of the classic problems of logic, a puzzle that had resisted all attempts at a solution for two thousand years: The Liar Paradox.

The liar paradox

The Liar Paradox, generally credited to the Greek philosopher Epimenides, asks us to consider the individual who stands up and says, "This assertion is false." The question is, is this assertion, then, true or false? Is the speaker telling the truth or lying? There are two possibilities: The speaker is either telling the truth or lying. Let's look at each possibility in turn. To clarify the analysis, let L stand for the sentence uttered.

If the speaker is telling the truth, then the assertion must be true. According to what L says, that means that the speaker is uttering a falsehood. In other words, the assertion is a falsehood. But that can't be the case, since we started out by supposing that the speaker was telling the truth. So this case is contradictory.

Now let's look at the case where the speaker is lying. That means that the assertion is false. According to what L says, that means that the speaker must be telling the truth. Again, we are in a contradictory situation.

It is an inescapable paradox: If the speaker is telling the truth, then he or she is lying; if the speaker is lying, then he or she is telling the truth.

Until recently, there was no known solution to this paradox. At the heart of the paradox seems to be its self-referential nature. Certainly, the argument that leads to the paradox makes heavy use of the fact that the utterance of L refers to that very utterance. But self-reference alone cannot be the culprit. There is nothing inherently wrong with self-reference. It happens all the time, and often in polite company. People frequently talk about themselves. A group of people in conversation at a dinner party can talk about the dinner party, making such remarks as, "This is a very interesting conversation." And how about the self-referential sentence "This sentence has exactly six words." Attempts to resolve the paradox by analyzing self-referential statements did not succeed.

Nor did approaches that concentrated on the notion of truth and falsity, the other key ingredient of the paradox. One such attempt at a resolution was to suppose that there is a third possibility besides the assertion being true or false: It could be undetermined. But the paradox arises again, like the Phoenix from the ashes, when someone stands up and says, "This assertion is false or undetermined."

Presumably, then, the paradox depends on the particular combination of self-reference and a claim about truth and falsity. Certainly, there was no shortage of logicians who thought this was the case. But it was not until Jon Barwise and John Etchemendy applied the formal techniques of situation theory in 1986 that the problem was finally resolved.

The real root of the paradox was neither self-reference nor truth, but an unacknowledged context. Once you take proper account of the context in which the Liar sentence is uttered, there is no more a paradox than there is a genuine conflict between the American who thinks that June is a summer month and the Australian who thinks June is a winter month. Here, laid bare, is what the Liar Paradox really amounts to.

(Escape point: The discussion of the Liar Paradox is fairly technical. Readers uncomfortable with technical analyses should skip ahead to the next section. Nothing further in our account depends on this section.)

Person a stands up and says, "This assertion is false." As before, let L denote the sentence uttered. The first question to ask is what exactly the speaker refers to by the phrase "This assertion." It cannot be the sentence L itself. Sentences are just strings of symbols, and a string of symbols is neither true nor false; it's just a string of symbols. Rather, what the speaker is referring to must be the assertion (or claim) being made by uttering the sentence. Let's call that assertion p (for proposition). In other words, a's utterance of the phrase "This assertion" refers to the claim p.

It follows that, in uttering the sentence "This assertion is false," a is making the claim 'p is false'. But we already used p itself to denote the claim made by a. Hence p and 'p is false' must be one and the same. I'll write this as an equation and give it a number to refer to later:

$$p = [p \text{ is false}]. \tag{1}$$

Now, the claim p made by a's utterance concerns the truth of p. But, as we have already observed, if we want to be able to decide whether a particular claim is true or false, we need to be careful about the context in which the claim is made. In other words, in making the assertion—which is about that very assertion—*a* must be making implicit reference to the context in which the assertion is made. Let *c* denote that context.

Thus, *a*'s utterance of the phrase "This assertion" refers to the claim that *p* is true in the context *c*. Using the notation of situation theory, this can be written as:

$$c \models p.$$

In other words, *p* must *be* the same as $c \models p$, since both are what *a* refers to by uttering the phrase "This assertion." So we have established a second equation:

$$p = [c \models p]. \tag{2}$$

Having sorted out what *a* is talking about, it's time to see whether *a*'s assertion is true or false.

Suppose first that *a*'s assertion is true. In other words, *p* is true. Using formula (2), we can express this as

$$c \models p. \tag{3}$$

By formula (1), we can replace *p* in formula (3) by [*p* is false] to obtain:

$$c \models [p \text{ is false}]. \tag{4}$$

Now we have a contradiction: Formula (3) tells us that *p* is true in the context *c* and formula (4) tells us that *p* is false in the same context *c*. Notice that there is no question of a Pacific Time–Eastern Time or America–Australia context difference here to explain the conflict. The context is the same in both cases, namely, *c*. The contradiction is inescapable, just as if we suddenly discovered it was simultaneously 4 o'clock and 7 o'clock in San Francisco. The only possible way out of this dilemma is that *a*'s claim cannot be true, since that is the supposition that got us to the contradiction.

So much for the case when we assume that *a*'s claim is true. Now let's look at the case where *a*'s claim is false. In other words,

$$p \text{ is false.}$$

But wait a minute. What is the context for this statement? This question did not arise in the previous case, since we knew the context for *p*; it was *c*. But nothing we know provides a context for the statement '*p* is false'.

You might feel that *c* is itself the appropriate context. After all, *c* is the context in which *a* makes the assertion, and to which the assertion implicitly refers. Fair enough, let's see what happens if we do make this assumption. Then,

$$c \models [p \text{ is false}].$$

By formula (1), this can be rewritten as

$$c \models p.$$

And now we are in the same contradictory situation as we were in the previous case. On that occasion, the conclusion was that a's claim cannot be true. But this time the conclusion is different: Namely, that c cannot be the appropriate context. Just as the knowledge that if a person in country X says truthfully that June is a winter month leads us to conclude that country X is not America, so too on this occasion, if a's claim is false, then we can conclude that the context for that claim being false cannot be c.

You have to be a bit careful with the comparison of the above scenario with the Australia example. The situation c is indeed the context for a's utterance. At issue is what is the context for making the new statement that a's original utterance is false. What the above argument shows is that *that* context, whatever it is, cannot be c.

So, when proper attention is paid to context, the Liar Paradox ceases to be a paradox. In saying "This assertion is false," the individual a is making a claim that refers (implicitly) to a particular context, $c,$ the context in which the sentence is uttered. If the claim is true, then it is true in the context $c,$ and that leads to a contradiction. So the claim must be false. But the context for making the observation that the claim is false cannot be $c,$ since if it were, then that too leads to a contradiction.

In other words, what was previously regarded as a paradox has turned into a discovery, or *theorem,* about contexts. A person a who stands up and says (in context c), "This assertion is false," is making a false statement. However, the fact that the statement is false cannot be asserted in the same context c. Admittedly this is a fairly odd conclusion. Then again, the original sentence of the Liar 'Paradox' is a pretty odd thing for anyone to say.

There is a particular irony about the way the Liar Paradox was finally put to rest. The paradox was first formulated by a logician in ancient Greece, at the time when the Greeks were starting to develop a theory of reasoning and truth (i.e., logic) that was independent of context. And yet, more than two thousand years later, we are able to recognize that Epimenides's argument is really about the crucial role played by context in discussing reasoning and truth. In short, a proper analysis of both communication or reasoning cannot be carried out without taking into account the context.

But the study of phenomena freed of all context is at the very heart of Cartesian science—that great investigative tradition that began with Plato and achieved almost total domination in science and philosophy with the work of Galileo and Descartes. Indeed, it was out of that very tradition that situation theory itself was developed. Jon Barwise, who first introduced the theory around 1980, was a mathematical logician—the most Cartesian variety of Cartesian scientists. Equally Cartesian was the work that followed Barwise, as a number of linguists and mathematicians (including Barwise himself) developed the mathematics of situation theory to the point where it could be used to investigate the influence of context on meaning.

What no one realized at the time was that they had set course on a path that would lead eventually to questions about the very suitability of the scientific method for the investigation of human reasoning and communication. Descartes's legacy was about to be brought into question.

11

GOODBYE, DESCARTES

Mathematicians wish to treat matters of perception mathematically,
and make themselves ridiculous . . . the mind . . . does it tacitly, natu-
rally, and without technical rules.

—Blaise Pascal[1]

LEAVING THE OMEGA

Modern logic tries to capture the patterns of reasoning, and, to some extent, the patterns of language required to formulate a logical argument, in
a pure fashion, isolated from context. But remember that this approach
has been the dominant one only for the last three hundred years or so.
Until the rise of what we call the scientific method in the seventeenth century, logic was regarded largely as one aspect of rhetoric—a study of how
one person's argument could convince another. That was certainly the
way Aristotle regarded logic. Plato disagreed, condemning the Sophists's
use of rhetoric as "making the worse arguments appear the better." But it
was Aristotle's view that predominated. For the Romans, a study of logic
was just one part of their training for public office. Likewise, when logic
was introduced as one of the mainstays of higher education, with the rise
of the universities in the twelfth century, it was as part of the overall
training for the mind.

---

1. From Pascal's *Pensées*, published in 1670. This quotation gains much of its strength
from the fact that Pascal was one of the most famous mathematicians of all time. Among
his mathematical achievements is that he was one of the two people who independently
founded the subject of probability theory, the other founder being Fermat.

However, in the seventeenth century, leading thinkers such as Galileo (in natural science) and Descartes (in philosophy) spearheaded a rapid change toward the 'isolationist' approach advocated by Plato. For these scholars, the only knowledge worth pursuing was that which could be expressed by precise, eternal, context-free rules that captured general patterns. So successful was this revolution—and it was a revolution—that even to this day, the word *rhetoric* carries a negative connotation, implying the use of cheap debating tricks to make up for a lack of honest, logical argument.

The contemporary philosopher Stephen Toulmin, in his book *Cosmopolis,* likens the course of post-seventeenth-century human thought to the Greek letter omega (Ω). He writes:

> The formal doctrines that underpinned human thought and practice from 1700 on followed a trajectory with the shape of an Omega, i.e. "Ω". After 300 years we are back close to our starting point. Natural scientists no longer separate the "observer" from the "world observed," as they did in the heyday of classical physics. . . . Descartes' *foundational* ambitions are discredited, taking philosophy back to [that of an earlier era]. (p. 167, emphasis in the original.)

The Cartesian approach—with its pinnacle role for mathematics—was extremely successful. It led to all of today's science and technology. But that very success led us around the loop of the omega. Our inability to breach the logic and language walls has forced us to go back to the view advocated by Aristotle—to put reasoning and communication back into context, the context where a person reasons, and the context where two people communicate. It is time to leave the omega. We need to look beyond logic.

Beyond Logic

The following problem appears in many books in one form or another. You are to imagine you are a member of a jury evaluating a claim arising from a hit-and-run driving case. A taxi driver is accused of having hit a pedestrian late one night and having fled the scene. The entire case against the taxi company rests on the evidence of one witness, an elderly man who saw the accident from his window some distance away. The elderly man says that he saw a blue taxi hit the pedestrian. In trying to establish her case, the injured person's lawyer establishes the following two facts:

1. There are only two taxi companies in town, the Blue Cab Company and the Black Cab Company. On the night in question, 85% of all taxis on the road were black, and 15% were blue.
2. The witness has undergone an extensive vision test, under conditions similar to those on the night in question, and has demonstrated that he can successfully distinguish a blue taxi from a black taxi 80% of the time.

If you were on the jury, how would you decide?

If you are at all typical, faced with eyewitness evidence from an on-looker who has demonstrated that he is right four times out of five, you might be inclined to declare that the pedestrian was indeed hit by a blue taxi, and hence, you would find against the Blue Cab Company. Indeed, if challenged, you might say that the odds in favor of the Blue Cab Company being at fault were exactly 4/5, those being the odds in favor of the witness being correct on any one occasion.

The facts are quite different. Based on the data supplied, the mathematical probability that the pedestrian was hit by a blue taxi is only 0.41, or 41%. Less than half. In other words, the pedestrian was *more* likely to have been hit by a black taxi than a blue one. The error in basing your decision on the accuracy figures for the witness is that this ignores the overwhelming probability, based on the figures, that *any* taxi in the town is likely to be black. If the witness had been unable to identify the color of the taxi, but had only been able to state—with 100% accuracy, let us suppose—that the accident was caused by a taxi, then the probability that it had been a black taxi would have been 85%, the proportion of taxis in the town that are black. So, *before* the witness testifies to the color, the chances are low—namely, 15%—that the taxi in question was blue. This figure is generally referred to as the *prior probability*, the probability based purely on the way things are, not the particular evidence pertaining to the case in question. When the witness then testifies as to the color, that evidence *increases* the odds from the 15% prior probability figure, but not all the way to the 80% figure of the witness's tested accuracy. Rather, the reliability figure for the witness's evidence must be *combined* with the prior probability to give the real probability. The exact mathematical manner in which this combination is done is known as *Bayes's law*. The details are not important here, but the probability works out to be 41%.

The most common alternative version of what is, at heart, the same problem, asks you to weigh your chances of survival if a blood test with an 80% likelihood of being correct gives a positive result for a fatal illness having a 15% rate of occurrence in the population. Most people cannot do this.

The moral many writers try to draw from problems like these is that human beings are innumerate, and as a result are not always able to make rational decisions. "Improve our math classes in the schools," say these experts, "and we will all be better equipped to make sound judgments." Now, improving school mathematics instruction may or may not have a beneficial effect on society. But the fact that the vast majority of people get the taxicab/fatal illness problems 'wrong' is not an argument in favor of teaching mathematics, and it certainly does not show that 'innumerate' people make poor judgments. What these particular examples show is that there can be a big difference between rational behavior and numerically or logically based behavior. The jurist who assigns damages against the Blue Cab Company might display a form of innumeracy, but he or she could still be acting rationally. Indeed, the jurist probably is acting rationally. Here's why.

First, let's be clear about what the use of Bayes's law tells us in this case. Providing that the stated proportions of blue and black taxis, namely, 15% blue and 85% black, is uniform throughout the town (or at least that these figures are reliable in the region where the accident occurred), then the 41% figure for the chance of the pedestrian being hit by a blue taxi is accurate. Given the right circumstances, Bayes's law is totally correct. So, assuming that the various figures quoted are reliable, the probability that the Blue Company is at fault is indeed a mere 0.41, and chances are the Black Company is to blame. Clearly, there is more than enough reasonable doubt here, and a rational jurist to whom this application of Bayes's law is explained should act accordingly.

On what basis, then, do I claim that the jurist—who, ignorant of the use of Bayes's law, decides against the Blue Company—can be said to be acting rationally? Well, over thousands of years of evolution, human beings have learned to make decisions that are beneficial—beneficial firstly to themselves and their nearest and dearest, then to others in the society. Only very rarely are they in full possession of enough information to make what an analyst would declare is the 'best' decision. Typically, humans have to make decisions based on very limited information, quite often only the information provided by their own senses—sight, sound, or smell. During the course of our evolutionary history, we have become very good at making optimum decisions based on such evidence. Those that were not adept at identifying potential danger often did not survive long enough to pass on their genes. Moreover, sensory perception, such as seeing, hearing, or smelling, has a conscious immediacy that gives us overwhelming faith in information we acquire in that way, far more than information we read or are told about. Seeing is particularly strong in this regard. Thus, both on evolutionary grounds and our own conscious experience, we tend to put great significance on information acquired first hand through sight, and what is more, it is entirely rational to do so.

It is entirely consistent with our rational tendency to rely on information acquired by seeing something to likewise rely on information that is directly reported to us by others who have acquired it by seeing. "I saw it with my own eyes," amounts to a personal guarantee of truth when someone reports something he has seen. In contrast, neither evolution nor our own experience has equipped us to have a 'feel' for highly abstract information based on numerical data about a large population we cannot possibly see. The information that 15% of the taxicabs in the town are blue and 85% are black and that their distribution through the town is uniform is mathematically precise but entirely abstract—we do not *see* it.

In our daily lives, though we are constantly faced with evaluating information and making decisions (in many cases, decisions on which our lives quite literally depend, such as crossing the street, driving a car, etc.), we rarely do so on the basis of statistical data of the taxicab variety. It is then hardly surprising that most of us, when faced with the kind of problem facing the jurist in the taxicab case, tend to downplay evidence based on statistical data and put great significance on eyewitness accounts. In the taxicab case, it is undoubtedly wrong to reason that if a series of tests show that the eyewitness is right four out of five times, then the probability of what he says being true on the occasion in question is also 4/5. But it is not at all *irrational* to reason in this way. As a jurist, you could only be accused of irrationality if, faced with a clear explanation of the application of Bayes's law to the case, you refuse to change your original evaluation of the eyewitness's evidence.

A similar phenomenon lies behind the tendency of most people to have trouble with the Monty Hall problem, discussed in Chapter 1. Recall the scenario: You are a contestant in the game show, and the host, Monty, has put you in front of three doors. You are told that behind one of them is a chest containing ten thousand dollars and behind each of the other two doors is a banana. You have to pick one door, and you get to keep what you find behind it. Monty knows where the money is, but you do not. Monty first asks you to choose a door. You tell Monty your choice but do not get to open your chosen door. Instead, Monty opens one of the remaining two doors to reveal a banana. Now, Monty makes you an offer: Do you want to stick with your original choice of doors, or would you rather switch to the other unopened door? It will cost you ten dollars to make the switch.

As discussed in Chapter 1, the most common response people give when presented with this scenario is that it does not make any difference to their chances of winning the money whether they change their original choice, so they decide not to pay the ten dollars to make the switch. However, the fact is that switching doors *doubles* your chances of winning the ten thousand dollars; the odds increase from the initial 1 in 3 of your first choice to a very favorable 2 in 3.

Once again, though people who believe it makes no difference to switch are completely wrong, they are not being irrational. Evolution and everyday experience have equipped us with an ability to make rapid, on-the-spot judgments of odds, although not the numerically precise odds of probability theory and statistics. Rather, faced with a situation involving a choice between two courses of action, A and B, we often evaluate the situation in the form "A is preferable over B," or "B is to be preferred over A," or "it makes no real difference." Sometimes we can be more confident in such an evaluation, judging, say, A to be "much more preferable" than B. Such on-the-spot evaluations are almost always based on the information that is the most recent and immediately at hand. Given our evolutionary history and our lifetime experience, when faced with having to make a choice between alternatives, it is entirely rational to make judgments of this kind.

The scenario presented to us by Monty Hall is fairly complex. To reason correctly, we have to take account not only of the situation with which we are presented, namely, two doors, behind one of which is a substantial prize, but also of the events that led up to that moment of choice. Virtually nothing in our evolutionary history or our daily experience has prepared us to make a judgment of that kind. Indeed, what both evolution and our experience have taught us is to ignore complicating factors and make our judgment on what appears to be the most significant feature of the situation. Faced with a car heading toward us on the highway on our side of the road, we swerve to the right (unless we are in, say, Britain, Japan, or Australia), assuming the other driver will do likewise. There may be other factors that would dictate an alternative course of action, but in that moment, we do not even consider them. We react to the single most salient feature of the situation. To the average Monty Hall contestant, the framework for the decision is simply that of being presented with two doors, behind one of which there is a prize. Everything else is ignored. On most occasions, the strategy of ignoring everything else would be appropriate. In the absence of the events leading up to

Monty's offer, there is indeed nothing to distinguish between the two doors, and a rational person would therefore opt not to waste ten dollars on switching. A Monty Hall contestant who chooses not to switch is undoubtedly making a poor choice, given the mathematical facts. However, considering the highly contrived nature of the challenge, that contestant is not being irrational.

THE PUZZLE OF RATIONALITY

Why do we behave the way we do? Why do we say the things we do, and what makes us understand things said to us the way we do? No one theory can answer these questions. A complete answer, if such were possible, would involve a psychological study, a sociological study, a logical study, a linguistic study, a moral/philosophical study, a historical study, a biological study, and who knows what other kinds of study. However, by providing a framework within which human cognitive activity can be examined, a *theory of context* (such as situation theory) can throw some light onto human rationality. In particular, it can enable us to explain the distinction between logical behavior and rational behavior.

Different contexts carry with them different rules of behavior. A first attempt at a definition of rationality might describe a person behaving rationally if he or she acts in a manner consistent with the rules of behavior that prevail in the context in which the person is currently situated. This is very much a notion of *relative* rationality—rationality in a context. In the example of the hit-and-run court case discussed in the previous section, the juror who reasons that the Blue Cab Company is very likely to blame, based on the testimony of the eyewitness, is reasoning according to a set of rules that prevail in what one might call the everyday reasoning and acting situation. This reasoning system—which is almost entirely unconscious and instinctive—is one that evolution and personal history have developed to a point where it is extremely reliable. In the courtroom, it is part of the job of the defense lawyer to convince the jury that, because of the particular circumstances of the case under consideration, the logic of everyday reasoning is not appropriate and that justice demands logic of a different kind, what we might call a statistician's logic.

Similarly, in the Monty Hall quiz show, the optimal reasoning process for the contestant uses mathematical reasoning, not the common-sense reasoning we use in an everyday context.

Different contexts also account for the apparent irrationality of the respondents to the French survey we discussed in Chapter 1, who were asked to rank the factors they regarded as important for happiness and then rank the factors that contributed to unhappiness. You may recall that the most common factor cited as important for happiness was another person. Lower down on the list came money, and good health came last. On the other hand, poor health was regarded as the single most significant cause of unhappiness.

The happiness ranking was almost certainly done in a 'normal context'. In such a context, good health is generally assumed, and the respondents saw no reason to rank it highly. Unhappiness, on the other hand, is an 'abnormal' situation that generally has a cause. Thus, when faced with the second question, they looked for factors that do not hold in the normal context and *which would cause* the resulting situation to be one in which they were unhappy. In this exercise, they ranked poor health the most significant factor.

There is, then, no irrationality in the respondents' responses. The two rankings were not inconsistent responses to two versions of what was essentially the same task; rather they were performing quite different tasks in response to the two questions.

A similar explanation also accounts for your seemingly illogical behavior when faced with attending the concert in bad weather, also described in Chapter 1. Here, again, are the two scenarios. In the first scenario, you have purchased a $100 ticket and will attempt to get to the concert even if it means a long and difficult drive in bad weather. In the second scenario, you are offered a free $100 ticket on the morning of the concert but decline it on account of the weather. Your net cost in both cases is $100, so your different behavior in the two scenarios seems illogical.

Again, your behavior in both scenarios is perfectly rational. Your different behavior is due to the different contexts under which you make your two decisions. In the first scenario, your purchase of the ticket establishes a context for your actions in which attending the concert is a highly significant event. That context will prevent you from making commitments to do other things at the time of the concert and will include goals and intentions to perform various actions necessary in order for you to attend. In short, the context will have shaped your actions for the time leading up to the concert. Having established the context as a frame for your actions—having *committed* to that context—you are understandably reluctant to abandon it. In contrast, with the second scenario there is no such context. You might have harbored a desire to attend, but having made no plans to do so, your context for action does not involve any commitment to attend.

One key, then, to understanding everyday reasoning is to abandon Descartes's decontextualized approach and take account of the context. The result is neither a completely mathematical nor a rule-based account. So it isn't logic. And you won't get very far in trying to program a computer to reason in the manner described. (In fact, you'll get a bit further than you would using conventional AI techniques, but that's all.) But it does appear to bear some relation to what we actually do when we reason.

Likewise, taking account of context enables us to explain the puzzles about language presented in Chapter 1.

UNDERSTANDING LANGUAGE

The puzzle, remember, is to explain how it is that we understand the sentences in each of the following sets in very different ways.

Safety goggles must always be worn inside the building.
Dogs must always be carried on the escalator.

John Smith to marry Mary Jones.
Retired priest to marry Bruce Springsteen.

Time flies like an arrow.
Fruit flies like an apple.

Noam set off on a trip to the beach. The car ran out of gas.
Noam set off on a trip to the beach. The car was still in the repair shop.

The boys drank two cups of cocoa because they were cold.
The boys drank two cups of cocoa because they were warm.

Susan saw the man in the park with a dog.
Susan saw the man in the park with a statue.
Susan saw the man in the park with a telescope.

The sun was already setting when a small sail boat slipped into the harbor.
Linguistics is a fascinating subject that interests a number of mathematicians.

In most of the above groups, the statements are superficially quite similar, and yet we interpret them in very different ways. The groundwork for an explanation of the distinctions was laid in Chapters 8 and 9. Adopting the informational stance, we can put the various relevant ideas together into a single explanatory framework.

For the sake of this discussion, I shall assume that each statement is presented in written form. The discussion of Chapter 9, in particular, concentrated on verbal conversation, but many of the ideas presented there apply to written statements. As before, I shall use the terminology of situation theory, although my account is not particular to any specific theory.

The key in each case is to take due account of the context in which the statement is made or the situation the statement refers to (either implicitly or explicitly).

The first pair of sentences involves instructions. Both sentences make an explicit reference to the situation to which they pertain—being inside the building in the first case and riding on an escalator in the second. In the context of being in the building, what the first directive tells you to do is to wear safety goggles at all times. However, the context is important. Once you leave the building, the directive ceases to have any relevance for you.

The second instruction says that when you are in the context of riding on an escalator with a dog, you should carry the dog. The directive only applies when you are riding on an escalator. Moreover, since it makes reference to a dog, the instruction can only apply to a person who is accompanied by a dog, and it only applies during the period when the person and the dog are actually on the escalator.

Though a more formal, situation-theoretical account of this pair of examples is actually quite a bit more involved than I have indicated, the key point I am trying to make is that the two contexts involved are very different, and that fact alone is enough to account for the very different ways the two statements are normally interpreted.

The remaining examples are all statements; that is, they provide information by making claims about some aspect of the world.

Any statement makes a claim about some situation. The person making the claim must somehow make it clear what that situation is. In the case of a spoken statement, there are various ways the speaker can achieve this end: pointing with a finger, nodding the head, casting an eye in the appropriate direction, relying on a previously established context, or simply being in the appropriate situation. And of course, a speaker can always articulate the context, saying "Around here . . . ," or "In the park . . . ," or "Last week . . . ," for example. In the case of a written statement, there are fewer options, depending on the medium involved. In the case of the examples in our list, all are presented free of context, other than being used as examples in this book.

Very often, the context appropriate for the interpretation of a particular statement results from a merging, or amalgamation, of two or more pre-existing contexts. For example, interpretation of the statement *John*

Smith to marry Mary Jones involves two contexts: a general world-knowledge context comprising everyday social and legal knowledge about marriages and a more specific John Smith-and-Mary Jones context. As we discussed in Chapter 9, present-day linguists would refer to the former context as background, which the statement itself brings into the common ground that it creates between the writer and the reader. Hence the statement has meaning even if you, as the reader, have no knowledge of Smith and Jones, though if you do have such knowledge, the statement will put that knowledge, as well, into the common ground. The knowledge about marriage brought into the common ground provides you with an interpretation of the actual roles played by Smith and Jones in the situation described by the statement. In contrast, the second statement in this particular pair, *Retired priest to marry Bruce Springsteen*, evokes a quite different context. The background context about marriage remains the same, being brought into the common ground by the statement. However, the reference to Bruce Springsteen, a very well-known singer, evokes a context that precludes the interpretation in which the priest and the singer play the same roles in the marriage as Smith and Jones in the first example. On the other hand, the facts in the background context concerning marriage provide an alternate and very natural role for the retired priest, so you have no more difficulty interpreting this statement than you do the previous one.

It is likewise the evocation of an appropriate context in each case that precludes any confusion between the interpretations of the two sentences *Time flies like an arrow* and *Fruit flies like an apple*. In the former case, the context is a linguistic one—the sentence is a well-known figurative use of language. The latter sentence evokes a context of general knowledge concerning insects.

It has to be admitted that there is nothing in this account that tells you *how* a particular statement evokes the appropriate context. Neither situation theory nor any other theory of contexts is a theory of human cognition. Such theories provide frameworks for the study of information flow. They do not even attempt to explain how the human mind manages to create or identify the context appropriate for a particular utterance with such apparent ease.

Turning to the utterances

Noam set off on a trip to the beach. The car ran out of gas.
Noam set off on a trip to the beach. The car was still in the repair shop.

we can pay attention to the ethnomethodologists who tell us that people use social and behavioral norms to provide some of the orderliness of the activities they observe. In his seminal baby-and-mommy paper, discussed in Chapter 9, Sacks formulates a maxim intended to capture such a use of a social norm:

> If one sees a pair of actions which can be related via a norm that provides for the second given the first, where the doers can be seen as members of the categories the norm provides as proper for that pair of actions, then (a) see that the doers are such members, and (b) see the second as done in conformity with the norm.

In plain, everyday language, what this says in the case of the first of the above utterances is that, since there is an 'obvious' connection between the second sentence and the first, the natural reading of these two sentences assumes that connection. In particular, it should be assumed that Noam set off by car. The same conclusion follows from Grice's relevancy maxim—why else mention the car? The second utterance can be treated analogously, except that in this case the natural reading is that Noam did not travel by car. For both examples, the context that is evoked has a causal, or explanatory, structure. Conformity to some normative, explanatory structure is one of the ways that a particular sequence of sentences creates a scene in the mind of the reader or listener.

It would belabor the point too much to examine each of the remaining sets of examples in any detail. The bottom line is that examples of the kinds considered seem puzzling only when presented out of context, such as in books on language. In ordinary everyday life, we normally hear and read such sentences without any sense of confusion. When used normally, language evokes or takes advantage of an appropriate context. Any attempt to understand how language works should therefore pay proper attention to that context. Context is not an additional feature to be incorporated 'at the end' into a theory of language, communication, and reasoning, after the bulk of the analysis has been done. Rather, context is a central feature of language use and of actual reasoning. The situation is not the same as in, say, classical mechanics, where it is possible to obtain a good theory of motion by first ignoring friction, and then adding it in as an extra term in the equations.

It is an attempt to take account of context from the very beginning that typifies much of the present-day research into language, communication, and reasoning. The inclusion of context into the analysis eliminates many of the traditional puzzles about language and reasoning. But this is not the end of the story, nor even the beginning of the end. Context raises a whole host of new puzzles. One of the most significant is how two people engaged in conversation manage to fix up the same context and maintain it as a common ground. A growing number of experts believe that finding ways to address these new puzzles will involve a rethinking of what we mean by a scientific theory—or, at least, what scientists traditionally mean by that phrase. That brings us to the last part of this account.

GOODBYE, DESCARTES

It is perhaps unfair to blame Descartes for an entire analytic tradition. Why not "Goodbye, Plato" or "Goodbye, Galileo" or goodbye to any one of generations of scientists and philosophers? On the other hand, it is surely a measure of Descartes's greatness and the significance of his ideas that his name is so often used to refer to certain aspects of the scientific tradition that have reigned for so long. Recall, for example, that Chomsky used the term *Cartesian linguistics* to refer to his own work on syntactic theory. And *Descartes' Error* is the title of a 1994 book by the neurologist Antonio Damasio, which examines the role played by the emotions in human reasoning, a thesis I will refer to presently.

To begin at the beginning, the scientific tradition to which it is time to say goodbye has identifiable roots with Thales, around 600 B.C., the Pythagoreans a hundred years later, and Plato and Aristotle around 350 B.C. It is to the ancient Greeks that we owe the notion that mathematics provides a key to understanding the physical and mental worlds. The classical liberal arts, the forerunner of today's liberal arts education, were dominated by mathematical thinking: The *quadrivium*—arithmetic, geometry, music, and astronomy—was based on number and quantity, and the *trivium*—grammar, rhetoric, and dialectic—was bound up with formal logic.

In the case of the trivium and the behavior of humans, there is no obvious reason to assume that a mathematical approach will lead to great insight, and in the case of music, to this day, mathematics can hardly be said to have provided more than a part of the explanation as to what distinguishes 'music' from mere 'noise'. However, the success of mathematics in astronomy and, later, the study of the physical word in general, was dramatic. As a result, it is hardly surprising that mathematics came to occupy a pivotal role in what is generally known today as the rational, or scientific, method.

After its initial flowering, Greek civilization was largely destroyed by the conquests of the Romans and the Mohammedans, and it was not until around 1500 A.D.—the Renaissance period—that the Greek ideas began to surface once again. The rebirth was not without difficulty. During the intervening years, southern European culture had been dominated by the Roman Catholic Church, who declared off limits any attempt to provide a mathematically based explanation of the universe. To Christians of the Middle Ages, the universe was the result of God's work, according to God's plan, and it was not for man to provide a Greek-style, 'natural' explanation of its inner workings. The mathematicians and scientists of the Renaissance attempted to sidestep the conflict by the introduction of a new doctrine, namely, that God had designed the universe according to mathematical principles. Since it was, according to Catholic belief, of great importance for man to search out and understand God's will and creations, this maneuver enabled the mathematicians of the sixteenth and subsequent centuries to engage once again in the pursuit of a mathematically based understanding of the universe, this time as a religious—or at least religiously motivated—activity.

Inspired by religious zeal, the scientists of the late sixteenth and early seventeenth centuries carried out what has been described as the scientific revolution. The rapid growth of science was accelerated by various events, among them geographic exploration and the discovery of new lands, both aided by the invention of the compass; the invention of the telescope and the microscope; and Copernicus's reintroduction of the heliocentric theory of the universe. However, with the last of these events, mathematics and science were suddenly brought into direct conflict with the Church once again. At that time, the only argument in favor of the theory that the Earth moves around the Sun was that the mathematics is much simpler than if you assume the Sun moves round the Earth. But the ruling Catholic doctrine of the day held that the Earth was the center of the universe and to support the heliocentric theory was an act of heresy. As a result, when Galileo Galilei, the great Italian champion of the heliocentric theory, published his observationally based findings on the planetary system in 1632, he titled the work *Dialogue Concerning the Two Major Systems of the Universe.* He also included a foreword declaring that the heliocentric theory was merely a figment of the imagination which just happened to provide a fairly simple mathematical explanation of the observations made by himself and by his famous contemporary, Johannes Kepler. However, though he discussed both theories, his own preference for the heliocentric theory was apparent, and before long Galileo was forced to recant his views. In 1663, his book was banned, a ban that was not lifted until 1822.

The modern scientific method, based on observation, mathematical measurement and description, and logical analysis, owes much to Galileo and his contemporaries Francis Bacon (1561–1626) and René Descartes

(1596–1650). "The great book of nature can be read only by those who know the language in which it is written," declared Galileo, continuing, "[a]nd this language is mathematics." In a similar vein, Descartes wrote that he "neither allows for nor hopes for principles in physics other than those that lie hidden in geometry or in abstract mathematics, for in this way all phenomena of nature will yield to explanation, and a deduction of them can be given."

Galileo saw the role of the scientist as focused on measurement and the discovery of descriptive, quantitative formulas, rather than the formulation of causal explanations obtained by philosophical reflection. In many ways, Galileo and Bacon were each an early epitome of the 'nononsense, down-to-earth, practical scientist' of the twentieth century.

Descartes, in contrast, was in many ways an early forerunner of today's 'applied philosopher'. Though he believed that all science could be reduced to mathematics, Descartes made very little use of mathematics in his own work, and his only substantial contribution to mathematics was his famous *La Géométrie,* in which he created analytic (a.k.a. Cartesian) geometry. This work was included as an appendix in his great philosophical work *Essais Philosophiques,* published from 1637 onward. Though this work, along with that of Galileo, Bacon, and others, established the modern scientific approach to knowledge, Descartes's ultimate interest was elsewhere, namely, the nature of human thought and what it is to know something—an interest reflected in his oft-repeated remark "I think, therefore I am."

Descartes's major essay on the scientific method, "Discourse on the Method of Properly Guiding the Reason in the Search of Truth in the Sciences," was published in 1637. Stripped to its bare details, Descartes's method consisted of (1) accepting only what is clear in one's own mind, beyond any doubt; (2) splitting big problems into smaller ones; (3) arguing from the simple to the complex; and (4) checking when one is done.

Descartes believed that his method, the method of science and mathematics, could be applied to the inner world of the mind as well as to the outer world of the physical universe. He wrote, "The long concatenations of simple and easy reasoning which geometricians use in achieving their most difficult demonstrations gave me occasion to imagine that all matters which may enter the human mind were interrelated in the same fashion."

In large part because of the enormous influence Descartes had on the development of modern science—Newton, in particular, was influenced by him—Descartes's views have led to numerous attempts to develop mathematical sciences of language and reasoning modeled on physics—

attempts that continue to this day. The belief is that, once we have identified the right features—the equivalents of the length, mass, velocity, acceleration, force, momentum, inertia, and so forth, of physics—we can develop a mathematical theory of language and/or reasoning that is every bit as rigorous and precise as physics. In such a science of the mind, as much as in physics, mathematics will be both "maidservant and queen," to use a phrase that was common in the less gender-sensitive years of the first half of the twentieth century.

For Descartes, the mind and the brain–body are separate entities. The mind is an abstract entity that resides in the physical brain. Mathematics can be used to explain the workings of that abstract mind. *Dualism* is the name given to this fundamental separation of mind from body. For the student of language and reasoning who works in the dualist tradition, there are two distinct domains: the subjective, internal world of the mind, and the external world, an objective reality made up of things that bear properties and stand in relation to one another. It is assumed that there are objective facts about the external world that do not depend on the interpretation—or even the existence—of any person. We make our way in the world by acquiring information about those things and constructing an internal representation, or mental model, of the external world. Thinking is a process of manipulating those internal representations. Cognition is based on the manipulations of the internal representations. Language is a system of symbols composed into patterns that stand for things in the world.

One of the major puzzles that arises from the dualist view of the world is the so-called mind–body problem: How can our abstract, internal thoughts and intentions about action cause the physical motion of our bodies?

So deeply rooted has Descartes's dualist view become in present-day science—and indeed in much of our present-day world view—that it is widely believed that it is only a matter of time before familiar looking, mathematical sciences of reasoning, language, and communication are developed. Furthermore, any theory—of cognition, language, society, or whatever—that does not fit the expectations of Cartesian science runs the risk of being dismissed, at least by many scientists, as not completely respectable.

However, despite its extensive and pervasive acceptance, in recent times, a number of philosophers have seriously challenged Cartesian dualism—Husserl, Heidegger, Ricoeur, Gadamer, Merleau-Ponty, Sartre, Mead, Dewey, Habermas, Wittgenstein, Dreyfus, and others. So too have a number of biologists and neuroscientists, among them Maturana, Varela, and

Damasio. Within the last decade or so, some leading figures in the computer world have also begun to question the Cartesian view on which much of computer science is based: Winograd and Flores, with their 1987 book *Understanding Computers and Cognition,* Lucy Suchman, with her book *Plans and Situated Action,* which also appeared in 1987, and others.

One of the first people to try to move away from the dualist position was the German philosopher Martin Heidegger. In his book *Being and Time,* published in 1962, Heidegger investigated the subject known as *phenomenology* (introduced by Husserl), which seeks to understand the foundations of everyday experience and action. Phenomenology challenges some of our basic assumptions about ourselves and the world, in the same kind of way as does the sociologists' ethnomethodology, which came later. According to Heidegger, it is wrong to adopt a simple objective stance, where the primary reality is an objective physical world, and it is likewise wrong to take a simple subjective stance, where your thoughts and feelings are the primary reality. Rather, neither can exist without the other, and you have to consider both together, as a single whole. In your normal, everyday life, says Heidegger, you do not adopt a detached, 'rational' view of what you do; you simply act. If you think about your actions in a detached, rational way at all, you do so after the event, perhaps because something went wrong and you decide to reflect on what you did. Since this is the way we actually experience the world, moment-to-moment, Heidegger insists, the detached Cartesian view is misleading and, far from leading to a deep understanding of our existence and our actions, will, in fact, prevent us from achieving an adequate understanding.

For instance, we approach every situation from a prior context that inescapably shapes and prejudices the way we encounter and react to that situation. Because this is how things always are, because we are never in the position of a completely detached observer with no prior experiences—we are never a clean slate if you like—we should not regard prejudice as a condition that leads us to interpret the world falsely. Our prior experiences are a necessary condition for us to interpret the world at all. Interpretation is always relative to prior experiences. Trying to strip away all context is an investigative strategy that can lead to a way of understanding ourselves and the world that may, on occasion, be useful. However, we should not confuse this investigative strategy with the way things 'really are'.

Coming from a very different intellectual background, the biologist Humberto Maturana argues that the dualist view of cognition obscures its complex biological nature and in so doing creates a misleading view of thought and communication. In their 1980 book *Autopoiesis and Cognition,* Maturana and his student Francesco Varela describe living systems (such as organisms) in terms of *autopoiesis,* a technical notion introduced by Maturana to describe the way the different parts of a living system interact to produce what we call life. Rather than view the system as 'acquiring information' by forming an internal representation, they argue, we should concentrate on the ongoing changes to the system brought about by constant interaction with the environment. Communication between two such systems should not be regarded as a transmission of information but as a form of coupling between them.

For Maturana, it is misleading to think of a single, isolated 'state' of an autopoietic system. You have to consider both its environment and its history. In particular, the mind cannot be understood in isolation from the body, a point discussed further in the book *The Embodied Mind,* written by Varela, Thompson, and Rosch and published in 1991.

The year 1991 also saw the appearance of the book *Consciousness Explained,* by the philosopher Daniel Dennett, in which he presented arguments to show that the phenomenon of consciousness can only be understood by looking at the way the components of a complex system interact with each other over a period of time.

Another recent 'attack' on dualism comes from the neurologist Antonio Damasio. In his 1994 book *Descartes' Error,* he argues that the emotions play a crucial role in human reasoning. While he acknowledges that allowing the emotions to interfere with our reasoning can lead to irrational behavior, Damasio presents evidence to show that a complete absence of emotion can likewise lead to irrational behavior. Damasio's evidence comes from case studies of patients for whom brain damage—either by physical accident, stroke, or disease—has impaired their emotions but has left intact their ability to perform 'logical reasoning', as may readily be verified by using standard tests of logical reasoning skill. Take away the emotions, and the result is a person who, while able to conduct intelligent conversations and score highly on standard IQ tests, is not at all rational in his or her behavior. Such people will often act in ways highly detrimental to their own well being. Damasio's evidence shows that, when taken to its extreme, the Cartesian idea of a "coolly rational person," who reasons in a manner unaffected by emotions, is an oxymoron. Truly emotionless thought leads to behavior that by anyone else's standards is quite clearly irrational.

And there is more of the same from other sources. It is all relatively new and almost all controversial. Science never provides 'right' answers.

At most, a scientific theory might gain universal or almost universal acceptance among the scientific community as the best explanation available at the time. With science in the making, controversy is far more common than agreement. In the case of investigations into human rationality, so deeply is the Cartesian dualist view ingrained in the psyche of twentieth-century Western man that any theory that challenges that view is bound to have a hard time of it. But for all that we may rail against it, in much the same way that our ancestors could not accept that the earth was round, the evidence continues to mount that the answers to the age-old questions concerning the nature of thought, communication, and action will not be found until we go beyond the boundaries imposed by the legacy of Plato, Aristotle, Descartes, and all the other great thinkers in that two-thousand-year intellectual tradition.

PLATO'S CAVE

It is a mark of the truly great thinkers that, even when their ideas and beliefs are being challenged and maybe in part abandoned, their thoughts can still be of great relevance. This is certainly true of Plato at a time when some of his views are being questioned. In Book Seven of *The Republic*, Plato describes the nature of human knowledge by means of the simile of the cave. He adopts his familiar form of an imaginary dialogue, which he prefaces with:

> I want you to go on to picture the enlightenment or ignorance of our human conditions somewhat as follows. Imagine an underground chamber, like a cave with an entrance open to the daylight and running a long way underground. In this chamber are men who have been prisoners there since they were children, their legs and necks being so fastened that they can only look straight ahead of them and cannot turn their heads. Behind them and above them a fire is burning, and between the fire and the prisoners runs a road, in front of which a curtain-wall has been built, like the screen at puppet shows between the operators and their audience, above which they show their puppets. . . .

> Imagine further that there are men carrying all sorts of gear along behind the curtain-wall, including figures of men and animals made of wood and stone and other materials, and that some of these men, as is natural, are talking and some not.

Having thus set the scene, Plato begins his imaginary dialogue as follows:

> An odd picture and an odd sort of prisoner.

They are drawn from life, I replied. For, tell me, do you think our prisoners could see anything of themselves or their fellows except the shadows thrown by the fire on the wall of the cave opposite them?

How could they see anything else if they were prevented from moving their heads all their lives?

And would they see anything more of the objects carried along the road?

Of course not.

Then if they were able to talk to each other, would they not assume that the shadows they saw were real things?

Inevitably.

And if the wall of their prison opposite them reflected sound, don't you think that they would suppose, whenever one of the passers-by on the road spoke, that the voice belonged to the shadow passing before them?

They would be bound to think so.

And so they would believe that the shadows of the objects we mentioned were in all aspects real.

Yes, inevitably.

The passage goes on to examine how the prisoners would react if they were suddenly freed from the cave and able to make their way to the outside world.

As with any great writing, Plato's simile of the cave has been subjected to a wide range of interpretations. For the scientist, and for those who would seek to understand the scientist's pronouncements, the story has a plain message to tell. A scientific theory, or indeed any other kind of theory of ourselves or of the world, can provide at most a shadowy outline of reality. If the light suddenly shines brighter, we may be able to see some shadows more clearly, and to distinguish as different shapes that once seemed to be one, but they are still just shadows.

From different parts of the cave the prisoners will see different shadows of the same object, and so too our different theories—the different human ways of knowing—can give different ways of understanding a particular phenomenon. Some of those shadows may be particularly good, providing a picture that has considerable internal logic. But still they remain shadows, not the real thing, and it is always possible that the view of reality they present is misleading. From our privileged viewpoint as observers of the scene both inside and outside Plato's cave, it would clearly appear foolish for the prisoners to squabble among themselves as to whose view—whose theory—is the best one. Their best chance of being able to grasp the true picture is to listen to what each of the others sees from his vantage point, and try to think of a 'reality' that could give rise to all of those different shadows.

In real life, who best understands a flower? The person who sees it with her own eyes, growing in the field? The photographer who chooses the best light and the best angle in order to transfer its beauty onto film? The painter who captures its subtleties on canvas? The poet who captures its beauty in words and likens it to aspects of the human condition? The blind person who perceives it by scent and touch? The musician who sees it swaying in the breeze and captures its motion in a melody? The botanist who knows how it germinates and grows? The biochemist who understands the chemical processes that keep it alive and give it color? The biologist who knows what insects depend on the flower in order to breed and survive? The mathematician who writes down equations that describe the flower's symmetry? Surely, there is no one way to view and to understand a flower, nor even a unique 'best' way. There may be ways that are more suited to a particular *purpose,* but that is another issue. In terms of understanding an aspect of our world, the more ways we have to understand a flower, the greater will be that understanding. The poet or the painter who remains ignorant of chemistry, biology, and mathematics is as deprived in his or her vision and understanding of the flower as the scientist who is blind to the flower's beauty.

One of the things that distinguishes human beings from other animals is that we are tool builders. We construct tools to help us understand and control our environment and to help us achieve our goals. Many of those tools are physical—hammers, spears, knives, projectiles (from stones to bullets to guided missiles), automobiles, cooking utensils, ovens, telephones, computers, aircraft, and so on. But we also construct and use conceptual tools. Language is one such tool. The various art forms may also be viewed as conceptual tools—drama is surely by far the most powerful means to influence people's most fundamental views of life and to inform them of the human condition. Other conceptual tools are our theories of physics, chemistry, biology, mathematics, psychology, sociology, and so forth.

Used skillfully, each of the tools in our conceptual toolkit can help us to get a better sense of what might lie beyond the walls of Plato's cave. But what if there is no world outside the cave? Built in to Plato's story is his fundamental belief that there is an ultimate truth, a genuine real world. You may interpret that as being 'God's realm', to which we will never have more than a shadowy access, at least in this life, or you may think of it as a physical reality, the understanding of which is the ultimate goal of science. For the prisoners in the cave, unless there is a chance of escape, it does not really matter whether there is anything beyond the walls. The most they can hope for is to formulate better and better 'pictures' that provide them with a way to understand what their eyes and ears tell them. Whether there is an outside world—an absolute standard—against which to compare that picture is, for the prisoners, a purely speculative question and a matter ultimately of belief.

In our attempts to understand both the physical world and the human world of reasoning, language, and communication, we are all prisoners in the cave. Whether there is or is not an outside world—an absolute answer—is, in all practical senses, irrelevant to our attempts to achieve that understanding. The best we can do is to keep looking at the shadows on the wall in as many different ways, and from as many different angles, as we can. Cartesian science and mathematics have taken us a long way in our understanding of the physical world. They have also provided us with significant—though hitherto far less useful—insights into the world inside our minds. But there is growing evidence that, when it comes to the human and cognitive sciences, we are reaching the limits of the understanding that can be achieved through the traditional tools and methods of science and mathematics.

Soft mathematics

Many scientists and mathematicians, trained in the traditions of their fields, throw up their hands in horror upon hearing someone claim that we need to look for ways of understanding that go beyond the limits of the traditional methods of science and mathematics and that challenge some of the basic assumptions of science going back to Plato, Aristotle, Descartes, Galileo, and Bacon. Used to the tidy compartmentalizations of traditional science, they generally put such suggestions into the 'fringes of science' bag, along with astrology, New Age medicine, California hot-tub encounter groups, Zen philosophy, space aliens in UFOs, and what have you. Most readers who know anything about the subject would probably be uncomfortable putting Zen philosophy in with astrology and space aliens, and believers in New Age medicine might object to their inclusion too. But to the dyed-in-the-wool physical scientist, all of the pursuits mentioned share the same, 'unscientific' flavor and as such are dismissed as irrelevant pastimes that cannot possibly lead to any real understanding of the universe or the people and other life forms in it.

For the record, I am neither a believer in nor a follower of any of the 'fringe' practices listed above. But, along with a significant and steadily growing number of individuals trained in the traditional sciences and mathematics, I have gradually come to realize that, tradition aside, in trying to develop an understanding of mind and language, we have probably come up against the limits of the traditional frameworks. I don't think this necessarily means that there cannot be sciences of the mind and language, nor does it mean that there will be no role in such sciences for mathematical and other traditional scientific methods. But it does mean that the new sciences will almost certainly have a different look and feel to them.

The role played by mathematics in the new sciences will almost certainly be that of maidservant, not queen. In fact, I doubt that there will be a great deal of scope for applications of much, if any, of the mathematics that exists today. Far more likely, it seems to me, is that it will be the *mathematical method* that is important—looking for the underlying patterns, representing them using mathematical symbols, and examining those patterns as represented by the symbols. It was the mathematical approach that was so effective in developing the physical sciences, where mankind uncovered the underlying patterns of nature. And it was the mathematical approach that led to present-day logic, where the patterns under investigation were those of formal reasoning, and much of current linguistics, such as Chomsky's investigations into the patterns of syntax.

The patterns identified and studied in the new sciences of mind and language will involve contexts, which in general can only be partially specified. As a result, the new sciences will involve a mixture of mathematical reasoning and the less mathematically formal kinds of reasoning used in the social sciences. A reasonable name for such reasoning would be soft mathematics, by analogy with the existing distinction between the hard sciences, such as physics and chemistry, and the soft sciences, such as sociology and psychology.

Soft mathematics does not yet exist. The situation theory introduced in Chapter 8 is one of a number of attempts to develop such a mathematical theory. Judged in terms of its mathematical content, soft mathematics will be very simple, much like the mathematical content of Aristotle's theory of the syllogism. In the case of Aristotle's logic, those simple beginnings led eventually to a considerable body of genuinely deep mathematics, and the same may happen with soft mathematics. But that is for the future to determine, and it is certainly not the yardstick by which the enterprise should or will be judged.

Many, perhaps most, of today's mathematicians find it hard to accept the current work in soft mathematics as 'mathematics' at all. However, a number see as inevitable not only its development, but also its eventual growth into an established branch of mathematics. The following words are those of one of the pillars of the present-day mathematical establishment, Gian-Carlo Rota. Rota is no mathematical lightweight. He is a Professor of Applied Mathematics and Philosophy at the Massachusetts Institute of Technology, a Fellow of the Los Alamos National Laboratory, and a member of the United States National Academy of Sciences. The quotation is taken from the preface to the book *Discrete Thoughts,* a collection of articles on mathematics and computing assembled by Rota and two other highly regarded mathematicians, Jacob Schwartz and Mark Kac, published in 1985:

> Sometime, in a future that is knocking at our door, we shall have to retrain ourselves or our children to properly tell the truth. The exercise will be particularly painful in mathematics. The enrapturing discoveries of our field systematically conceal, like footprints erased in the sand, the analogical train of thought that is the authentic life of mathematics. Shocking as it may be to a conservative logician, the day will come when currently vague concepts such as motivation and purpose will be made formal and accepted as constituents of a revamped logic, where they will at last be allotted the equal status they deserve, side-by-side with axioms and theorems.

Just what you take Rota's paragraph to mean depends on how you read that phrase *revamped logic.* Given a mathematical reading, Rota seems to be predicting the eventual success of the Cartesian approach in the mental realm, a success I have argued to be unachievable. But if you understand the term in the spirit of soft mathematics, where other kinds of analysis stand alongside—and blend in with—mathematics, then Rota's words echo the suggestions I am making in this chapter.

In part because it abandons so many of the cherished scientific traditions of Plato, Galileo, Descartes, and Co., soft mathematics has yet to be embraced by much of the existing scholastic establishment. Research in the new field is not supported on a substantial scale by any university department of mathematics, computer science, linguistics, sociology, or indeed of any established discipline. Nor is support provided by any of the traditional public research funding agencies such as America's National Science Foundation. (The exceptions are the industry-related public organizations such as Japan's MITI and Britain's Department of Trade and Industry, both of which have supported some research in this area. And some work has been done as parts of larger projects funded by the European Community.) Occasionally, established university researchers are supported by their departments to do such work, but that is a different matter, since researchers with a good track record will generally receive some support from their home institution to carry out any investigation. By far the greatest support has come from industry and related private funding agencies, whose criteria for evaluating research is very different from universities and public agencies. The reason why companies such as Xerox and IBM support such research is that what concerns them is not how a particular research project measures up against an existing mathematical standard, computer science standard, or linguistics standard, but whether the project addresses the obstacles that stand in the way of the development of the technological products they manufacture and whether the project offers any prospects of overcoming those obstacles. Others showing increasing interest in the new sciences are the large industrial organizations whose management and workforce are spread across a number of locations, often a continent apart. For those companies, the development and maintenance of effective means of communication is the key to their survival.

If you want to see where the new sciences are developing, then, it won't do any good to look in any single university department or, indeed, in any one geographic location. You have to step back and see what is being done by small teams of one, two, or three individuals at universities and industrial research laboratories all over the world. The new sciences are not being *created;* they are *emerging.* And they measure themselves not by any of today's scientific yardsticks, but by the needs of tomorrow's technology.

WHAT IS UNDERSTANDING?

Whether motivated by pure human curiosity or by the needs of commerce or industry, the purpose of any scientific investigation is to increase our understanding. But what exactly *is* understanding? In what way is our understanding increased if it requires mastery of intricate theories of physics, chemistry, mathematics, or whatever—theories that may themselves be difficult to understand? And what of the closely related notion of explanation? What constitutes an explanation of some phenomenon?

The first observation we wish to make is that understanding and explaining are *relative:* They both involve relating observations of the phenomenon concerned to what is already known and understood.

The phenomenon of electricity provides a good illustration. Indeed, electricity is quite like information in some respects: Though we can measure it in various ways and can observe some of its effects, we cannot see or touch it. How does the human mind come to understand and explain something as abstract as electricity?

The answer, surely, is by means of a metaphor, or at least an understanding that is rooted in metaphor. The metaphor used most commonly is that of flowing liquids. As children, we all become familiar with water, and in particular, its flow properties. This familiarity is achieved in an intimate and tactile manner, as we play in it, wash in it, swim in it, shower in it, pour it through tubes and from container to container, and observe it flow from the tap having passed through the water pipes into our homes. By direct feel we learn to distinguish low pressure from high, the effect of squeezing together the end of a garden hose, and so forth. Based on such childhood experiences, we can then readily conceptualize electric current flowing through a wire as similar to water flowing through a pipe, with amperage corresponding to the diameter of the pipe and voltage corresponding to pressure. Indeed, this is a standard way for middle school or high school teachers to try to explain the behavior of electric current.

Once this basic flowing liquid metaphor has been adopted, the next step in our understanding of electric current comes from observing those points at which the behavior of electricity *differs* from that of the metaphor; for instance, we learn that electric current is not subject to gravity in the way water is. Then, subsequently, we may merge, or even replace, the simple water metaphor with another one, namely of particles (electrons) flowing along the wire. At this level, the metaphor becomes fairly sophisticated, since particles (a defined notion) called *electrons* constitute a significant part of the metaphor used by physicists in order to study the universe. At this level, the metaphor becomes a mathematical one.

Thus, *understanding* a certain phenomenon amounts to:

1. the construction of a suitable metaphor;
2. the identification of the points where the metaphor fails; and
3. the construction of a suitably detailed description of the phenomenon, a description based on the metaphor but sufficiently abstract to transcend the limitations that the metaphor imposes.

In the cases of the metaphors we utilize to understand scientific and technical phenomena, the abstract description in step 3 is usually in mathematical terms, or else scientific terms that are themselves rooted in mathematics.

Successful educational tools and software systems often make ingenious use of metaphors that throw us back to the everyday physical world with which we are so familiar. The windows (pages)-desktop-document-folder-filing cabinet-trashcan display of the Apple Macintosh computer is a now-classic example of such a metaphor.

And of course, the very talk of *information flow, flow charts,* et cetera, is itself a metaphorical way to approach communication and computation.

Though the example considered, electricity, begins with a metaphor rooted in everyday human experience, namely, water flowing through a pipe, the elaboration and augmentation of that initial understanding required to produce sufficient understanding to support the activities of, say, an electrical engineer, requires the framework of mathematics and physics. To understand the phenomenon of electricity to that degree, it is necessary to start out with an adequate knowledge and understanding of the relevant mathematics and physics—for that is the framework relative to which electricity may be understood and based on which a technical explanation of the phenomenon may be given.

A particular, and important, consequence of the above considerations is that what constitutes an adequate explanation of a particular phenomenon depends, in a fundamental way, on the shared conceptual framework and associated value system of the persons providing and receiving the explanation. By the phrase *associated value system* is meant the following. Providing an explanation is a social activity that depends on the shared (background) knowledge of the participants. Where the required background knowledge includes technical knowledge or expertise, say mathematics, physics, psychology, or sociology, there is an associated value system: The mathematicians have criteria that determine what constitutes 'correct', 'acceptable', or 'good' mathematics, and likewise for the sociologists and for the other disciplines. What constitutes an acceptable or adequate explanation of a phenomenon for a sociologist may not be an acceptable or adequate explanation to a mathematician, and vice versa; indeed, in practice, it is highly unlikely that the explanation for the one will be acceptable to or adequate for the other.

THE SOFT MATHEMATICIAN'S TOOLBOX

To most people familiar with applications of mathematics, mention of a *mathematical treatment* of a domain such as reasoning or communication suggests some form of *reductionism,* where everything is reduced to some initial collection of abstract, mathematical objects. For most of its development, classical logic was of this kind. More recently, almost all attempts to develop mathematical theories of natural language have likewise been reductionist in nature. However, this is not at all what soft mathematics is about.

The evidence presented in the previous chapters should have made you very skeptical that any reductionist, mathematical theory of everyday reasoning or of human–human communication is feasible, even in highly restricted domains. Soft mathematics involves a new role for mathematics—or, if you prefer, for mathematical techniques. The use of mathematics in the physical sciences, especially in physics, is of an all-embracing theory (in many cases involving differential equations, for instance). The physical scientist uses mathematics as a conceptual erector set, constructing an elaborate framework, a skeleton on which the flesh of the theory may be built. The justification for such an approach is that it has, over the centuries, proved extremely useful. Soft mathematics, in contrast, is captured far better by the analogy of a toolbox. Mathematical techniques are used as if they were screwdrivers and gauges (or scalpels and thermometers, if you prefer a medical example), used to tease apart various aspects of the data and to probe for unclear or even inconsistent points in our initial understanding.

What does a soft mathematics analysis look like? In this book, I have written about mathematics and linguistics but have not actually 'done' any mathematics or linguistics, and the same is true for soft mathematics. The description I gave of the resolution of the Liar Paradox in Chapter 10 can be sharpened up into a soft mathematics argument using situation theory as the underlying mathematical framework. The argument has two aspects: the genuinely mathematical parts and those parts of the argument that cannot be formalized in mathematics. The analysis to identify the role played by context in an utterance of the Liar sentence is of the latter, nonmathematical kind. The only way to understand the role played by context is to obtain and examine linguistic evidence. The valuation system against which this part of the argument is evaluated is that of linguistics. The 'mathematical' parts of the analysis can, in this example, be made as mathematically rigorous as you wish. In fact, in their book *The Liar,* published in 1987, Barwise and Etchemendy present the mathematical part of the resolution of the Liar Paradox with full mathematical rigor, just like any mathematical proof in algebra or geometry.

Likewise, each of the brief descriptions of the key contextual issues involved in the various linguistic puzzles given earlier in this chapter can be developed into a soft mathematics analysis using situation theory as the underlying mathematical framework. And again, it is possible to make the mathematical part as mathematically rigorous as you like or to make the linguistic or sociological part of the argument as substantial as desired in terms of data-based linguistic or sociological analysis.

In terms of mathematical content, in all the examples of soft mathematics analyses to date, it seems to be possible to make the mathematical parts as mathematically formal as you like. A key issue is whether it serves any purpose to do so. Complete mathematical rigor is one of the two principal valuation criteria in mathematics—the other being the far less precise measure of mathematical aesthetics. To qualify as good mathematics, a mathematical argument has to be completely rigorous. But for soft mathematics, the evaluation system is different. There, the goal is to use mathematics together with other kinds of reasoning to gain and increase our understanding of various complex human phenomena that in all likelihood cannot be fully described using the formal systems of mathematics. If the analyst suspects that there is something dubious or problematic about a particular point of a soft mathematics analysis, then it is probably sensible to increase the level of mathematical precision at that point and see if there is a flaw in the logic of the argument. However, given the complexity of even the simplest example of everyday human reasoning or human–human communication, too much mathematical precision simply swamps the analysis in pages of complex formulas. Then, far from increasing our understanding, the resulting analysis simply obscures the issues of concern.

The soft mathematics approach is very different from most past attempts to use mathematics in the study of reasoning and communication, which have for the most part been firmly rooted in the 'erector set' paradigm. This is, in particular, characteristic of all work on reasoning and natural language in AI. Nevertheless, the toolbox role for mathematics, that I am calling soft mathematics, is, I believe, the role that mathematical techniques will increasingly have to play in the realm of reasoning and communication. The evaluation of scientific work using soft mathematics will require the development of a quite new value system, one motivated—at least initially—more by the needs of technology than by any existing scientific paradigm.

Mathematics is unique in the high degree of precision it can offer in a particular study, but that precision comes at a high price in terms of simplification. The simplification involved in the use of mathematics—the amount that has to be discarded or ignored—makes it an inappropriate basis for a comprehensive theory of reasoning and communication of the kind that was envisaged by many from the 1950s through the 1970s. But to conclude on this basis, as some sociologists and linguists have, that the use of the precise tools of mathematics has no place in the study of language, is to turn one's back on an extremely powerful product of three thousand years of human intellectual development. The surgeon's scalpel and the nurse's thermometer do not in themselves provide an overall understanding of human physiology or the key to a healthy life, but when used properly, with precision and on the right occasion, they can contribute greatly to both goals. A growing number of people are coming to believe that the techniques of soft mathematics will find an analogous application in achieving a scientific understanding of everyday reasoning and communication.

SELECTED FURTHER READING

The books listed below—some of which are referred to in the text—all provide useful sources of information to extend the discussion presented in this book.

The book by Kneale and Kneale [27] is the classic account of the history of logic. There are a number of introductory-level books on mathematical logic, for example, the book by Enderton [17].

Chomsky's original treatise [7] is still one of the best accounts of his original work. Pinker's book [30] is the place to look for an excellent general introduction to Chomsky-style contemporary linguistics. Sampson [36] gives a broader overview of linguistics.

There are any number of introductory texts on artificial intelligence, for instance, Rich [34]. Dreyfus [14] and Dreyfus and Dreyfus [15] provide the countercase.

Treatises on ethnomethodology tend to be hard going. Suchman [38] gives some indications of the subject. Coulter's compendium [9] provides a range of articles of varying levels of difficulty.

Clark [8] provides a very readable account of various aspects of psycholinguistics, particularly, the structure of conversations.

Dretske [16] is one of the first books that proposes the development of a theory of information, and it underpins what I have called the informational stance toward reasoning and communication. It is highly readable.

Situation theory is described in Devlin [12] with detailed applications of the theory in Barwise [1], Devlin and Rosenberg [13], and Gawron and Peters [20].

Good introductions to cognitive science are provided by Gardner [18] and Johnson-Laird [25].

The account of the myths of Hopi time and Eskimo snow words is taken from Geoffrey Pullum's excellent and amusing book [32].

Despite the title, this book is not about Descartes. Rather, he is used largely to identify a paradigm. But for those who want to know more about him, there is Keeling's classic book, *Descartes* [26].

Other than that, just go by the title.

BIBLIOGRAPHY

[1] Barwise, J. *The Situation in Logic,* Stanford: CSLI Publications (Stanford University), 1988.

[2] Barwise, J. and Perry, J. *Situations and Attitudes,* MIT Press, 1983.

[3] Barwise, J. and Etchemendy, J. *The Liar: An Essay in Truth and Circularity,* Oxford University Press, 1987.

[4] Bickerton, D. *Language and Human Behavior,* University of Washington Press, 1995.

[5] Boden, M. A. (ed.). *The Philosophy of Artificial Intelligence,* Oxford University Press, 1990.

[6] Boole, G. *An Investigation of the Laws of Thought on Which are Founded the Mathematical Theories of Logic and Probabilities,* Dover, 1958.

[7] Chomsky, N. *Syntactic Structures,* Mouton (The Hague), 1957.

[8] Clark, H. *Arenas of Language Use,* CSLI Publications (Stanford University), 1992.

[9] Coulter, J. (ed.). *Ethnomethodological Sociology,* Edward Elgar (UK), 1990.

[10] Damasio, A. *Descartes' Error: Emotion, Reason, and the Human Brain,* Grosset/Putnam, 1994.

[11] Dennett, D. *Consciousness Explained,* Little, Brown, 1991.

[12] Devlin, K. *Logic and Information,* Cambridge University Press, 1991.

[13] Devlin, K. and Rosenberg, D. *Language at Work: Analyzing Communication in the Workplace to Inform Systems Design,* CSLI Publications/Cambridge University Press, 1996.

[14] Dreyfus, H. *What Computers Still Can't Do,* MIT Press, 1993.

[15] Dreyfus, H. and Dreyfus, S. *Mind Over Machine: The Power of Human Intuition and Expertise in the Era of the Computer,* The Free Press, 1986.

[16] Dretske, F. *Knowledge and the Flow of Information,* Blackwell, 1981.

[17] Enderton, H. *A Mathematical Introduction to Logic,* Academic Press, 1972.

[18] Gardner, H. *The Mind's New Science: A History of the Cognitive Revolution,* Basic Books, 1985.

[19] Garfinkel, H. *Studies in Ethnomethodology,* Prentice–Hall, 1967.

[20] Gawron, J. M. and Peters, M. *Anaphora and Quantification in Situation Semantics,* CSLI Publications (Stanford University), 1990.

[21] Grice, H. P. "Logic and Conversation," in Cole, P. and Morgan, J. (eds.), *Syntax and Semantics 3: Speech Acts,* Academic Press, 1975.

[22] Gumpertz, J. and Hymes, D. (eds.). *Directions in Sociolinguistics, The Ethnography of Communication,* Holt, Rinehart and Winston, Inc., 1972.

[23] Hofstadter, D. W. and Dennett, D. C. *The Mind's I: Fantasies and Reflections on Self and Soul,* Basic Books, 1981.

[24] Jackendoff, R. *Semantics and Cognition,* MIT Press, 1986.

[25] Johnson-Laird, P. *The Computer and the Mind: An Introduction to Cognitive Science,* Harvard University Press, 1988.

[26] Keeling, S. V. *Descartes,* Oxford University Press, 1934, 1968.

[27] Kneale, W. and Kneale, M. *The Development of Logic,* Oxford University Press, 1962.

[28] Pascal, B. *Pensées,* Paris, 1670. Garnier-Flammarion (Paris), 1976.

[29] Partridge, D. and Wilks, Y. (eds.). *The Foundations of Artificial Intelligence: A Sourcebook,* Cambridge University Press, 1990.

[30] Pinker, S. *The Language Instinct,* William Morrow, 1994.

[31] Plato, *The Republic,* many editions, e.g., Norton (New York), 1985.

[32] Pullum, G. *The Great Eskimo Vocabulary Hoax and Other Irreverant Essays on the Study of Language,* University of Chicago Press, 1991.

[33] Putnam, H. "The Meaning of 'Meaning'," in Gunderson, K. (ed.), *Language, Mind, and Knowledge,* University of Minnesota Press, 1975.

[34] Rich, E. *Artificial Intelligence,* McGraw-Hill, 1983.

[35] Sacks, H. "On the Analyzability of Stories by Children," in [22].

[36] Sampson, G. *Schools of Linguistics,* Stanford University Press, 1980.

[37] Searle, J. *The Construction of Social Reality,* The Free Press, 1995.

[38] Suchman, L. *Plans and Situated Actions: The Problem of Human Machine Communication,* Cambridge University Press, 1987.

[39] Toulmin, S. *Cosmopolis: The Hidden Agenda of Modernity,* University of Chicago Press, 1990.

[40] Winograd, T. and Flores, F. *Understanding Computers and Cognition: A New Foundation for Design,* Addison-Wesley, 1987.

INDEX